TWENTIETH-CENTURY
BLAKE CRITICISM

GARLAND REFERENCE LIBRARY
OF THE HUMANITIES
(VOL. 285)

TWENTIETH-CENTURY BLAKE CRITICISM
Northrop Frye to the Present

Joseph P. Natoli

GARLAND PUBLISHING, INC. • NEW YORK & LONDON
1982

Library of Congress Cataloging in Publication Data

Natoli, Joseph P., 1943–
 Twentieth-century Blake criticism.

 (Garland reference library of the humanities ; v. 285)
 Bibliography: p.
 Includes index.
 1. Blake, William, 1757–1827—Bibliography.   I. Title.
II. Series.
Z8103.N37   1982   [PR4147]   016.821'7   82-15400
ISBN 0-8240-9326-7

Printed on acid-free, 250-year-life paper
Manufactured in the United States of America

For My Wife, Elaine

CONTENTS

PREFACE

Although this bibliography will be of use to all who read Blake's work and seek an overview of recent commentary, it is primarily designed for college students. It differs from G.E. Bentley's *Blake Books* (item 5) in a number of ways, not the least being that the present work is restricted to commentary, criticism, and scholarship on Blake's work. Bentley's work, on the other hand, is a descriptive bibliography, a thorough examination of Blake's writings, and a listing of commentary up to April 1975.

My work is restricted to the period from the publication of Northrop Frye's *Fearful Symmetry* (item 157) in 1947 to 1980. I have selected Frye's book as a beginning point because it represents the first attempt to treat Blake's work as a coherent whole susceptible to a literary exegesis. It might therefore be considered *the* work which has inspired a twentieth-century, basically North American, exhaustive, academic study of Blake, although commentators have gone on to rebel against Frye the father figure.

In an effort to give my work a handbook-like quality and thus render it more useful to students, the criticism is divided according to eleven classifications. Annotations summarize arguments (if indeed arguments are presented), readings, comparisons, hypotheses, discoveries, etc. Each chapter is preceded by an introductory essay in which I survey the chapter and attempt to guide the student through the chaff and into the kernel. An index lists authors of articles and books, authors-as-subjects, titles of works, and subjects.

This bibliography does not include:

1. primary works, either poetry or pictorial art, except insofar as they are considered reference tools and are therefore listed in the Reference section;

2. comments on editions of primary works;

3. foreign-language items;

ix

4. new appearances of earlier books unless they are revised;

5. listings of conferences, slides, concerts, plays, musical
adaptations, tapes, and exhibits;

6. exhibit and library catalogs;

7. dissertations not listed in *Dissertation Abstracts International.*

In addition, no attempt has been made to list *all* appearances of
cited essays, or *all* reviews of books listed in the bibliography.

The following works were referred to in compiling this bibliography:

Studies in English Literature 1500–1900, 1960– , bibliographic
essay, "Recent Studies in the 19th Century";

English Language Notes, 1965– , romantics bibliography;

The Romantic Movement Bibliography, 1936–1970. Edited by
Elkins and Forstner. A master cumulation from *ELH, Philological Quarterly, English Language Notes*;

Philological Quarterly, 1926–1975, bibliographic essay, "The
Eighteenth Century: A Current Bibliography";

The Eighteenth Century: A Current Bibliography. New Series, Edited by R. Allen. 1975 and 1976 volumes published;

MLA International Bibliography;

Annual Bibliography of English Language and Literature;

Year's Work in English Studies;

Index to Book Reviews in the Humanities;

Cumulated Index to Little Magazines;

Humanities Index;

British Humanities Index;

Art Index;

Essay and General Literature Index;

Art and Humanities Citation Index;

Dissertation Abstracts International.

The student of Blake must be directed especially to Bentley's
Blake Books and to *Blake: An Illustrated Quarterly (BIQ). BIQ* was
from 1967 until 1977 titled *The Blake Newsletter.* In 1976, *BIQ*
began an annual bibliography under the direction of Thomas
Minnick. In 1979 this bibliography became "Blake and His Circle: A Checklist of Recent Scholarship." This annual bibliography
is a continuing source of Blake bibliography for the student.

Bentley's *Blake Books* supersedes the earlier Bentley and Nurmi *A Bibliography of Blake* (item 2) as well as Keynes's descriptive bibliography, *A Bibliography of William Blake* (item 55) and Keynes and Wolf's *William Blake's Illuminated Books: A Census* (item 56).

I would like to clarify the arrangement of three chapters. In the chapters "Blake's Influence," "Sources and Analogues," and "Critical Comparisons" I have tried to categorize three basically different kinds of essay. The chapter on influence represents a category of works in which arguments are made for Blake's influence on a particular author or school of thought or sensibility. "Sources and Analogues" considers authors and schools of thought which illuminate Blake. I argue, however, that while it is frequently possible to speak of Blake's influence on, say, Yeats, because direct evidence outside a conjunction of analogous ideas in the works exists, it is not worthwhile to pursue sources and influences of and upon Blake's work. The best "source" studies actually describe common experiences and illuminating analogues. Unlike the "Sources and Analogues" chapter, the "Critical Comparisons" chapter includes items which are not intended simply to illuminate Blake but to be mutually illuminating. Authors compared and contrasted to Blake in this section may obviously have been influenced by him, or may have influenced him, and therefore the student must realize that my little system of categories breaks down, as all systems should, at some point. But there is, I sincerely believe, more benefit in drawing this barest circumference of order than not. Items which cannot be classified easily under one heading are cross-referenced in other chapters. The index is to be used as an offensive tool against categories which become barriers. Book reviews are listed directly after books reviewed and are designated by (rev.). No attempt was made to include all book reviews. I included all I saw except those which were obviously superficial. The reader is encouraged to use *Book Review Digest, Book Review Index* and *Current Book Review Citations* to gather additional reviews. I cite those appearances of articles which I was able to find most easily. I presume that ease will extend to the reader.

I would like to thank the following people for making my task easier: Patricia Giles, Head, Reference Department, Merrill Bertrong, University Librarian, Richard Murdoch, Rare Books

Librarian, Wake Forest University; Norman Hoyle, School of Library and Information Science, SUNY at Albany; Roger Berry, Rare Books Librarian, University of California, Irvine; Julia Johnson and Barbara Bergeron, Garland Publishing. I am grateful to Mary Lynn Johnson, Coe College, for pointing out some factual and typographical errors in the manuscript.

I also received some very helpful comments from Hazard Adams, John E. Grant, Morton D. Paley, and Robert Essick regarding the past, present, and future state of Blake studies. The following items were also brought to my attention: Johnson and Grant's *Blake's Poetry and Designs* (Norton Critical Edition), Diana Hume George's *Blake and Freud* (Cornell University Press, 1980), Leopold Damrosch, Jr.'s *Symbol and Truth in Blake's Myth* (Princeton University Press, 1980), Pamela Dunbar's *William Blake's Illustrations to the Poetry of Milton* (Oxford University Press, 1980), *Night Thoughts* (Oxford: Clarendon, 1980) (edited by John E. Grant, Rose Tolley, and Erdman), Zachary Leader's *Reading Blake's Songs* (Routledge, 1981), and Martin Butlin's *The Painting and Drawings of William Blake*, a catalogue raisonné, Yale University Press, 1981. In the near future we are to have a hundred-page survey of Blake scholarship by Mary Lynn Johnson for the fourth edition of the MLA's *English Romantic Poets: A Review of Research and Criticism*.

INTRODUCTION

Early in the course of reading and annotating the mass of Blake scholarship and criticism produced since the publication of Frye's *Fearful Symmetry* in 1947, I discovered numerous comments ranging from dogmatic and obtuse to bitchy and belligerent to reverent and hortatory. Somewhere in between were the bewildered. Since it is in the nature of a bibliographer to list, I shall list some of these comments, not only to register the various levels of Blake reaction in the twentieth century but also to give the student of Blake just embarking on a voyage into Blake interpretation an introduction to the winds of various issues, concerns and feelings.

> Blake died in 1827 at the age of seventy. But it has taken more than a hundred years for competent scholars to know and appreciate him. As late as 1910, when the famous 11th edition of the Encyclopedia Britannica appeared, the item about the poet Blake finished him off in a single sentence. "With the publication of *Songs of Experience* Blake's poetic career, so far as ordinary readers are concerned, may be said to close."— John C. Ransom. "Blake Triumphant." *New York Review of Books*, October 23, 1969, 4–5.

> The phenomenon of Blake's art is awesome. The past twenty-five years have witnessed his emergence from a second-rank eighteenth century pre-romantic poet to one of the six major Romantic poets. As recently as twenty years ago *The English Romantic Poets* (1950), edited by Thomas M. Raysor and sponsored by the MLA, could in a review of scholarship in the Romantic period exclude Blake. And only twelve years ago a companion volume, *The Major English Romantic Poets* (1957), edited by Clarence D. Thorpe, Carlos Baker

and Bennett Weaver, discussing the pertinence of the "chief English Romantic poets" continued to remain silent on Blake! But the circles of destiny roll with accelerating omnipotence as the century advances, bringing Blake ever more rapidly to his apotheosis. Currently he is sitting in coronation as the pre-eminent poet of the period, the touchstone of Romanticism, necessitating our re-evaluation of the age and our re-interpretation of his great contemporaries in the light of his apocalyptic vision.—Max Schulz. *Eighteenth Century Studies*, IV (1971), 223–229.

. . . currently Blakean fundamentalism is being replaced, as a centre of interest, by an appreciation of the other major poets in the romantic movement.—J.R. Watson. "The Romantics." *Critical Quarterly*, XXI (1979), 3–15.

Perhaps the first thing to say is that while the revelation according to Frye is still very much alive and well, the road to revisionism, perhaps even to excess, has already been well travelled. Younger Blakeans have for some time now been chipping away at the tablets and erecting golden calves of their own. The assumption that Blake's life work is a unity impervious to major chronological changes in attitude and idea; the belief that the key to Blake is to be found in archetypal interpretations of his mythic system; the notion that he consistently attributed to creativity and to works of art themselves a supreme value—these and other interpretative premises have ceased to appear axiomatic. Some even have ceased to appear true.—Spencer Hall. "Some Recent Directions in Blake Studies—A Review Essay." *Southern Humanities Review*, X (1976), 172.

Frye distorts Blake by making a thorough idealist and a clerical obscurantist out of him. The Blake who has been the centre of so much idealistic criticism since 1947 is Frye's Blake, the poet of visionary imagination and a guide to Christian interpretations of literature. Frye's Blake has so little to do with the world in which he lived and so other worldly that one cannot help wondering whatever happened to the politically and socially active poet. . . ."—Pauline Kogan. *Northrop Frye: The High Priest of Clerical Obscurantism.* Montreal: Progressive Books, 1969.

. . . I quite realize how often the popular estimate of Blake is sounder in perspective than the scholarly one. Scholars will assert that the famous 'Jerusalem' hymn is crypto-anglo-Israelitism or what not; but when it was sung in front of Transport House at the Labour victory of 1945 the singers showed that they understood it far better than such scholars did. Scholars will assert that the question in "The Tyger" "Did he who made the lamb make thee?" is to be answered with a confident yes or no; yes if Blake is believed to be a pantheist, no if he is believed to be a Gnostic. Most of those who love the poem are content to leave it a question, and they are right.—Northrop Frye. "Blake After Two Centuries," *English Romantic Poets: Modern Essays in Criticism*, 55–67 (item 154).

The trouble with Blake is that there is too much obscurity in his critics.—Cleanth Brooks. Quoted in *Yale Review*, LXIII (1974), 590.

My study of Blake has led to the conclusion that to the degree that one regards Blake's art as an object of analysis and interpretation, to the degree that any criticism fosters such a view, to that degree has Blake been misused . . . misread. To regard Blake's vision of life as an object of study or perception is to transform it into a shadow of death. Thus he designed his work to be a means of vision in us, to "rouze" our faculties to act the way his had been roused.—Jerome McGann. "The Aim of Blake's Prophecies and the Uses of Blake Criticism." *Blake's Sublime Allegory* (item 118), 3–21.

... can his home-brewed mythology really interest anyone who isn't thinking of writing a book about it?—John Jump. *Critical Quarterly*, XIII (1971), 87–88.

Blake was an important and original poet, but he appears to have attracted the wrong kind of critic, especially in recent years. . . . The ordinary reader does not need to be introduced by elaborate commentaries to the lives of Urizen and Luvah and Tharmas and Urthona. He needs first of all a general description of what Blake did.—Benjamin Sankey. "A Preface to Blake." *Spectrum*, IV (1960), 108–112.

There isn't one book one can recommend as a guide, either on Blake in general, or even on *Songs of Innocence and of Experience*. In fact, it is one's responsibility to warn the student against being hopeful of light and profit to be got from the Blake authorities and the Blake literature. More than that, he should be told unequivocally that none of the elaborated prophetic works is a successful work of art.—F.R. Leavis. "Justifying One's Valuation of Blake." *William Blake: Essays in Honour of Sir Geoffrey Keynes* (item 240), 66–85.

Blake refused to go to school on the ground that he couldn't stand the discipline. About the work of this poet—immensely gifted though he was—two theories are tenable. One is that after the death of his brother Robert his memory became dangerously out of control, so that when he thought he was writing from intuition he was in fact recalling the books of mystical philosophy he had ransacked in earlier years. The other theory is that starved of experience, knowledge and subject matter, Blake went in cold blood to these same philosophers and versified them, more or less clumsily, into what we now know as the Prophetic Books. I will leave the probabilities for the Intentionalists to sort out. What concerns the reader is that for most of his life Blake was producing masses of obscurity which generations of scholars have at-

tempted, with varying degrees of success, to explain.—
Philip Hobsbaum. "The Romantic Dichotomy." *British
Journal of Aesthetics*, XVI (1976), 32–45.

Thirty years ago when I was doing Blake in graduate
school there were few people who thought the prophetic books could possibly mean anything to ordinary
men. . . . Since that time Blake has fared better. People
have given up the idea that he was a madman who
wrote a few good short poems and many bad long
ones.—Thomas Merton. "Blake and the New Theology." *Sewanee Review*, LXXVI (1968), 673–682.

I am sure that I am not the only reader of poetry who
finds himself in a state of permanent uncertainty about
William Blake, unable either to fit him comfortably in
the sequence of great English poets or to exclude him
therefrom with an easy conscience. This uncertainty is
not due to the eccentricity of his opinions—were those
of Shelley or Yeats any less eccentric?—but to the sheer
unreadability of his major works. But one could never
leave him alone.—Patrick Cruttwell. "Blake, Tradition, and Miss Raine." *Sewanee Review*, XXIII (1970),
133.

Wordsworth, who had the advantages which Blake
lacked, has little to say to us today; and he, after all,
produced just as much bad verse as Blake.—Arland
Ussher. "The Thought of Blake." *Dublin Magazine*,
XXIII (1948), 23–32.

No one (to invoke only recent events) who joined
SNCC in Mississippi or the draft-resistance movement
or the early consciousness-raising sisterhoods, no one
who took part in the spontaneous mass movements of
1968 in Paris or Prague, will doubt the possibility of an
apocalypse of fraternity. Of such a possibility, though
expressed in terms not easily available to us today,
Blake is our chief poet and prophet.—Michael Ferber.
"Blake's Idea of Brotherhood." *PMLA*, XCIII (1978),
438–447.

How important an artist is William Blake? If the present age is the age of any one artist of the English present or past, it is, surely, the Age of Blake.—J.R. Harvey. "Blake's Art." *Cambridge Quarterly*, VII (1977), 129.

As the cash nexus shut down over human culture like a net, strangling all other values but profit, the poets and novelists reacted—Blake understood. Sade, Hegel, Kierkegaard, the philosophers of alienation, all to a greater or lesser degree fail where Blake succeeds.— Kenneth Rexroth. *The Elastic Retort*. New York: Seabury, 1971.

Are those who write about Blake mad or not? According to Blake's newest critics everything he said—which is in itself complicated enough—means something other than what it appears to mean, indeed often several different things at the same time.—Anthony Blunt. "Blakomania." *Yale Review*, LXI (1972), 305–306.

Had he been a Catholic, he might have been canonized by now. It is not just that he was once thought mad and is now adjudged sane, beautiful, and prophetic, but that his vision, dazzling, and hyperbolic, suddenly seems so applicable (let us eschew "relevant") to our heaviest problems of the here and now: how to live, what to do, mental space, utopian possibilities, who owns the park. . . . What would be useful is a little red book of Quotations from Chairman Blake to help the masses understand the dimensions of his thought.— Frederic V. Grunfeld. "Quotations from Chairman Blake." *Horizon*, XIV (1972), 106–111.

William Blake has probably suffered more strange and extreme reinterpretations than any other major artist. His life and works have exercised the wisest and the dottiest of commentators. Many have interpreted him in their own image. . . . He has been cast as the purest, most ascetic spirit of Neoclassicism and as the wildest apostle of Romanticism.—*Times Literary Supplement,* Feb. 17, 1978, 212.

Of the writing of books about Blake in the last score of years there seems to be no end, to say nothing of reproductions of his works and articles in what are known in the mills of academia as "learned journals." Blake has become an industry.—Edwin Wolf. *Fine Print,* V (1979), 60–61.

Ideas that inhabit poems as living things do not explain the poems as much as they create them, and that is why exegetical and interpretative books on Blake's poetry are rarely without profit.—Marius Bewley. "Blake and Some Recent Critics." *Sewanee Review,* XVII (1964), 278–285.

I am afraid that the halting approach of the academy can do little for the splendor of Blake's spiritual genius. This kind of genius is too foreign to the minor tensions and traps of conventional scholarship, which are not quite equal to allowing or holding the greatness of a true and valiant soul. The horses of instruction have never made it evident that they are wiser than the tygers of wrath.—Frank O'Malley. *Review of Politics,* IX (1947), 183–204.

[Students] need close critical analyses and evaluations of individual works.—Anon. *TLS,* March 20, 1969, 308.

If he [the critic] is not careful, he only succeeds in imposing a Urizenic scheme, a unified system which fixes a self-contained vision, and so represents the opposite of everything Blake stood for, however accurate the allusions and relations may be . . . sometimes a feeling arises that we are faced with a self-perpetuating industry . . . the driving force in the writing of essays may become the need to maintain a scholarly *esprit de corps*, a mutual activity in which we must all join, rather than a respect for Blake himself. . . .—W.H. Stevenson, *Blake Studies*, II (1969), 91–97.

It is necessary that this wall [the camp wall of regular Blakeans] be breached periodically if Blake is not to become a remote cult image, familiar only to a coterie of initiates.—Robert Wark. *Blake: An Illustrated Quarterly*, XII (1978–79), 211–212.

Our caviar was cheap then as there were few competitors who had developed a palate for it, but now the hordes who used to snack on loaves and fishes have become intrigued and so our one time reasonable delicacies have become as outré as Perigord truffles stuffed with Beluga.—Ruthven Todd. "Two Blake Prints and Two Fuseli Drawings with Some Possibly Pertinent Speculations." *Blake Newsletter*, V (1972), 173–181.

In Blake's case there is a deepcut disparity of attitudes between English and North American critics. English readers see an immediate point in Blake's commentary on the London of his time. . . . And English critics find it natural to read his work in the context of the English eighteenth century. . . . For Americans, on the other hand, whose civilization has been dominated less by an imaginative history than by an interlinked set of ideas and ideals, Blake's Urizen . . . has been a more compelling figure.—Anon. "Some Anglo-American Divergencies in the Appraisal of William Blake." *Times Literary Supplement*, Dec. 25, 1969, 1471.

From then on [after the First World War] the floodgates were open. Blake was shown to be a Hindu, a mystic and a Christian heretic, a Freudian and a Jungian, a Communist and a nationalist, an expressionist and a surrealist; there was no school of thought or art, past or present, with which he was not found to have some affinities. Every line that he wrote was dissected and loaded with interpretation.—Anthony

Blunt. "Blake and the Scholars: I." *New York Review of Books*, Oct. 28, 1965, 22–23.

It would be instructive, perhaps amusing, to promote a symposium in which scholars would be asked in turn to state simply Blake's opinions on religion, politics and sex. The many apparent self-contradictions in Blake's own work would immediately come to light; and the audience would be left wondering whether Blake was an orthodox Christian or an uncompromising rebel against religious forms; a preacher of free love, or a firm upholder of the marriage contract.—John Beer. "Blake and His Readers," *Blake's Humanism*, 25 (item 76).

A student who leaves Blake's work and approaches the criticism may do so in the hope of having obscurities illuminated. It is as if the string Blake has unwound suddenly disappears or threatens to disappear and a Virgilian guide must be found. This annotated bibliography of Blake criticism in the twentieth century has been prepared to assist just such a student. But it is obvious from the above quotations that there are questions regarding the degree to which Blake's work can be illuminated, especially the later books, and the ways in which Blake interpreters go about interpreting Blake.

The Pragmatics of Reading Blake

There is a pragmatics of Blake study that involves time invested and profit extracted. In fact, it has been a key concern with a variety of Blake commentators for the entire thirty-four years this bibliography surveys. My own assumption is that students take from Blake according to their own needs, interests and capacities and that a tabulation of debits and credits is purely an individual enterprise. I hope that a very early reward of Blake study would be a replacement of a cash-nexus mentality with something more humanly oriented.

The Blake that is comprehended by any individual reader is inevitably that individual's Blake. That comprehension is something very different from the quest made by the total corpus of Blake scholars and critics for a definitive introduction, a definitive biography, a definitive exegesis. The degree to which Blake's entire work can be reduced to uniform, systematic comprehensibility does not affect the degree to which his work has an effect upon any individual reader. The discursive cannot be substituted for the non-discursive. The quest for a common ground, for an objective Blake, for comprehensible, communicable themes, *is* the academic quest. It is engaged as enthusiastically with poets as with philosophers, with painters as with physicists. And yet, there is no objectively understood Blake; there is only Blake understood by someone. The work will always have an effect. Effects which are the results of not striving to locate and define Blake's work may be productive by virtue of encountering a greater proportion of one's own mind than Blake's work. Since we are all, as individual readers, variously encountering our own minds, the only question pertains to how we make our reading of Blake's work efficient. Effects which are the results of staying closely with Blake's work, reliable text and commentaries, are most efficient if one is indeed reading Blake. When we read Blake, we are committed to that reading. We are committed to reading what others have said, to locating a reliable text. We are committed to locating Blake's work as it exists outside our own minds. *We* intend to read *Blake*— a dialogue of reader and work to be read.

In this dialogue of Blake's work and the reader of Blake's work, the exegetist of the work goes on as if the individual reader did not have determining priorities. And it cannot be otherwise. Whether or not the priorities of the reader are acknowledged, the exegesis of the work goes on. It is only when an attempt is made to impose uniformly a supposed definitive, objective exegesis on the individual reader that the inviolability of an equal dialogue must be asserted. Unfortunately, Blake-in-the-classroom is too often a uniformly perceived Blake for the purpose of uniform evaluation of response. One of the purposes of this bibliography is to provide students with a guide to Blake studies so they can select in accordance with their interests. Thus, a bibliography such as this becomes a means by which to break through the circumference of a possibly too Urizenic, institutional presentation. It is hoped that, most often, it will complement Blake-in-the-classroom. Whether or not a student of Blake who comes to this bibliography is enrolled in a course which includes Blake, this bibliography can aid the student in coming to terms with Blake's work.

Neither the poetry nor the pictorial art *is* the commentary, and the failure to find a precise equation for the two should not exasperate the student nor lead to the conclusion that Blake's work is incomprehensible and therefore meaningless. The reader who intends to read Blake does not read with less of the imagination, emotion and senses than of reason. There are really two instances when a reader's comprehension of Blake may go on in the absence of commentary or in opposition or partial opposition to commentary: when Blake's work is merely a vehicle by which one is transported back into one's own mind, and when an imaginative-emotional-sensuous-rational comprehension of Blake's work is achieved. In this latter instance, comprehension has gone beyond commentary. Only Blake's poetry and pictorial art represent such comprehension. But the commentary that does exist is an aid to locating Blake's work and therefore an aid to enabling a reader to achieve what Blake would call a "fourfold" understanding.

If my reading of thirty-four years of commentary has produced any one single effect, it is this: there is an overall unity of perception of Blake's work which extends to what it is and what it is worth to us, if not to what it means in purely rational terms.

The Politics of Blakean Criticism

In order to come fully to terms with a literary text, a student approaches commentary. It is doubtless true that when a student approaches Blake commentary, he or she feels at first compelled to seek commentary for the commentary. I think this is true because one has to learn the language of the myth in which Blake's work is housed. There are countless proper names in Blake which any critic may call up in the interpretation of any one of Blake's works. A try at commentary on "The Fly" or "Laughing Song" may send the unsuspecting reader reeling. Characters and actions of the later works are often used to gloss the early and middle works.

Before discussing the various ways Blake commentators divide themselves, I should like to comment on Blake's obscurity. Regardless of how accessible on the levels of imagination, emotions and senses any individual may find Blake's work, it is true that his work is difficult to reduce to a lucid, discursive exegesis. It is difficult to decipher Blake, to work Blake out like a puzzle. Nor is Blake a puzzle read by a cabbalistic coterie of devotees, however puzzle-like his work may seem and however esoteric Blake commentary may seem. I maintain that Blake's work is difficult-to-reduce and that the faculties which are called upon by his work are not commonly exercised nor are they the basis of critical exposition.

In order to put Blake together on this strictly expository level, Blake commentators frequently present ingeniously subtle, ornate interpretations or exhaustively particularized exegeses in which both the reader and the writer assuredly lose sight of the whole. In regard to the whole, Bentley asserts that ". . . the most interesting part . . . is effable and eluctable . . . (*Blake Books*, p. 37). I read this to mean that the whole of Blake is difficult-to-reduce, to make effable and eluctable, and therefore the most interesting part of Blake, for the interpreters, is the portion that can be interpreted, that can be reduced. I have serious problems with this view, although I firmly believe in the worthiness of clarifying Blake where he can be clarified. It seems indisputable to me, however, that in order to either illuminate or interpret Blake, various ineluctable, ineffable aspects of his work are "bracketed" out.

A student who approaches the commentary must realize that he or she is not only approaching something different from Blake's work but also less than Blake's work. As a last word on Blake's obscurity, I would say that just as there is no understanding of Blake without someone, some individual, understanding, there is no difficulty without some individual experiencing that difficulty. Who could disagree that Blake is the number one choice in our own Urizenic time for people to have difficulty with?

An artist who remolds, imaginatively, his own age and its traditions and then produces poetry and engravings and paintings within that recreated world is an artist who will attract a wide variety of commentators. Even that number is extended if we recall that Blake believed he was, in his work, laying down a string that his reader could follow to paradise, regeneration. The "academics" look down at the "lunatic fringe," those hapless souls who "believe in" Blake's vision. There are also those, like N.O. Brown and Theodore Roszak, who apply Blake to the contemporary malaise like aspirin for fever. Allen Ginsberg invokes Ginsberg's Blake as a protector and founding father of uncircumscribed exuberance and spontaneity. Thomas Altizer finds Altizer's Blake to be a premature observer of God's absence. Kathleen Raine's Blake is a Blake who accepts the baton of the "perennial philosophy" and at the appropriate time passes it on. Northrop Frye's Blake is a hot poetic crucible of archetypes inherited from literary ancestors and bequeathed to literary progeny. Harold Bloom's Blake deliberately misread everyone. T.S. Eliot's Blake did not read enough. Middleton Murry's Blake is a Christian-Marxist. English critics go about trying to fit Blake into their own eighteenth century while some American critics wrestle with Blake's message to America and others turn to Blake as a worthy subject for their shiny new critical surgery. While Frye and Adams, among others, advocate a non-developmental view, Gillham and Paley are spokesmen for a "developmental" view. Bindman and W.J.T. Mitchell feel that Blake breaks with the tradition of *ut pictura poesis* while Hagstrum has argued he follows it. For Erdman, social and political forces are determining in Blake's work. For Frye, Blake's art need only be glossed by art. Blake is either easily explained by referring to Thomas Taylor, Boehme, the Antinomians, etc., or is completely different, transforming everything that came before into something totally unique. In the middle are those who find varying degrees of transformation of sources by Blake.

This variety of approaches and interpretations can be frustrating, exasperating. It means that Blake is the kind of artist who cannot be totally reduced to rational paraphrase, but is nonetheless inspiring over a very wide range. The total canon of Blake commentary does not provide a single, unified view of Blake. It does not even come close to this, although there is a hard core of Blake scholars who mistake a rigorously constructed Trojan horse left outside the Blakean walls for a successful infiltration and victory over what lies within. We have a concordance, a dictionary, a descriptive bibliography (revised three times), any number of enumerative bibliographies, two Blake journals, biographies, letters, facsimiles (being produced by an English Blake Trust and an American Blake Foundation), two worthy editions of Blake's poetry and prose, all the illuminated work in one inexpensive volume, all the engravings in one volume, and a catalogue raisonné on the way.

I think these are useful tools. If I did not, I would not have put countless hours into the preparation of this particular bibliography. I think these are useful tools that enable one to come as close as possible to Blake's work. In the dialogue of a reader reading Blake, coming as close as possible to Blake is precisely one-half of making Blake one's own.

BIBLIOGRAPHY

CHAPTER ONE

REFERENCE WORKS AND BIBLIOGRAPHIES

G.E. Bentley's *Blake Books* (item 5) covers Blake criticism
and scholarship from Blake's own time to 1975. A supplement published in *Blake: An Illustrated Quarterly*, XI, 2 (1977), 137-
177, extends that coverage to 1977. *Blake Books* is an expansion
and revision of Bentley and Nurmi's *A Blake Bibliography* (item
2). More than half of *Blake Books* is descriptive bibliography,
covering not only editions of Blake's writings but reproductions
of drawings and paintings and commercial engravings. Thomas L.
Minnick, bibliographer for *Blake: An Illustrated Quarterly*
(*BIQ*), compiles an annual bibliographic update of Blake studies
entitled "Blake and His Circle: A Checklist of Recent Scholarship." *BIQ* has published some interesting bibliographies, including Mary Lynn Johnson's "Choosing Textbooks for Blake
Courses: A Survey & Checklist." This checklist includes sections
on "Guidebooks, Introductions & Study Aids" as well as "Facsimiles & Reproductions Inexpensive Enough for Classroom Use."
As to complete editions of Blake, a student can choose between Erdman's edition (item 38) and Keynes's (item 54). Bentley's *William Blake's Writings* (item 18) is in two volumes; the
first volume includes numerous plate designs. Erdman's *The
Illuminated Blake* (item 41) includes "all of William Blake's
illuminated works with a plate-by-plate commentary." The plates
are black and white, but the edition is relatively inexpensive.
This *Illuminated Blake* should be for the student a companion
volume to the Erdman, Bentley or Keynes editions of the writings.
David Bindman's *The Complete Graphic Works of William Blake*
(item 19) includes all of Blake's designs but does not include
Blake's engravings after other artists. Essick and Easson's
William Blake: Book Illustrator (item 32) is concerned with
this aspect of Blake's engraving. Bindman's book contains the
illustrations to *Job*, the *Grave*, Virgil and Dante as well as
Blake's own illuminated works. Martin Butlin is preparing a
catalogue raisonné of Blake's drawings and paintings which,
according to Robert Essick, who has read the proofs of the
work, "should be the most important work on Blake as an artist
ever."

Since commentary restricted to Blake's writing is becoming more and more frowned upon, a student of Blake must make an effort to incorporate a "reading" of Blake's designs together with a reading of his poetry. Fairly inexpensive facsimiles are being offered by the William Blake Trust and the American Blake Foundation. *Blake Books* contains facsimile items in the descriptive bibliography sections.

Erdman's *Concordance* (item 35) should be referred to upon all occasions when a student feels drawn to Damon's *A Blake Dictionary* (item 24). Damon's *Dictionary* is indeed *his* dictionary and should be read as an exegetical rather than as a reference work. *The Letters* (item 52) and both Gilchrist's biography (item 309) and Wilson's biography (item 351) must be considered essential reference material. Other biographical studies will be discussed in Chapter Three. G.E. Bentley's *Blake Records* (item 10) is a sourcebook of biographical data and most definitively fills gaps found in narrative accounts of Blake's life.

1. Bentley, G.E., Jr. "William Blake 1757-1827." *New Cambridge Bibliography of English Literature*, II. Edited by George Watson. Cambridge, 1971, 615-636.

2. Bentley, G.E., Jr., and Martin K. Nurmi. *A Blake Bibliography; Annotated Lists of Works, Studies, and Blakeana*. Minneapolis: Minnesota University Press; London: Oxford University Press, 1964. 393pp.

    Bibliography superseded by Bentley's *Blake Books* (item 5). Everything in this early bibliography is incorporated in *Blake Books* and extended, especially the descriptive bibliography of Blake's works.

    2a. Erdman, David V. (rev., *A Blake Bibliography*). *Journal of English and Germanic Philology*, LXIV (1965), 744.

        "As mines of information go, this new compendium is exceptionally copious, efficiently organized, and certain to establish itself as an indispensable companion to the study of Blake once the initial unfamiliarity and oddness have been overcome."

3. Keynes, Geoffrey. (rev., *A Blake Bibliography*). *Book Collector*, XIV (1965), 250, 253.

        Considers the arrangement, the bibliographic excellencies, etc., and finally concludes that the book is an asset.

4. Bentley, G.E., Jr. "A Supplement to G.E. Bentley, Jr. and Martin K. Nurmi, *A Blake Bibliography* (1964)." *Blake Newsletter*, II (1968), 1-29.

5. Bentley, G.E., Jr. *Blake Books*. Oxford: Clarendon Press, 1977. 1079pp.

   Terminus for this work is about April 1975. The descriptive bibliography of Blake's writings, Part I, is much more elaborate than the earlier *A Blake Bibliography* (item 2). Brief annotations accompany more than 75 percent of the enumerative bibliography items.

6. Eeles, Adrian. (rev., *Blake Books*). *Times Literary Supplement*, Jan. 27, 1978, 100.

   "Here [the Biography and Criticism section] the result is dispiriting rather than impressive, so immense is the literature, so computerized and uncritical the presentation."

7. Essick, Robert N. (rev., *Blake Books*). *Blake Newsletter*, XI (1977-1978), 178-199.

   "*Blake Books* will be accepted as the standard bibliography in its field and will remain so for many years."

8. Bentley, G.E., Jr. "A Supplement to *Blake Books*." *Blake Newsletter*, XI (1977-1978), 137-177.

   This supplement takes *Blake Books* up to March 31, 1977.

9. See item 2a.

10. Bentley, G.E., Jr. *Blake Records*. Oxford: Clarendon Press, 1969. 678pp.

    Attempts to list all references to Blake made by his contemporaries. This minutely particularized calendar of Blake's life lacks the narrative continuity necessary in a biographical work. It is, however, a prodigious example of what it intends to be: a foundation for a future biography.

11. Brennan, Norman. (rev., *Blake Records*). *Blake Studies*, IV (1971), 103-107.

    Bentley's volume took fifteen years to compile. "... a truly major contribution to Blake scholarship."

12. Erdman, David V. (rev., *Blake Records*). *English Language Notes*, IX (1971), 27.

    It's very difficult to disparage a work which is the result of Herculean scholarly labors.

13. Gilbert, Thomas. (rev., *Blake Records; Blake and the Nineteenth Century* [item 363]; *Blake's Visionary Universe* [item 83]). *English*, XIX (1970), 66–67.

    Bentley's work is considered prodigious; Dorfman has presented a few comments on some interesting areas and Beer's effort is decent.

14. Peter, John. (rev., *Blake Records*). *Malahat Review*, XV (1970), 121–122.

    Why does Bentley leave out all the rumors and scandal about Blake? All that makes the thing readable for the general public.

15. Schulz, Max F. (rev., *Blake Records*). *Eighteenth Century Studies*, IV (1971), 490–492.

    "... an accessible, verified documentation of the known facts of Blake's life and of the financial and legal data of his art dealings."

16. Bentley, G.E., Jr. "Blake Scholars and Critics: Commentators and Exhibitions." *University of Toronto Quarterly*, XL (1970), 86–101.

    Surveys some recent critical works and lists various Blake exhibitions.

17. Bentley, G.E., Jr. "Blake Scholars and Critics: The Texts." *University of Toronto Quarterly*, XL (1970), 274–287.

    Reviews a number of Keynes's texts: *The Letters of William Blake, The Gates of Paradise, Europe* and *Songs of Innocence and Experience*.

18. Bentley, G.E., Jr. *William Blake's Writings*. Oxford: Clarendon Press, 1978.

    Volume I: "Engraved and Etched Writings"; Volume II: "Writings in Typography and in Manuscript."

18a. Bentley, G.E., Jr. "Geoffrey Keynes's Work on Blake: *Fons et Origo*, and a Checklist of Writings on Blake by Geoffrey Keynes, 1910–1972." *William Blake: Essays in Honour of Sir Geoffrey Keynes* (item 240).

19. Bindman, David. *The Complete Graphic Works of William Blake*. London: Thames and Hudson, 1978.

    "I have set out to reproduce every printed design by Blake as well as their major variants. I have included virtually all the prints which Blake designed but did not engrave himself but have omitted almost all of Blake's engravings after other artists."

20. Butlin, Martin. "Cataloguing William Blake." *Blake in His Time* (item 149), 77-90.

    Discusses his problems in putting together a catalogue raisonné of Blake's works.

21. Candela, Gregory. "A Checklist of Recent Blake Scholarship." *Blake Newsletter*, VI (1973), 11-15.

22. Connolly, Thomas E. "Songs of Innocence, Keynes (1921) Copy U, Keynes-Wolf (1953) Copy U." *Blake Newsletter*, VII (1974), 88-89.

    A note on an addition to the standard bibliographic description.

23. Curran, Stuart. "Recent Studies in the Nineteenth Century." *Studies in English Literature 1500-1900*, XIV (1974), 638-668.

    This is a yearly appraisal which includes an assessment of Romantic work published that year. Duplicates *Year's Work in English Studies* in regard to purpose and format, but since the *SEL* survey is necessarily selective and adapted to the varying interests of the authors, there is no real duplication here. This item is included as a representation of *SEL*'s review of nineteenth-century literary criticism and scholarship. "It is only fair to say ... that about one quarter of the books surveyed here have no compelling reason for their publication.... In the Romantic period, except for the continuing pell-mell rush into the Blakean Eden from whose gates Frye dislodged the Covering Cherub some time back, the achievements of the year are editorial...."

24. Damon, S. Foster. *A Blake Dictionary*. Providence, R.I.: Brown University Press, 1965; rpt. New York: E.P. Dutton, 1971; rpt. Boulder, Colo.: Shambhala Press, 1979.

There is no entry for "Contrary or Contraries," the metaphysical basis, as Nurmi has shown, of Blake's work. Neither will one find an entry for "Energy" or "Evil" or "Good"--to mention a few. "Christ" and "Reason" get less space than an obscure place name or a minor character. Nevertheless, the book identifies vast numbers of Blake allusions. An index to this work is provided by Morris Eaves in *Blake Studies*, III (1970), 69-85; this index is included in the 1979 reprint.

25. Anon. (rev., *A Blake Dictionary*). *Papers on Language and Literature*, II (1966), 274-282.

Damon's stupendous work adds to the rich contribution he has already made.

26. Anon. "Blake More or Less" (rev., *A Blake Dictionary; A Blake Bibliography* [item 2]). *Times Literary Supplement*, Sept. 2, 1965, 756.

Damon's work on Blake's symbols has unfortunately not been revised since 1924. Bentley and Nurmi do not measure up to Keynes since they are sometimes brash where he was gracious, etc.

27. Ellsworth, R.C. (rev., *A Blake Dictionary*). *Queen's Quarterly*, LXXVIII (1971), 635.

"While those more interested in the moral, social and aesthetic aspects of Blake may question this assumption [mysticism is most important] *A Blake Dictionary* will remain one of the essential works that any student of Blake must consult."

28. Erdman, David V. (rev., *A Blake Dictionary*). *Journal of English and Germanic Philology*, LXV (1966), 606-612.

Damon presents his own evaluations of Blake's symbols rather than a summary of scholarly consensus. "... the most strikingly 'fresh' interpretations are independent not only of other interpretations but of solid textual or biographical or bibliographical support."

29. Grant, John E. (rev., *A Blake Dictionary*). *Philological Quarterly*, XLV (1966), 533-535.

"I expect to be learning from it for the rest of my life."

30. Luke, Hugh J. (rev., *A Blake Dictionary*). *College English*, XXVII (1966), 516.

    An indispensable work, although there are some errors of fact.

31. Raine, Kathleen. "Once More, O Ye Laurels" (rev., *A Blake Dictionary*). *Sewanee Review*, LXXIII (1965), 711-719.

    "No reader who has seen the essential nature of symbolic discourse for what it is can be satisfied ... by Professor Damon's dictionary."

32. Easson, Roger R., and Robert N. Essick. *William Blake: Book Illustrator. A Bibliography and Catalogue of the Commercial Engravings*. Volume I: Plates Designed and Engraved by Blake. American Blake Foundation, 1972. Volume II: Plates Designed or Engraved by Blake, 1774-1796. Memphis, Tenn.: The American Blake Foundation, 1979.

33. Eaves, Morris. "A List of the Entries in Damon's *Blake Dictionary*." *Blake Studies*, III (1970), 69-85.

    "... Damon's work is handicapped by the absence of either a table of contents or an index." Supplements item 24.

34. Erdman, David V. "Blake." *English Poetry: Select Bibliographical Guides*. Edited by A.E. Dyson. London: Oxford University Press, 1971.

35. Erdman, David V. *A Concordance to the Writings of William Blake*. Ithaca, N.Y.: Cornell University Press, 1967.

    36. Pagliaro, Harold E. (rev., *A Concordance to the Writings of William Blake*). *Computers and the Humanities*, IV (1970), 283-285.

        "It seems unfortunate that Erdman could not have used his own edition of Blake as the basic text."

37. See item 34.

38. Erdman, David V., ed. *Poetry and Prose of William Blake*. Commentary by Harold Bloom. Garden City, N.Y.: Doubleday/Anchor, 1965.

An edition noted for original Blake punctuation and for Bloom's commentary, 807–889.

39. Moore, Richard. "Two New Editions of Blake" (rev., *Poetry and Prose*). *Poetry*, CXI (1968), 263–266.

"I prefer the Erdman volume because the paper is thicker, the printing better, and there is an interpretive as well as a textual commentary. Blake's bizarre punctuation is also kept in Erdman's text—which I think is desirable; one senses the rebellious engraver in every line."

40. Erdman, David V. "A Temporary Report on Texts of William Blake." *William Blake: Essays for S. Foster Damon* (item 256).

Report on textual work and description of remaining problems.

41. Erdman, David V. *The Illuminated Blake*. Garden City, N.Y.: Anchor Press, 1974. 416pp.

Does not present all the variants as Bindman does (item 19) but instead selects the clearest copies. Erdman's notes "attend to the fold of meaning that seems uppermost, yet [take] notice of Blake's workshop symbolism whenever it visibly links illustrations and text." These are black and white reproductions.

42. Chayes, Irene. (rev., *The Illuminated Blake*). *ELN*, XIII (1975), 29–30.

"Erdman's commentary is once more a model of meticulous observation and description, especially in reference to the tiny, marginal and interlinear designs."

43. Ferguson, James B., and F.N. Paris. "1972–73: A Bibliography of Blake Scholarship in the United Kingdom." *Blake Newsletter*, VII (1973), 44–46.

44. Foreman, Foster, et al. "A Checklist of Blake Scholarship October 1970–March 1972." *Blake Newsletter*, V (1972), 214–219.

45. Frost, Everett. "A Checklist of Blake Slides." *Blake Newsletter*, IX (1975), entire issue.

46. Frye, Northrop, and Martin K. Nurmi. "William Blake."
    English Romantic Poets and Essayists. Edited by Carolyn
    and Lawrence H. Houtchens. New York: New York Univer-
    sity Press, 1966.

    Frye wrote an earlier version of this essay for the
    1957 edition. The present collaboration contains an
    Addendum discussing the critical works since 1956. The
    most recent work discussed in that addendum was published
    in 1964. Bentley's "Blake's Reputation and Interpreters"
    in *Blake Books* (item 5) supplements this essay.

47. Gorham, Laura. "A Checklist of Blake Scholarship: June
    1969-September 1970." *Blake Newsletter*, IV (1970),
    51-59.

48. Gross, Rochelle C., and C.M. Henning. "Dissertations on
    Blake: 1963-1975." *Blake: An Illustrated Quarterly*,
    XI (1977), 54-59.

49. Hall, Spencer. "Some Recent Directions in Blake Studies--
    A Review Essay." *Southern Humanities Review*, X (1976),
    172-177.

    A review of some recent Blake publications which really
    serves as an opportunity for the author to chip away at
    both new and old golden calves of Blakean criticism.

50. Hoover, Suzanne. "Fifty Additions to Blake Bibliography:
    Further Data for the Study of His Reputation in the
    Nineteenth Century." *Blake Newsletter*, V (1972), 167-
    172.

51. Johnson, Mary Lynn. "Choosing Textbooks for Blake Courses:
    A Survey & Checklist." *Blake Newsletter*, X (1976),
    8-26.

52. Keynes, Geoffrey, ed. *The Letters of William Blake*.
    Cambridge: Harvard University Press, 1970. 224pp.;
    London: Rupert Hart-Davis, 1956, 1968; Oxford: Claren-
    don Press, 1980.

53. Keynes, Geoffrey. "William Blake (1757-1827)." *Cambridge
    Bibliography of English Literature*, V. Edited by F.W.
    Bateson. Cambridge, 1957, 425-428.

54. Keynes, Geoffrey, ed. *The Complete Writings of William
    Blake with Variant Readings*. London: Oxford University
    Press, 1966.

55. Keynes, Geoffrey. *A Bibliography of William Blake*, 1921; rpt. Kraus, 1969.

    This is a descriptive bibliography of Blake's works which also includes reproductions of designs, lists of Blake marginalia, commentary, chronological ordering of works and almost everything else which one considers pertinent to Blake studies. Bentley in *Blake Books* (item 5) acknowledges the timelessness of Keynes's work: "Naturally new copies of Blake's books have turned up since 1921, as well as new letters and new marginalia, but the bibliographical outlines of our knowledge of Blake are those which Keynes established" (33).

56. Keynes, Geoffrey, and Edwin Wolf II. *William Blake's Illuminated Books: A Census*. New York: Grolier Club, 1953; rpt. Kraus, 1969.

    Supplements Keynes's *Bibliography* (item 55). Both are encompassed by Bentley's *Blake Books* (item 5).

57. Lister, Raymond. "W.B. Yeats as an Editor of William Blake." *Blake Studies*, I (1969), 123-138.

    Yeats-Ellis edition of Blake is poor, but a "school for Yeats's soul." "... Yeats's commentaries on Blake need separate treatment to be dealt with adequately, for it is complex and involved."

58. Minnick, Thomas L., et al. "Blake and His Circle: A Checklist of Recent Scholarship." *Blake: An Illustrated Quarterly*, XIV (1980), 85-93.

59. Minnick, Thomas. "A Checklist of Recent Blake Scholarship." *Blake Newsletter*, X (1976), 59-62.

60. Morgan, Richard. "A Handlist of Works by William Blake in the Department of Prints and Drawings of the British Museum. With Supplementary Notes by G.E. Bentley." *Blake Newsletter*, V (1972), 223-258.

61. Roberts, Peter. "On Tame High Finishers of Paltry Harmonies: A Blake Music Review and Checklist." *Blake Newsletter*, VII (1974), 91-99.

    Reviews Blake-inspired music, including the work of Ralph Vaughan Williams.

62. Taylor, Ron. "A Checklist of Recent Blake Scholarship."
     Blake Newsletter, VIII (1975), 146-158.

63. Trawick, Leonard M. "The Present State of Blake Studies."
     Studies in Burke and His Time, XII (1971), 1784-1803.

     Review of important Blake scholarship which includes
     evaluations and suggestions for future study. In 1971,
     Trawick felt that more attention should be given to the
     poems themselves than to contemporary parallels of Blake's
     vision. Linguistic study should furnish tools to study
     Blake's poems as autonomous objects of art.

64. White, William. "A Blake Bibliography: Review with Addi-
     tions." *Bulletin of Bibliography*, XXIV (1965), 155-156.

65. See item 351.

CHAPTER TWO

ESSAY COLLECTIONS AND INTRODUCTORY WORKS

Because of the variety of approaches to Blake, it is difficult, as F.R. Leavis has stated, to recommend a single introduction to Blake's work. It seems to me, however, to be a matter more of levels of exposure or degrees of introduction than of whether there is one single work which "introduces" a student to all that Blake represents. Part of what a student will be introduced to is indeed the dissension among Blake commentators regarding such topics as the importance of various sources in Blake's works, the precise nature of Blake's composite art, the presence or absence of development in Blake, the degree to which Blake is a man of his times, employing myth to respond to it, or employing myth in an effort to transcend it, or both. What does the importance that Blake places in generation and the body really mean in relation to various notions we have from mysticism to apocalyptic humanism, with some form of Christianity lying between? Are there Eastern influences or not? Is Blake's view of women either sex chauvinist or liberated or both? To what degree is Ginsberg's and Roszak's and Brown's Blake of the sixties a valid Blake? Do we best approach Blake by ignoring extra-literary determinants and by referring only to literary archetypes? What are real inconsistencies, divorced from ambiguities, ironies and meaningful paradoxes in Blake's later work? To what extent has the unfolding of Blake in the latter part of the twentieth century damaged him unalterably? What are the real strengths and weaknesses of Blake's work? Will there ever be a middle ground in Blake reaction or will there always be Blakeans and non-Blakeans? The questions I think are still very many. Are there more and different kinds of questions we ask concerning other poets? Are there, in contrast with other poets, a superordinate number of questions that need answering in regard to Blake study? Perhaps the study of Blake produces questions whereas the reading of Blake does not.

I suggest that a very good introduction to commentary on
Blake is the bibliographic essay. In other words, before one
can select an introductory work, an overview of Blake commentary must be approached. See Northrop Frye and Martin Nurmi's
"William Blake" (item 46). Frye's "Blake After Two Centuries"
(item 154) provides the reader with some context regarding
Blake commentary. See also "Blake's Reputation and Interpreters"
in Bentley's *Blake Books* (item 5). Current, ongoing bibliographic appraisals can be found in *Studies in English Literature*, Autumn issue, and in *Year's Work in English Studies*
(annual).

Regarding the obviously packaged introductory works, I
would avoid initially Raine's *William Blake* (item 249) since
she presents a highly debatable view as a commonly held view;
Gillham's *William Blake* (item 175) since he sees *Milton*,
Jerusalem and the *Four Zoas* as complete failures; Kettle's
William Blake (item 196) since it is highly reductionist in
favor of his view of Blake as revolutionary; Paananen's
William Blake (item 224) since it seems to me to be both
superficial and misguided for an introductory work; Malcolm
Muggeridge's "William Blake" (item 217) since it is too much
Muggeridge's Blake; Norman Nathan's *Prince William B* (item
218) since it is a good example of a tract written by a Blake
disciple; and Davis's *William Blake: A New Kind of Man* (item
293), which is representative of a kind of *new* work which
would have been considered less than contributive a hundred
years ago.

There are works which are less dangerously misleading
and to varying degrees helpful. Klonsky's *William Blake*
(item 201) is very much Klonsky's Blake but the color reproductions are fine and his commentary is often interesting.
Beer's *Blake's Humanism* (item 76) and his *Blake's Visionary
Universe* (item 83) suffer from a lack of coherent apprehension
of the whole of Blake's work and are best attacked via their
indexes. Jack Lindsay's *William Blake* (item 204) is more a
readable biography than a sufficient introduction to the
themes. However, if one holds the view that an introduction
to the man is an important introduction to the work, then
biographies of Blake should certainly be considered. Gilchrist's
biography (item 309) is recommended above all others. Harris's
Monarch Notes work, *The Poetry of William Blake* (item 184),
oversimplifies. Blackstone's *English Blake* (item 99) and
Schorer's *William Blake: The Politics of Vision* (item 1682)
have been surpassed in some ways and yet remain works I would
recommend, with reservations based on their age, as worthy
introductions. Holloway's *Blake: The Lyric Poetry* (item 187)
is very brief, restricted to the *Songs* but worthwhile.

The final category of works I would recommend should enable the student to get close to Blake's work either because the author doesn't have a system to impose upon Blake or because if he or she does, the reader can both benefit from and dispose of that system. If indeed a man sees in accordance with what he is, there are Blakean commentators who come to Blake alive not only intellectually but imaginatively as well. Although Frye's Blake is indeed Frye's Blake, Bloom's Bloom's, etc., Blake is enhanced to a much greater degree than he is lost. Ultimately, the provocation and stimulation we receive from the Blake criticism we come to must accrue to the benefit of Blake. It is a feather in Blake's cap that he has attracted Frye, Bloom, Adams, Erdman, Raine, Merton, Altizer, Brown, Roszak, Ginsberg, Jung, Cary, Shaw, Yeats, Auden, Swinburne, Rossetti, Chesterton, Middleton Murry, Damon and Keynes.

Two general tributary essays I would recommend at the outset are Bronowski's "A Prophet for Our Age" (item 107) and Erdman's "The Bravery of William Blake" (item 138). According to Hazard Adams "... the best introductory statement about Blake is still Northrop Frye's essay 'Blake's Treatment of the Archetype' [item 162], which appeared 30 years ago in *English Institute Essays* 1950...." Bloom's essay "William Blake" (item 105) is fine as is Erdman's "Blake: The Historical Approach" (item 129).

In regard to books, I would urge the student to go at Frye's *Fearful Symmetry* (item 157) in stages, certainly approaching the chapter entitled "The Case Against Locke" without trepidation. *Fearful Symmetry* should perhaps be joined by Paley's *Energy and the Imagination* (item 229) and Erdman's *Blake: Prophet Against Empire* (item 130). Bloom's *Blake's Apocalypse* (item 101) is a good explication of selected passages of Blake, and his commentary for the Erdman edition (item 38) follows the same pattern.

Martin Nurmi's *William Blake* (item 220) is more recent than the above and is both balanced and readable, although he does not discuss the pictorial art. Morton Paley's *William Blake* (item 226) is well illustrated and Paley's commentary is fine. The major strength here is that the student is being introduced to both the poetry and the art. Mitchell's *Blake's Composite Art* (item 215) is the best single introduction to the nature and presentation of the composite art. A more chronological narration of Blake the artist is to be found in Bindman's *Blake as an Artist* (item 96).

66. Adams, Hazard. *William Blake: A Reading of the Shorter Poems*. Seattle: University of Washington Press, 1963.

Adams explores all the work which appeared between *Songs* and *The Marriage of Heaven and Hell* and the later prophecies. He holds the view, derived from Frye, that Blake's vision is one at all times. A brief bibliography of criticism on Blake's lyrics appears on pages 299-332.

67. Armens, Sven. (rev., *William Blake: A Reading of the Shorter Poems*). *Philological Quarterly*, XLIII (1964), 341-344.

"Both Gleckner [*The Piper and the Bard*] and Adams have fulfilled their intentions creditably."

68. Bateson, F.W. (rev., *William Blake: A Reading of the Shorter Poems*). *Review of English Studies*, XVI (1965), 226-227.

"... Mr. Adams's solid, scholarly study is welcome because it shows how, and how far, the Frye formula can in fact be *used*: the degree of its usefulness, that is, as a critical tool to elucidate Blake's obscurities."

69. Bewley, Marius. "Blake and Some Recent Critics" (rev., *William Blake: A Reading of the Shorter Poems*). *Hudson Review*, XVII (1964), 278-285.

"The chief fault of this book is one that he [Adams] shares with many excellent Blake commentators: lack of critical economy. Meanings are hammered out with the ruthless determination of Los at the forge creating Urizen's backbone." Adams believes that any period in Blake's work can be called upon to clarify any other period, thus the numerous references which Bewley dislikes.

70. Gleckner, Robert F. (rev., *William Blake: A Reading of the Shorter Poems*). *Journal of English and Germanic Philology*, LXIII (1964), 802-805.

"It is simply wrong to assume, as Adams seems to do, that Blake's vision of the system was clear and complete, but that he deliberately chose not to express it in the *Poetical Sketches*, to express it only in 'fragments' and 'phases' in the *Songs* and later lyrics, and fully in the prophecies."

71. Grant, John E. (rev., *William Blake: A Reading of the Shorter Poems*). *Modern Language Quarterly*, XXV (1964), 356-364.

Mentions a Unitarian-Divisionist faction in Blake
criticism. The Unitarians believe that "all his
subsequent ideas and images are latent in his very
early work." The Divisionists believe that Blake
changed and refer to biographical data. Adams is
a Unitarian.

72. Henn, T.R. (rev., *William Blake: A Reading of the
     Shorter Poems*). *Modern Language Review*, LX (1965),
     97-99.

     "This laborious, worthy, and painstaking book
     is not without its virtues."

73. Nurmi, Martin K. (rev., *William Blake: A Reading
     of the Shorter Poems*). *Criticism*, VII (1965), 110-
     112.

     Suggests that Adams presupposes that "there was
     relatively little development in his [Blake's]
     thought except in the sense that he gained a clearer
     and fuller insight into the meaning of the struc-
     ture of images comprising the system he was try-
     ing to express." This view "minimizes the distinc-
     tion between the lyrics and the prophecies."

74. Austin, D. "Threefold Blake's Divine Vision, Intention
     and Myth." *The Binding of Proteus*. Edited by M.W. McCune,
     T. Orbison and P.M. Withim. Lewisburg, Pa.: Bucknell
     University Press, 1980, 79-96.

     Argues for a consideration of wholeness and intention
     in Blake rather than an excessive orientation to the
     parts of his work.

75. Battenhouse, Henry M. "William Blake." *English Romantic
     Writers*. Great Neck, N.Y.: Barrons, 1958.

     A very superficial presentation of Blake. No indication
     that the bulk of Blake's work is even known by the author.

76. Beer, John. *Blake's Humanism*. Manchester: University of
     Manchester Press; New York: Barnes & Noble, 1968.

     "We must study the total context of that work if we
     want to see it as anything more than an obscure land-
     scape lighted by periodic flashes; and we must sometimes
     do this in order to get the full effect of the 'flashes'
     themselves."

77. Adelman, Clifford. "The Dehumanization of William
     Blake" (rev., *Blake's Humanism*). *Cambridge Review*,
     LXXXIX (1968), 549-550.

     Beer's *Coleridge the Visionary* was a much better
     book than this on Blake. Beer treats the poetry as
     a product of experiences and not as an experience
     itself; and gets locked into a thematic organiza-
     tion which circumscribes Blake too narrowly.

78. Anon. (rev., *Blake's Humanism*). *Times Literary Sup-
     plement*, June 27, 1968, 680.

     "It is a pleasure to find a Blake study as good
     as Dr. Beer's.... Since Bernard Blackstone's
     English Blake [item 99] there has been nothing
     published which fills this need so well."

79. Baine, Rodney M. (rev., *Blake's Humanism; Blake and
     Tradition* [item 1096]; *The Letters of William
     Blake* [item 52]). *Georgia Review*, XXIV (1970),
     38-45.

     Beer has not aligned himself with any of the
     predominant schools of Blake interpretation.
     Raine's work is irritating because it implies we
     cannot read Blake unless we know her obscure
     sources. Keynes corrects Blake's punctuation.

80. Bottrall, Margaret. (rev., *Blake's Humanism*). *Critical
     Quarterly*, X (1968), 400.

     "The significance of his symbols does not re-
     main constant, because he was forever exploring
     the possibilities of human achievement...." Beer
     is a non-aligned critic.

81. Hirst, Desiree. (rev., *Blake's Humanism*). *Blake
     Studies*, I (1967), 98-101.

     Hirst is a Neoplatonist and Beer definitely
     points out his "freedom" from such prejudices.
     The review follows accordingly.

82. Taylor, Clyde. (rev., *Blake's Humanism*). *Criticism*,
     XI (1969), 100-101.

     "The book's failure to crystallize for the
     reader a whole view of Blake is perhaps related
     to its author's feeling that Blake's vision is
     itself not a whole one."

83. Beer, John. *Blake's Visionary Universe*. Manchester:
     Manchester University Press; New York: Barnes & Noble,
     1969.

     A disjointed assessment of "Blake's visionary universe,"
     as undefined a term as his "Blake's humanism." This is
     neither a good introduction nor a careful analysis. Ameri-
     can critics have not been satisfied by Beer's attempts
     here and in *Blake's Humanism* (item 76) to make Blake
     indisputably comprehensible.

84. Baine, Rodney M. (rev., *Blake's Visionary Universe;
     Blake Records* [item 10]; *Blake: Prophet Against
     Empire* [item 130]; *Blake's Apocalypse* [item 101];
     Energy and the Imagination [item 229]). *Georgia
     Review*, XXIX (1971), 238-241.

     Beer's work is well balanced and can be used
     if Blake and Frye are heavy reading. Bentley's
     book is the most important of the year. Erdman's
     book is not well revised. Paley's is thorough.

85. Bottrall, M. (rev., *Blake's Visionary Universe*).
     Critical Quarterly, XII (1970), 286-287.

     "In the first [*Blake's Humanism*, item 76] our
     attention is particularly focused on the earlier
     writings, which manifest so powerfully Blake's
     concern for social justice, and for political and
     personal freedom. In the second [*Blake's Visionary
     Universe*] Blake's mythmaking is the central topic...."

86. Chayes, Irene H. (rev., *Blake's Visionary Universe*).
     Blake Newsletter, IV (1971), 87-90.

     A close attack on "Beer's way of looking at
     Blake's pictures ...," citing specifics. "... a
     literate new reader who previously had only glanced
     at the poems undoubtedly would gain enlightenment
     from Beer's commentary...."

87. John, Brian. (rev., *Blake's Visionary Universe*).
     Blake Studies, IV (1971), 107-110.

     "'The elusive visionary dimension' Beer finds
     lacking in *Poetical Sketches* sometimes eludes him
     in his own study of the Prophetic Books, and one
     needs to supplement this work with reference to
     other Blake criticism."

88. Scott, R.E. (rev., *Blake's Visionary Universe*).
Library Journal, XCV (1970), 1370.

"All the chapters are good and the ones on the
prophetic books superb."

89. Stevenson, W.H. (rev., *Blake's Visionary Universe*).
Durham University Journal, New Series, XXXII
(1970), 74-75.

Unsuccessful attempts to disentangle and to
clarify. "It is difficult to be sure what Blake's
'visionary universe' actually consisted of."

90. Tolley, Michael J. "A Superficial Vision." *Southern
Review* (Adelaide), IV (1971), 242-246.

This is really a review of John Beer's *Visionary
Universe*, which Tolley believes to be a hastily
published work which testifies to the low level
of British Blake scholarship.

91. Beer, John. "Blake, Mr. Tolley and the Scholarly Imagination." *Southern Review* (Adelaide), IV (1971), 247-255.

Tolley exhibited a noticeable lack of scholarly imagination in his review of *Blake's Visionary Universe* (see
item 90).

92. Bentley, G.E., ed. *William Blake: The Critical Heritage*.
London and Boston: Routledge & Kegan Paul, 1975.

93. Hoover, Suzanne R. (rev., *William Blake: The Critical
Heritage*). *Blake Newsletter*, X (1976-77), 89-90.

Three-fourths of the material here has appeared
in *Blake Records* (item 10). The introduction is
from the essay "Blake's Reputation and Interpreters."

94. Bentley, G.E. "William Blake's Protean Text." *Editing
Eighteenth Century Texts*. Edited by D.I.B. Smith.
Toronto: University of Toronto Press, 1968, 44-58.

Some of the special problems that the textual critic
of Blake encounters.

95. Bernbaum, Ernest. "William Blake." *Anthology and Guide
Through the Romantic Movement*. New York: Ronald Press,
1949.

An outdated, superficial guide.

96. Bindman, David. *Blake as an Artist*. Oxford: Phaidon; New
     York: E.P. Dutton, 1977.

     Attempts to take "an analytical view of Blake's art
     with particular emphasis upon its relationship to English
     art of his own time...."

97. Hagstrum, Jean H. (rev., *Blake as an Artist*). *Blake:
     An Illustrated Quarterly*, XII (1978), 64-67.

     "The author has ... given us not so much a new
     work of intellectual synthesis or of scholarship
     as another introduction to Blake's chief works
     with incidental comments on their personal and
     traditional contexts."

98. Spurling, John. (rev., *Blake as an Artist*). *New
     Statesman*, Nov. 18, 1977, 698.

     Scholarly, well written, but with sadly inade-
     quate illustrations.

99. Blackstone, Bernard. *English Blake*. Hamden, Conn.:
     Archon, 1949; rpt. 1966.

     Blackstone is very good at providing a readable proposal
     regarding Blake's cosmogony and theogony, and although
     much has been done in Blake scholarship and criticism
     since this work was written, it remains a good introduc-
     tion.

100. Clarke, Austin. (rev., *English Blake*). *Spectator*,
      CLXXXII (1949), 520.

      "Despite his belief that Blake was above all
      vulgar error, Dr. Blackstone can be a shrewd
      critic."

101. Bloom, Harold. *Blake's Apocalypse: A Study in Poetic
      Argument*. Ithaca, N.Y.: Cornell University Press,
      1963; rpt. 1970.

      Bloom runs through the poems almost line by line, in-
      terpreting, tying together and generally acting as a fine
      guide through the Blake text. He quotes lines continu-
      ously with the confidence that they are worthy of the
      reader's attention--at least as worthy as his commentary.

102. Erdman, D.V. (rev., *Blake's Apocalypse*). *Philological
      Quarterly*, XLIII (1964), 448.

      "... a helpful vade mecum for all of us...."

103. Grant, John E. "Blake on Blooms-day" (rev., *Blake's Apocalypse*). *Yale Review*, LII (1963), 591-598.

"Despite some shortcomings, it should immediately be recognized as the standard book-length introduction to Blake's poetry, at least for serious readers who wish to study all of Blake's work."

104. Rose, Edward J. (rev., *Blake's Apocalypse*). *Western Humanities Review*, XXV (1971), 362.

"All in all, *Blake's Apocalypse* is a book written in the right spirit. It benefits from Professor Bloom's ability to establish an essentially sound context that includes a sympathetically true feeling for Romanticism."

105. Bloom, Harold. "William Blake." *The Visionary Company: A Reading of English Romantic Poetry*. New York, 1961; Garden City, N.Y.: Doubleday, 1963; Ithaca, N.Y., & London: Cornell, 1971.

Argues that Blake, like Keats, Byron, Shelley, Wordsworth and Coleridge, held that the theory of poetry is the theory of life. Discusses "Ode on the Poetical Character" as an introduction to the world in which Blake was born. Certainly a fine introductory section on Blake.

106. Bottrall, Margaret, ed. *William Blake: Songs of Innocence and Experience: A Casebook*. London: Macmillan, 1970.

Part Four: Recent Studies:
Wolf Mankowitz, "William Blake: *The Songs of Experience*"
C.M. Bowra, "Songs of Innocence and Experience"
Northrop Frye, "Blake After Two Centuries" (item 154)
Robert Gleckner, "Point of View and Context in Blake's Songs" (item 1672)
Martin K. Nurmi, "Blake's Revisions of 'The Tyger'" (item 1680)

107. Bronowski, Jacob. "A Prophet for Our Age: William Blake, 1757-1827." *Nation*, CLXXXV (1957), 407-411.

A good introduction written at the bicentenary of Blake's birth. "The likeness between our dilemma and that of Blake's time derives certainly from the changes set in motion by the development of machines in factories."

108. Bronowski, Jacob. *William Blake and the Age of Revolu-
     tion*. New York: Harper and Row, 1969. (c.1965; original-
     ly *William Blake: A Man Without a Mask*, 1944.)

     Like Erdman's *Blake: Prophet Against Empire* (item 130),
     this work attempts to place Blake in his own time, within
     a political, cultural and social framework. It is Bronow-
     ski's thesis that Blake couched his revolutionary message
     in esoteric symbolism in order to avoid the repercussions
     that he recognized only too well.

109. Cutler, Edward J. (rev., *William Blake and the Age
     of Revolution*). *Library Journal*, XC (1965), 3452.

     "Dr. Bronowski, combining a wide knowledge of
     history and economics with an equally impressive
     grasp of the Blake canon, first shows how the
     economic history of the times can be seen as
     the direct inspiration for many of Blake's meta-
     phors and then demonstrates the very real harm
     suffered by those of his contemporaries who made
     their criticism of the establishment too explicit."

110. Ward, Aileen. (rev., *William Blake and the Age of
     Revolution*). *Book Week*, Jan. 23, 1966, 4.

     "Bronowski is perhaps too impatient with Blake's
     later work; he sees Blake's development of a
     system of symbols as merely obscuring what he
     was trying to say through them, which was essen-
     tially a protest against the other systems of
     his time."

111. Bronowski, Jacob. "The Mystical Quest of William Blake."
     Literary Guide, LXIX (1954), 4-7.

     General, introductory but not superficial.

112. See item 107.

113. Buckley, Vincent. "Blake's Originality." *Melbourne
     Critical Review*, VII (1964), 3-21.

     The "system" people have ignored the originality of
     the poetry—*Songs of Experience* most notably.

114. Bullett, Gerald. "Blake." *The English Mystics*. London:
     Michael Joseph, 1950, 161-185.

     "Blake is the most thorough-going of all English
     mystics. For him the whole universe is a complex imagina-
     tive act."

115. See item 117.

116. See item 117a.

117. Clark, Kenneth. "Blake." *The Romantic Rebellion*. New
      York: Harper & Row, 1973, 147-176. Also published as
      Blake and Visionary Art (University of Glasgow Press,
      1973).

      Blake's system is a good muddle and Blake himself
      recognized Dante's superiority and therefore illustrated
      him well. Clark hasn't made much effort to come to terms
      with Blake.

      117a. Hagstrum, Jean H. (rev., *Blake and Visionary Art*
            [see item 117]; *The Romantic Rebellion*; *British
            Romantic Art*). *Blake Newsletter*, VIII (1975),
            143-144.

            Clark can go just so far with Blake since he
            considers Blake's thought a muddle. Lister's
            work contains many positive aspects.

118. Curran, Stuart, and Joseph A. Wittreich, eds. *Blake's
      Sublime Allegory: Essays on "The Four Zoas," "Milton,"
      and "Jerusalem."* Madison: University of Wisconsin
      Press, 1973.

      Jerome J. McGann, "The Aim of Blake's Prophecies and
      the Uses of Blake Criticism" (item 211)
      Joseph A. Wittreich, "Opening the Seals: Blake's Epics
      and the Milton Tradition" (item 1155)
      Ronald L. Grimes, "Time and Space in Blake's Major
      Prophecies" (item 465)
      Edward J. Rose, "Los, Pilgrim of Eternity" (item 543)
      Jean H. Hagstrum, "Babylon Revisited, or the Story
      of Luvah and Vala" (item 1673)
      Morton D. Paley, "The Figure of the Garment in *The
      Four Zoas, Milton*, and *Jerusalem*" (item 522)
      John E. Grant, "Visions in Vala: A Consideration of
      Some Pictures in the Manuscript" (item 1342)
      Mary Lynn Johnson and Brian Wilkie, "On Reading *The
      Four Zoas*: Inscape and Analogy" (item 1346)
      Irene Tayler, "Say First! What Mov'd Blake? Blake's
      Comus Designs and *Milton*" (item 1482)
      James Rieger, "The Hem of Their Garments: The Bard's
      Song in *Milton*" (item 1478)
      W.J.T. Mitchell, "Blake's Radical Comedy: Dramatic
      Structure as Meaning in *Milton*" (item 1475)

Roger R. Easson, "William Blake and His Reader in *Jerusalem*" (item 1382)
Stuart Curran, "The Structures of *Jerusalem*" (item 1377)
Karl Kroeber, "Delivering *Jerusalem*" (item 1397)

119. Adams, Hazard. (rev., *Blake's Sublime Allegory*). *Blake Newsletter*, VII (1973-74), 69-72.

The collection is not impressive. Close readings of the prophecies and an emphasis on the composite art.

120. Anon. (rev., *Blake's Sublime Allegory*). *Choice*, X (1974), 1715.

"... it reads as a unity, having sequence, continuity, and a cumulative effect."

121. Dorfman, Deborah. (rev., *Blake's Sublime Allegory*). *Philological Quarterly*, LIII (1974), 641-643.

"Represented here are the jargons of phenomenology, linguistics, structural anthropology, theology, radical politics, psychoanalysis, and analytical psychology, to name a handful."

122. Faulkner, Dewey. (rev., *Blake's Sublime Allegory*). *Yale Review*, LXIII (1974), 590-599.

"... there is enough 'darkness visible' in this volume to assure [Blake's] Satan that his dominion is indeed at hand."

123. Stevenson, W.H. (rev., *Blake's Sublime Allegory*). *Blake Studies*, VI (1976), 188-192.

A casual conglomeration in need of more organization. Vala's designs are discussed but not *Milton*'s or *Jerusalem*'s. Two authors interpret the same lines without referring to each other.

124. Daugherty, James. *William Blake*. New York: Viking Press, 1960. 128pp.

This book is directed to very young children.

125. Davies, Hugh S., ed. "Blake." *The Poets and Their Critics*. London: Hutchinson, 1962.

Excerpts from Blake's critics.

126. Drake, Constance M. "An Approach to Blake." *College
      English*, XXX (1968), 541-547.

      "... if the teacher and the student go to his work for
      an understanding of a poem and not a man or a system,
      then they will receive an emotional and intellectual
      experience."

127. Dumbaugh, Winnifred. *William Blake's Vision of America.*
      Pacific Grove, Calif.: Boxwood Press, 1971.

      Less said the better.

128. Edwards, Thomas. "The Revolutionary Imagination."
      *Imagination and Power: A Study of Poetry on Public
      Themes.* New York: Oxford University Press, 1971, 140-
      184.

      Blake's "system itself, as distinct from the feelings
      and insights it brings together, has too much of the
      improvisational and arbitrary about it to be as impres-
      sive as some modern exegesis makes it seem." Discussion
      of "London" and "The Human Abstract."

129. Erdman, David V. "Blake: The Historical Approach."
      Discussions of William Blake (item 182), 17-27.

      "The aim of the historical approach is to approximate
      Blake's own perspective, to locate, as nearly as we
      can, the moment and place in which he stood, to discover
      what he saw and heard in London's streets...."

130. Erdman, David V. *Blake: Prophet Against Empire.* Prince-
      ton: Princeton University Press, 1954; revised edi-
      tion, New York: Anchor, 1969. 546pp.

      Blake's thought and art in relation to the history
      of his own times. Develops the thesis that Blake's ob-
      scurantism was a radical's act of self-protection. The
      political rather than the visionary Blake is percep-
      tively presented here, although Erdman does not deny
      that these are "visionary politics."

     131. Anon. "Blake's Composite Art" (rev., *Blake:
           Prophet Against Empire; Blake Studies* [item
           197]; *Life of William Blake* [item 351]; *Blake:
           The Artist*; *Blake's Illustrations to the Poems
           of Gray* [item 912]; *Blake and Tradition* [item
           1096]; *Blake's Visionary Forms Dramatic* [item
           139]; *Energy and Imagination* [item 229]; *The*

Poems of William Blake). *Times Literary Supplement*, Dec. 10, 1971, 1537-1539.

Erdman's book is updated and so are Keynes's and Wilson's. Todd's book is "a handbook in the form of a factual year-by-year account of Blake's production, not attempting to interpret his work but describing Blake's special techniques in detail." Tayler "defines Blake's ... approach to illustration as one of vigorous critical reinterpretation." Raine subsumes the composite art within her thesis. Erdman and Grant have produced an excellent collection, and Paley's book is illuminating.

132. Beach, Joseph W. "Blake the Seer as Artist and Poet" (rev., *Blake: Prophet Against Empire*). *Sewanee Review*, LXII (1954), 527-534.

Erdman's is a volume "that must at once take its place as one of the most acute and reliable studies of Blake's allegory in his historical and 'prophetic' poems and *the* one most thorough study of this allegory in its political bearings."

133. Chayes, Irene. (rev., *Blake: Prophet Against Empire*). *ELN*, VIII (1970), 22.

A review of the 1969 revision in which most revisions are in the footnotes. "... still an unsurpassed account of the historical background...."

134. Frye, Northrop. (rev., *Blake: Prophet Against Empire*). *Philological Quarterly*, XXXIV (1955), 273-274.

"Mr. Erdman's book is almost a social history of England between 1760 and 1820, as seen from Blake's point of view."

135. Grant, John E. (rev., *Blake: Prophet Against Empire*). *Philological Quarterly*, L (1971), 407-408.

"It is not too much to say that no one should try to publish anything on Blake without having first studied this book."

136. Joost, Nicholas. (rev., *Blake: Prophet Against
      Empire*). *Poetry*, LXXXIV (1954), 364-365.

      "It is, of course, primarily a lengthy and
      detailed treatise for scholars and students of
      Blake's writing, and understandably it demands
      an intimate knowledge of that writing."

137. Rose, Edward J. (rev., *Blake: Prophet Against
      Empire*). *Blake Newsletter*, IV (1970), 48-49.

      "Were I asked to defend historical criticism,
      I should cite *Blake: Prophet Against Empire* as
      the best example of that kind of criticism I
      could name...."

138. Erdman, David V. "The Bravery of William Blake." *Blake
      Newsletter*, X (1976), 27-31.

      This is the introduction to the Signet Classic edition
      of *The Selected Poetry of Blake*, edited by Erdman.

139. Erdman, David V., and John E. Grant, eds. *Blake's Vision-
      ary Forms Dramatic*. Princeton: Princeton University
      Press, 1970.

      Martha W. England, "Apprenticeship at the Haymarket?"
      (item 1670)
      William F. Halloran, "*The French Revolution*: Revela-
      tion's New Form" (item 1367)
      W.J.T. Mitchell, "Blake's Composite Art" (item 889)
      Jean H. Hagstrum, "Blake and the Sister-Arts Tradi-
      tion" (item 843)
      David V. Erdman, "*America*: New Expanses" (item 1294)
      Michael J. Tolley, "*Europe*: 'to those ychain'd in
      sleep'" (item 1333)
      Robert E. Simmons, "*Urizen*: The Symmetry of Fear"
      (item 1322)
      Janet A. Warner, "Blake's Use of Gesture" (item 570)
      Eban Bass, "*Songs of Innocence and of Experience*:
      The Thrust of Design" (item 1532)
      Irene H. Chayes, "The Presence of Cupid and Psyche"
      (item 980)
      John Sutherland, "Blake and Urizen" (item 559)
      George Quasha, "Orc as a Fiery Paradigm of Poetic
      Torsion" (item 529)
      Irene Tayler, "Metamorphoses of a Favorite Cat" (item
      915)
      John E. Grant, "Envisioning the First *Night Thoughts*"
      (item 832)

Ben F. Nelms, "Text and Design in *Illustrations of the Book of Job*" (item 894)

Brian Wilkie, "Epic Irony in *Milton*" (item 1486)

Helen T. McNeil, "The Formal Art of *The Four Zoas*" (item 1354)

Henry G. Lesnick, "Narrative Structure and the Antithetical Vision of *Jerusalem*" (item 1399)

Kenneth R. Johnston, "Blake's Cities: Romantic Forms of Urban Renewal" (item 486)

Edward J. Rose, "'Forms Eternal Exist For-ever': The Covenant of the Harvest in Blake's Prophetic Poems" (item 538)

140. Blunt, Anthony. "Blakomania" (rev., *Blake's Visionary Forms Dramatic*; *Blake's Illustrations to the Poems of Gray* [item 912]). *Yale Review*, LXI (1971), 301-306.

The essays in Erdman-Grant conflict and no attempt is made by the contributors to reconcile or even acknowledge the divergent opinions of fellow contributors. Tayler's treatment of the illustrations is sensitive and perceptive.

141. Hirst, Desiree. (rev., *Blake's Visionary Forms Dramatic*; *Blake Studies* [item 197]). *Review of English Studies*, XXIV (1973), 95-99.

The Erdman-Grant collection is generally unsatisfactory since one poem is read in terms of another, scarcely any of the contributors know the language of Blake's symbolism (Hirst means Neoplatonic symbolism), and the heavy, technical Americanese is tiresome. Keynes's bibliographical labors have resulted in Blake's popularity, although he is popular in "hippie" circles for reasons other than bibliographical efforts on the part of Sir Geoffrey.

142. Paley, Morton. (rev., *Blake's Visionary Forms Dramatic*). *Blake Studies*, IV (1971), 93-99.

"... one of the major events of recent Blake criticism."

143. Essick, Robert N. "*Preludium*: Meditations on a Fiery Pegasus." *Blake in His Time* (item 149), 1-10.

Describes the art historical approach to Blake and the literary approach to Blake. Frye's approach is "toward a synchronic model wherein every work is part of a great, co-existing *corpus*." The art historian is aware of formal qualities while the literary scholar looks for meaning, iconography, in art. Cites the "verbal bias" of the literary scholars.

144. Essick, Robert N., ed. *The Visionary Hand: Essays for the Study of William Blake's Art and Aesthetics*. Los Angeles: Hennessey & Ingalls, 1973.

Laurence Binyon, "The Engravings of William Blake and Edward Calvert"
Anthony Blunt, "Blake's 'Ancient of Days': The Symbolism of the Compasses"
Allan R. Brown, "Blake's Drawings for the *Book of Enoch*"
C.H. Collins Baker, "The Sources of Blake's Pictorial Expression"
Piloo Nanavutty, "A Title Page in Blake's Illustrated Genesis Manuscript" (item 1679)
Northrop Frye, "Poetry and Design in William Blake" (item 825)
David V. Erdman, "The Dating of William Blake's Engravings" (item 805)
Hazard Adams, "The Blakean Aesthetic" (item 405)
Albert S. Roe, "A Drawing of the Last Judgment" (item 1681)
W. Moelwyn Merchant, "Blake's Shakespeare" (item 887)
Joseph Burke, "The Eidetic and the Borrowed Image: An Interpretation of Blake's Theory and Practice of Art" (item 1668)
Martin Butlin, "Blake's 'God Judging Adam' Rediscovered" (item 792)
Edward J. Rose, "'A Most Outrageous Demon': Blake's Case Against Rubens" (item 542)
W.J.T. Mitchell, "Poetic and Pictorial Imagination in Blake's *The Book of Urizen*" (item 1678)
Thomas H. Helmstadter, "Blake's *Night Thoughts*: Interpretations of Edward Young" (item 855)
John E. Grant, "Blake's Designs for *L'Allegro* and *Il Penseroso*" (item 837)
Judith Rhodes, "Blake's Designs for *L'Allegro* and *Il Penseroso*: Thematic Relationships in Diagram" (item 903)
Robert E. Simmons and Janet Warner, "Blake's 'Arlington Court Picture': The Moment of Truth" (item 908)

John E. Grant, "Redemptive Action in Blake's 'Arlington Court Picture'" (item 838)
Robert N. Essick, "Blake and the Traditions of Reproductive Engraving" (item 812)
Jenijoy LaBelle, "Words Graven with an Iron Pen: The Marginal Texts in Blake's *Job*" (item 1677)

145. Erdman, D.V. (rev., *The Visionary Hand*). *ELN*, XII (1974), 32.

Well edited but still a collection of reprints.

146. Minnick, Thomas L. (rev., *The Visionary Hand*). *Blake Newsletter*, VIII (1975), 130-132.

Attempts to redress the long neglect of Blake's art.

147. Welch, Dennis. (rev., *The Visionary Hand*). *Philological Quarterly*, LIII (1974), 646-647.

"While Essick's book reflects some indiscretion in its construction, it is nevertheless useful, and indispensable to every Blakean's library."

148. Wilkie, Brian. (rev., *The Visionary Hand*). *Blake Studies*, VI (1974), 204-208.

Chief value of this book is "to illustrate the variety of avenues one can take in approaching Blake's pictorial art...." The most prevalent approach is the iconographical, in which pictorial images are suspected of being symbols comprising some system.

149. Essick, Robert N., and Donald Pearce. *Blake in His Time*. Bloomington: Indiana University Press, 1978.

Hazard Adams, "Revisiting Reynolds's *Discourses* and Blake's Annotations" (item 265)
Bentley, G.E., Jr. "A Jewel in an Ethiop's Ear" (item 965)
Easson, Roger R. "Blake and the Gothic" (item 996)
Essick, Robert N. "*Preludium*: Meditations on a Fiery Pegasus" (item 143)
David Bindman, "Blake's Theory and Practice of Imitation" (item 968)
Anne K. Mellor, "Physiognomy, Phrenology, and Blake's Visionary Heads" (item 1067)

Joseph A. Wittreich, Jr., "Painted Prophecies: The
Tradition of Blake's Illuminated Books" (item 646)
Jean H. Hagstrum, "Romney and Blake: Gifts of Grace
and Terror" (item 1022)
Edward J. Rose, "The 'Gothicized Imagination' of
'Michelangelo Blake'" (item 1264)
Morton D. Paley, "'Wonderful Originals'--Blake and
Ancient Sculpture" (item 897)
Kay P. Easson, "Blake and the Art of the Book" (item
800)
Jenijoy LaBelle, "Blake's Visions and Re-Visions of
Michelangelo" (item 874)
Leslie Tannenbaum, "Blake and the Iconography of Cain"
(item 911)
Yvonne M. Carothers, "Space and Time in *Milton*: The
'Bard's Song'" (item 1459)

150. Ward, Aileen. (rev., *Blake in His Time*). *Words-
      worth Circle*, XI (1980), 160-162.

      The essays that succeed "are those that eschew
      flights of analogical or exegetical fancy and
      keep to the editorial program of relating Blake's
      visionary forms, both visual and verbal, to the
      minute particulars of his artistic and intellec-
      tual milieu."

151. Fairchild, B.H. *Such Holy Song: Music as Idea, Form,
      and Image in the Poetry of William Blake*. Kent, Ohio:
      Kent State University Press, 1980. See item 682.

      "... music--as idea, form or image--had in the *Songs*
      and the *Four Zoas*, as well as other poems, a central
      role in restoring the Golden Age to mankind, of carrying
      it through innocence and experience to a vision of
      apocalypse."

152. Fairchild, H.N. "Blake." Chap. III of *Religious Trends
      in English Poetry*. Vol III: 1780-1830. *Romantic Faith*.
      New York: Columbia University Press, 1949, 66-137.

      Points out the many contradictions in Blake's reli-
      gious views and attributes them to his failure to "think
      and even feel coherently on religious questions...."
      Blake is a worshipper of Jesus while at the same time a
      pantheist. Blake's Christianity is "a new firm trading
      under the old name."

153. Frye, Northrop. "Reflections in a Mirror." *Northrop Frye in Modern Criticism*. Edited by Murray Krieger. New York: Columbia University Press, 1966, 135-136.

    Some comments from Frye which relate to his "start" with Blake criticism.

154. Frye, Northrop. "Blake After Two Centuries." *English Romantic Poets: Modern Essays in Criticism*. New York: Oxford University Press, 1975.

    A good introduction to various reactions to Blake. An assortment of comments that any student would find interesting.

155. Frye, Northrop, ed. *Blake: A Collection of Critical Essays*. Englewood Cliffs, N.J.: Prentice-Hall, 1965.

    William J. Keith, "The Complexities of Blake's 'Sunflower': An Archetypal Speculation" (item 1049)
    Northrop Frye, "Blake's Introduction to Experience" (item 1563)
    Northrop Frye, "Poetry and Design in William Blake" (item 825)
    Irene Chayes, "Plato's *Statesman* Myth in Shelley and Blake" (item 979)
    Robert Gleckner, "Point of View and Context in Blake's Songs" (item 1672)
    Jean H. Hagstrum, "William Blake Rejects the Enlightenment" (item 1021)
    Martin Nurmi, "Fact and Symbol in 'The Chimney Sweeper' of Blake's *Songs of Innocence*" (item 1609)
    Hazard Adams, "'The Crystal Cabinet' and 'The Golden Net'" (item 1498)
    Harold Bloom, "States of Being: *The Four Zoas*" (item 1338)
    Anthony Blunt, "The First Illuminated Books" (chap. 4 of item 782)
    David V. Erdman, "Blake's Vision of Slavery" (item 1660)

156. Feldman, Burton. (rev., *Blake: A Collection of Critical Essays*). *Denver Quarterly*, I (1966), 155-156.

    Notes that most of the essays are reprints. Good collection. Frye's conclusions regarding the homogeneity of Blake's opinions may be appropriate only in regard to these Frye-selected essays.

157. Frye, Northrop. *Fearful Symmetry: A Study of William Blake*. Princeton: Princeton University Press, 1947, 1949, 1958, 1969; Boston: Beacon, 1962, 1965, 1967.

In attempting to unravel all of Blake's symbolism in this impressive work, Frye discovered what he considers to be various archetypal motifs, the Orc cycle, for example, which appear throughout literature. Thus, contemporary archetypal criticism has its origin in this Blake study. In regard to Blake scholarship, Frye held that Blake's vision was one throughout his career. His opening chapter on the eighteenth-century background is essential reading for all students of Blake.

158. Ames, Alfred C. "Escaping Selfhood" (rev., *Fearful Symmetry*). *Poetry*, LXXI (1947), 101-103.

"Frye, as no other before him, develops Blake as a typical poet; he intends his book to be not only a vade mecum for the students of Blake, but for the larger body of the students of poetry."

159. Frankenberg, Lloyd. (rev., *Fearful Symmetry*). *Saturday Review of Literature*, XXX (1947), 19.

"This is perhaps the height of discipleship."

160. McLuhan, Herbert M. "Inside Blake and Hollywood." (rev., *Fearful Symmetry*). *Sewanee Review*, LV (1947), 710-713.

"... Blake was not so much concerned with the visual and dramatic character of his imagery as with its intellectual meaning. So that reading Professor Frye is a more satisfactory thing for most of Blake than reading Blake himself...."

161. Sitwell, Edith. (rev., *Fearful Symmetry*). *Spectator*, CLXXIX (1947), 466.

"... this book, I believe, is the first to show the full magnitude of Blake's mind, its vast creative thought."

162. Frye, Northrop. "Blake's Treatment of the Archetype." *Discussions of William Blake* (item 182), 6-16.

What emerged from Blake, "one of the hottest poetic crucibles of modern times," was a poetry which consisted almost entirely of the articulation of archetypes.

163. Gardner, Stanley. *Blake*. New York: Arco, 1969. 160pp.

Confined to the poetry before 1794 and a continuation of Gardner's search for symbolism rather than myth in the lyrics. The Arco series claims to be straightforward, by which they apparently mean reductivist.

164. Harding, D.W. (rev., *Blake*). *Notes and Queries*, XVII (1970), 120.

Much to be modified and questioned here but perhaps little to be completely discarded.

165. Johnson, Mary Lynn. (rev., *Blake*). *Blake Studies*, III (1970), 94-98.

"Gardner dismisses the illuminations as secondary and inessential to the meaning of the poetry and almost completely ignores anything written after 1794."

166. Gardner, Stanley. *Infinity on the Anvil: A Critical Study of Blake's Poetry*. Oxford: Basil Blackwell, 1954. 160pp.

Concerned with Blake's symbolism, which he argues is most vigorously presented in his poetry, the lyrics, and not in the illustrations. Gardner feels Blake did nothing of poetic relevance after the *Book of Urizen*. The later works may have some interest to philosophers and psychologists.

167. Gaunt, William. *Arrows of Desire: A Study of William Blake and His Romantic World*. London: Museum Press Ltd., 1956. 299pp.

Blake is off-stage in this book, and the stage is set for historical milieu, though nothing really comes together. Very light on Blake's work itself.

168. Gillham, D.G. *Blake's Contrary States: The Songs of Innocence and of Experience as Dramatic Poems*. Cambridge: Cambridge University Press, 1966.

Treats the *Songs* divorced from later work—and thus postulates, questions or otherwise remains silent on matters elucidated by such references.

169. Bottrall, Margaret. (rev., *Blake's Contrary States*). *Critical Quarterly*, IX (1967), 189-190.

This work can "only be sustained by a determined disregard of literary and bibliographical evidence."

170. Davies, J.G. (rev., *Blake's Contrary States*). *Modern Language Review*, LXIII (1968), 206-207.

Maintains that this work is superior to Gleckner's (who tried to fit the poetry into a rigid system), Hirsch's, Gardner's and Wicksteed's.

171. Grant, John E. (rev., *Blake's Contrary States*). *Philological Quarterly*, XLV (1967), 329-330.

"As a scholarly book this is incompetent.... On one hand Gillham admits that the *Songs* must be read together for the light they shed on one another, but on the other he excoriates interpretations of them made in the light of Blake's prophecies because they become 'crushed beneath the weight of exegesis they cannot bear.'"

172. Griffin, Robert J. (rev., *Blake's Contrary States*). *Yale Review*, LVI (1967), 578-580.

Gillham, Hirsch and Gleckner have all published full-length works on the *Songs*, and they all believe that the *Songs* are the only Blake works susceptible to such study.

173. Nurmi, Martin K. (rev., *Blake's Contrary States*). *Journal of English and Germanic Philology*, LXVII (1968), 314-316.

Nurmi attacks Gillham's notion that Blake wrought well with the *Songs* but gave up the lyric gift to write incomprehensible prophecies.

174. Ure, Peter. (rev., *Blake's Contrary States*). *Review of English Studies*, XIX (1968), 83-85.

"One cannot help wondering what Blake would have made of emunctae nares of this kind, and of the attribution to him of poetical intentions which seem to lie so far outside the probable range of his idea about the character and function of poetry."

175. Gillham, D.G. *William Blake*. Cambridge: Cambridge University Press, 1974.

Intended as an introduction for the layman, this work is a lopsided appreciation of Blake. The *Songs* are Blake's masterwork while the later books are obvious failures.

176. Anon. (rev., *William Blake*). *Times Literary Supplement*, May 18, 1973, 1100.

> "He plays the well-worn game of quoting one or two of the least satisfactory passages from the Prophetic Books, along with some of the less illuminating comments of later critics, in order to persuade the reader that he need not bother with them at all...."

177. Ault, Donald. (rev., *William Blake*). *Philological Quarterly*, LIII (1974), 647-648.

> "... this book is a falsification of Blake in fundamental ways and should be recognized as such."

178. Luedtke, Luther. (rev., *William Blake*). *Blake Studies*, VI (1973), 98-103.

> Very much based on Gillham's *Blake's Contrary States* (item 168) but may encourage a reader to pursue independently the later works, despite Gillham's view of their irrelevance.

179. Ostriker, A. (rev., *William Blake*). *Blake Newsletter*, VIII (1975), 136-137.

> Believes Gillham is a horse of instruction who turns Blake and his work into horses of instruction.

180. Gleckner, Robert. *The Piper and the Bard*. Detroit: Wayne State University Press, 1959.

The *Songs* plus *Tiriel*, *Thel*, the *Marriage* and *Visions* are viewed by Gleckner as "the key elements of an organic and ever-developing 'system' that began with the seeds of innocence and resulted finally in the prophetic books." Close readings of the poems, paying particular attention to the identity of various speakers in the poems.

181. Rose, E.J. (rev., *The Piper and the Bard*). *Dalhousie Review*, XL (1960), 405-407.

> "Although the author is generally reliable,
> there are some serious misreadings of Blake's
> symbolism.... However, the book may prove valuable
> to those who are basically unfamiliar with Blake
> but feel the need to know a few things about his
> work beyond the usual platitudes of the antholo-
> gies."

182. Grant, John E., ed. *Discussions of William Blake*. Boston:
      Heath, 1961.

      Northrop Frye, "Blake's Treatment of the Archetype"
      (item 162)
      David V. Erdman, "Blake: The Historical Approach"
      (item 129)
      Peter F. Fisher, "Blake and the Druids" (item 1004)
      Northrop Frye, "Poetry and Design in William Blake"
      (item 825)
      Hazard Adams, "Reading Blake's Lyrics: 'The Tyger'"
      (item 1520)
      John E. Grant, "The Art and Argument of 'The Tyger'"
      (item 1575)
      Mark Van Doren, "On 'The Little Black Boy'" (item
      1643)
      John H. Sutherland, "Blake's 'Mental Traveller'" (item
      1506)
      Martin K. Nurmi, "On the *Marriage of Heaven and Hell*"
      (item 1440)
      Karl Kiralis, "A Guide to the Intellectual Symbolism
      in Blake's Later Prophetic Writings" (item 495)

      183. Bentley, G.E. (rev., *Discussions of William Blake*).
            Philological Quarterly, XLI (1962), 658-659.

            Represents some of the best essays of the
            1950s.

184. Harris, Eugenia. *The Poetry of William Blake*. Monarch
      Notes. New York: Monarch Press, 1965.

      This is an accessible work but it is reductive and
      therefore very often, especially in regard to the later
      books, misleading.

185. Harris, R.W. "The New Jerusalem and William Blake."
      Romanticism and the Social Order, 1780-1830. London:
      Blandford Press, 1969.

      This is not really an historical consideration but a
      survey, quick and light, of some of Blake's themes.

186. Hobsbaum, Philip. "The Romantic Dichotomy." *British
      Journal of Aesthetics*, XVI (1976), 32–45.

      "Blake is the archetypal Romantic who let go of a lyric
      gift in favour of didacticism and pseudo-prophecy."

187. Holloway, John. *Blake: The Lyric Poetry*. London: Edward
      Arnold, 1968.

      Relationships between Blake's lyrics and certain
      eighteenth-century traditions of thought and feeling. A
      good introduction to the *Songs*.

   188. Anon. (rev., *Blake: The Lyric Poetry*). *Times
         Literary Supplement*, March 20, 1969, 308.

         "... Mr. Holloway has performed his task with
         full respect for his author."

189. Hume, Robert D. "The Development of Blake's Psychology:
      The Quest for an Understanding of Man's Position in
      the World." *Revue des Langues Vivantes*, XXXV (1969),
      240–258.

      Blake expresses a developing understanding of the
      human condition in each of his prophecies.

190. James, D.G. "The Gospel of Hell." *The Romantic Comedy*.
      London: Oxford University Press, 1948.

      Believes that Blake's mind was confused and this led
      to the disorder in his work. Argues that Blake moved
      from a Christian belief to a naturalistic one. Written
      from a very rigid, though unfathomable, Christian view-
      point.

191. John, Brian. "William Blake: The Poet as Mental Prince."
      Supreme Fictions. Montreal and London: McGill-Queen's
      University Press, 1974, 15–74.

      Blake is in the vitalist tradition and Force is the
      major tenet of this tradition. This vital Force involves
      dialectic, energy, revelation and, frequently, apoca-
      lypse.

   192. Donoghue, Denis. (rev., *Supreme Fictions*). *Modern
         Language Review*, LXXII (1977), 155–156.

         "Throughout the book he takes his main terms
         from Stevens and from the version of Romanticism
         which Stevens defined, but the more earnestly

these terms are enforced, the more unsatisfactory
they appear."

193. Frosch, Thomas. (rev., *Supreme Fictions*). *Philo-
      logical Quarterly*, LIV (1975), 906-907.

      "The movement from Blakean energy and awakening
      to Carlylean Force and Heroism is thus one of
      externalization, and the Blake poem closest, in
      effect, to much of the spirit of Carlyle is 'The
      Tyger,' in which energy and greatness appear out-
      side an awed speaker."

194. Wagenknecht, David. (rev., *Supreme Fictions*). *Blake
      Newsletter*, IX (1975), 55.

      "Neither out far nor in deep."

195. Kettle, Arnold. "William Blake--No Chains." *Mainstream*,
      X (1957), 9-23.

      Interesting Marxist view of Blake the revolutionary.

196. Kettle, Arnold. *William Blake (1757-1827)*. Bletchley,
      Bucks., 1972. Arts: A Second Level Course: The Age of
      Revolution (The Open University), Units 21-22.

      This is really an extended syllabus with commentary.
      Kettle's paraphrasing of certain key statements in the
      Marriage leads the reader by the nose in spite of fre-
      quent disclaimers. Kettle's notion of revolution in re-
      gard to Blake is limited to the early Blake. It is this
      early Blake, the Blake of simple revolutionary change,
      that suits Kettle's intentions, although this leaves
      the reader only partially introduced to Blake.

197. Keynes, Geoffrey. *Blake Studies: Essays on His Life and
      Work*. Oxford: Clarendon Press, 1971.

      The first edition was published by Rupert Hart-Davis
      in 1949. There are twenty-nine essays written by Keynes
      in the 1971 edition. Previous essays were revised. These
      essays are quite varied, but the student will find them
      somewhat remote from basic questions one is likely to
      ask in regard to Blake's work, questions such as, what
      does Blake mean here? Rather, these essays represent
      the interests of a bibliographer trying to establish
      a Blake record that will be useful for future inter-
      preters.

198. Anon. (rev., *Blake Studies*). *Dublin Magazine*,
      XXIV (1949), 66-67.

>   "... everyone of these seventeen essays, con-
>   tributed to *The Times Literary Supplement* and
>   to various other publications during the past
>   forty years, contains matter of the highest in-
>   terest and importance...."

199. Hirst, Desiree. (rev., *Blake Studies*). *Review of
      English Studies*, XXIV (1973), 95-99.

>   Blake's popularity is not due to "hippy circles"
>   but to the bibliographical labors of Sir Geoffrey
>   Keynes.

200. Miner, Paul. (rev., *Blake Studies*). *Blake News-
      letter*, VIII (1975), 122-125.

>   "Sir Geoffrey is the primum mobile for Blake
>   scholars, and the second edition of *Blake Studies*
>   is further evidence that establishes his posi-
>   tion in this domain of scholarship."

201. Klonsky, Milton. *William Blake: The Seer and His Visions*.
     New York: Harmony Books, 1977. 142pp.

The author has attained an understanding of Blake via
an LSD trip. A very attractive book with fine color reproductions. Klonsky's commentary isn't LSD babble, nor
is he a dismissible Blakean zealot with his own personal
revelation of Blake's "message."

202. Spurling, John. (rev., *William Blake: The Seer and
      His Visions*). *New Statesman*, Nov. 18, 1977, 698.

>   "... blossoms into a useful short guide to
>   Blake's half-ludicrous, half-impressive universe."

203. Lea, F.A. *Voices in the Wilderness: From Poetry to
     Prophecy in Britain*. London: Bentham Press, 1975.

A rather disjointed account of Blake as one of the
exposers of the philosophy of "the greatest happiness
of the greatest number."

204. Lindsay, Jack. *William Blake: His Life and Work*. London:
     Constable, 1978; New York: George Braziller, 1979.
     334pp.

Blake struggled to "secularize" millenary religion, using a religious idiom since no other idiom of equal force was available in his day. His ultimate kinship is with the early Marx, though he rivalled Hegel's method with his own "symbolic constructions." This is a very readable biography with a "Foreword" that truly makes a reader want to know more about Blake.

205. Barfoot, C.C. "Current Literature 1978" (rev., *William Blake*). *English Studies*, LX (1979), 770-793.

"... a fully professional job."

206. Lister, Raymond. *William Blake: An Introduction to the Man and His Work*. London: Bell, 1968.

Lister, an artist, provides an interesting perspective.

207. Anon. (rev., *William Blake*). *Times Literary Supplement*, June 27, 1968, 680.

"This book is the fruit of a lifelong familiarity with all that concerns Blake and his circle; except the products of the academic supermarket."

208. Douglas, Dennis. (rev., *William Blake*). *Journal of the Australasian Universities Language and Literature Association*, XXXIII (1970), 126-127.

Unqualified approval.

209. Luddy, T.E. (rev., *William Blake*). *Library Journal*, XCV (1970), 2682.

"Lister's wide artistic experience brings a sensitive responsiveness to his study of the relationship between Blake's poetry and his pictures."

210. Pinto, Vivian de Sola. (rev., *William Blake; A Blake Dictionary* [item 24]; *A Concordance to the Writings of William Blake* [item 35]). *Modern Language Review*, 65 (1970), 153-155.

The *Dictionary* and the *Concordance* can't be denied; the Lister work has some problems, especially as an introduction.

211. McGann, Jerome J. "The Aim of Blake's Prophecies and the Uses of Blake Criticism." *Blake's Sublime Allegory* (item 118), 3-21.

    "To regard Blake's vision of life as an object of study or perception is to transform it into a shadow of death."

212. Malcolmson, Anne. *William Blake: An Introduction.* New York: Harcourt, Brace & World, 1967. 127pp.

    Really a selection of his poetry and art with some very slight commentary and a brief biographical sketch.

213. Margoliouth, Herschel M. *William Blake.* New York: Oxford University Press, 1961; rpt. 1967. 184pp.

    Generally an adequate, brief introduction which unfortunately places Blake in such categories as "The Rebel" and "The Prophet." Adheres to the view that a thorough knowledge of Milton and the Bible is needed in Blake study.

    214. Anon. (rev., *William Blake*). *Dublin Magazine*, XXVI (1951), 61-62.

        "Mr. Margoliouth ... examines simultaneously in the poetry and the pictures ... their subjects, treatment and symbolism."

215. Mitchell, W.J.T. *Blake's Composite Art: A Study of the Illuminated Poetry.* Princeton: Princeton University Press, 1978. 230pp.

    Disagrees with Hagstrum (item 845) regarding Blake's commitment to pictorialism. The principle of *ut pictura poesis* dominated eighteenth-century aesthetics, and Blake had a highly critical attitude toward the notions of the sister arts, notions which included a belief in superficial differences in mediums, similar techniques, and a notion of complementarity, a coupling of the two arts toward one purpose. Chapter One, "Blake's Composite Art," is one of the best introductions available.

    216. Frosch, Thomas. (rev., *Blake's Composite Art*). *Blake: An Illustrated Quarterly*, XIII (1979), 40-48.

        "A formalistic study which would be nicely extended by the use of an external perspective which would treat both an analysis of Blake's

composite art as well as a formalist discussion
of how it is expressed."

217. Muggeridge, Malcolm. "William Blake." *A Third Testament*.
     Boston: Little, Brown, 1976, 85-117.

     A very slight account, probably because it was a tele-
     vision script. Muggeridge wants to see the Christian,
     traditionally spiritual Blake and is willing to ignore
     the ambiguities and complexities.

218. Nathan, Norman. *Prince William B: The Philosophical Con-
     ceptions of William Blake*. The Hague: Mouton, 1975.
     164pp.

     Undocumented tract which attempts to discuss Blake's
     notions of God and Man. "Blake's narratives are set in
     the Times Square of the mind." And so is this book.

219. Nelson, John W. "Blake's Minor Prophecies: A Study of
     the Development of His Major Prophetic Mode." *DAI*,
     XXXI (1970), 3514A (Ohio State University).

     Development of themes and techniques in *America*,
     Europe, *Song of Los*, *Urizen* and *Book of Los*.

220. Nurmi, Martin K. *William Blake*. Kent, Ohio: Kent State
     University Press, 1976. 175pp.

     Does not discuss the art, but provides musical nota-
     tion for some lyrics. One of the better introductions,
     even though it does not consider the composite art.

     221. Erdman, D.V. (rev., *William Blake*). *ELN*, XIV (1976),
          31.

          "Recommendable to beginners."

     222. Zall, Paul. (rev., *William Blake*). *Blake News-
          letter*, IX (1975), 54-55.

          A book for beginners which does not consider
          Blake's art.

223. O'Neill, Judith, ed. *Critics on Blake*. Coral Gables,
     Fla.: University of Miami Press, 1970.

     Mark Schorer, "Blake's Imagery" (excerpt from item
     1682)
     Northrop Frye, "Blake's Treatment of the Archetype"
     (item 162)

David V. Erdman, "Infinite London: *The Songs of Experience* in Their Historical Setting" (excerpt from item 130)

John H. Sutherland, "Blake's 'Mental Traveller'" (item 1506)

Robert Gleckner, "Irony in Blake's 'Holy Thursday'" (item 1569)

George W. Digby, "Blake's Art: *Images of Wonder*" (excerpt from item 1669)

Anthony Blunt, "Vision and Execution in Blake's Painting" (excerpt from item 782)

R.D. Laing, "The Divided Self" (excerpt from item 710)

Peter Fisher, "Albion and Jerusalem" (excerpt from item 1005)

Herbert Read, "A Personal Influence" (excerpt from item 738)

Martin Price, "The Vision of Innocence" (excerpt from item 527)

224. Paananen, Victor N. *William Blake*. Boston: Twayne (G.K. Hall), 1977. 171pp.

The complexity of Blake's vision is slighted in this work which sees the *Book of Urizen* as establishing most of Blake's system. The *Marriage* is glossed over and the author concludes that Blake confidently relies on a Christian stance.

225. Rose, Edward J. (rev., *William Blake*). *Blake: An Illustrated Quarterly*, XIII (1977-78), 205-206.

"The Twayne *Blake* by Paananen cannot be taken seriously as a contribution to the study of Blake." Not even a good introduction.

226. Paley, Morton D. *William Blake*. Oxford: Phaidon Press; New York: E.P. Dutton, 1978. 192pp.

This work was intended to fill a need for an introduction to Blake's poetry and art in a large-format arrangement and containing a "sufficient number of plates to indicate the rich variety of Blake's production in different modes and in various media."

227. Wark, Robert R. (rev., *William Blake*). *Blake: An Illustrated Quarterly*, XII (1978), 211-212.

"... a praiseworthy attempt to provide access for people who are not inside the camp of regular Blakeans."

228.   Wolf, Edwin. (rev., *William Blake*). *Fine Print*,
       V (1979), 60-61.

       Paley "stokes the fires in one of the [Blake]
       factories."

229. Paley, Morton D. *Energy and the Imagination*. Oxford:
      Clarendon Press, 1970.

      "... proposes to study the thought of William Blake
      as it developed from the works of his early maturity
      through his great culminating statement, *Jerusalem*."
      This study traces its designated theme in an interesting
      fashion. Paley sides with those who believe Blake's
      system changed, developed. Argues for a transference
      of hero status from energy to the imagination.

      230.   Anon. (rev., *Energy and the Imagination*). *Choice*,
             VII (1970), 1042.

             "Paley's contribution here lies in his pre-
             sentation of analogues and historical sources
             for Blake's images and ideas: for example, Mir-
             cea Eliade's history of the cosmogonic myths of
             primitive societies may illuminate Blake's vision
             of possible escape for man from the cycle of
             history through the cycle itself."

      231.   Anon. (rev., *Energy and the Imagination*). *Philo-
             logical Quarterly*, L (1971), 409.

             "The reader is left at some distance from the
             works as aesthetic creations, and Paley is very
             cautious about offering any overview."

      232.   Gleckner, Robert F. (rev., *Energy and the Imagina-
             tion*). *Modern Language Quarterly*, XXXII (1971),
             326-328.

             "... demonstrates the development in the
             poetry and painting of Blake's ideas of energy
             and imagination, their seeming conflict early
             in his career, their interaction, and ultimately
             their marriage."

      233.   Grant, John E. (rev., *Energy and the Imagination*).
             ELN, IX (1972), 210-216.

             "After the bad books published recently by
             Beer and Miss Raine, it is a pleasure to read
             a good new interpretive book on Blake."

234. Howard, John. (rev., *Energy and the Imagination*).
     Blake Studies, III (1971), 197-199.

     "... a fine example of the history-of-ideas
     approach to Blake's work.... There are a few long
     explications of poems, and one would wish for
     more about *Jerusalem*, but Paley does not pretend
     to be exhaustive. What he provides is a frame-
     work for the reading of most of Blake's poems,
     a framework that is reflected in the thesis and
     structure of the book."

235. Jump, John D. (rev., *Energy and the Imagination*).
     Critical Quarterly, XIII (1971), 87-88.

     "... can his home-brewed mythology really in-
     terest anyone who isn't thinking of writing a
     book about it?"

236. Malekin, P. (rev., *Energy and the Imagination*).
     Review of English Studies, 22 (1971), 352-
     354.

     Compares Paley's views with Raine's and clas-
     sifies the former as a "modernist" and Raine and
     himself as traditionalists. Basic disagreement
     is with regard to Blake's view of body and soul,
     mind and matter.

237. Mayhead, Robin. (rev., *Energy and the Imagination*).
     English, XXII (1971), 59-62.

     Considers this work a trifle scholarly for the
     layman.

238. Paley, Morton, ed. *Twentieth Century Interpretations
     of the Songs of Innocence and of Experience*. Engle-
     wood Cliffs, N.J.: Prentice-Hall, 1969.

     Alicia Ostriker, "Metrics: Pattern and Variation"
     (excerpt from item 621)
     S. Foster Damon, "The Initial Eden"
     Martin Price, "The Vision of Innocence" (excerpt from
     item 527)
     David V. Erdman, "Infinite London" (excerpt from item
     130)
     Northrop Frye, "Blake's Introduction to Experience"
     (item 1563)
     Morton D. Paley, "Tyger of Wrath" (item 1613)
     Joseph H. Wicksteed, "The Blossom"

Harold Bloom, "Holy Thursday" (excerpt from item 101)
Mark Schorer, "Experience" (excerpt from item 1682)
Hazard Adams, "The Two Nurse's Songs" (excerpt from item 66)
Martin K. Nurmi, "Blake's Revisions of 'The Tyger'" (item 1680)
E.D. Hirsch, Jr., "The Human Abstract" (excerpt from item 1582)

239.   Essick, Robert N. (rev., *Twentieth Century Inter-pretations of the Songs of Innocence and of Experience*). *Blake Studies*, III (1970), 91-94.

"... a good place to start for students just launching into the vast amounts of critical and scholarly comment devoted to Blake's best known poems."

240. Paley, Morton D., and Michael Phillips, eds. *William Blake: Essays in Honour of Sir Geoffrey Keynes*. Oxford: Clarendon Press, 1973.

Michael Phillips, "Blake's Early Poetry" (item 1515)
David Bindman, "Blake's 'Gothicised Imagination' and the History of England" (item 780)
Michael J. Tolley, "Blake's Songs of Spring" (item 562)
Jean H. Hagstrum, "Christ's Body" (item 1020)
G. Wilson Knight, "The Chapel of Gold" (item 1675)
David V. Erdman, with Tom Dargan and Marlene Deverell-Van Meter, "Reading the Illuminations of Blake's *Marriage of Heaven and Hell*" (item 1429)
Janet Warner, "Blake's Figures of Despair: Man in His Spectre's Power" (item 934)
Morris Eaves, "The Title-Page of *The Book of Urizen*" (item 1316)
John Beer, "Blake, Coleridge, and Wordsworth: Some Cross-Currents and Parallels, 1789-1805" (item 1172)
Morton D. Paley, "William Blake, the Prince of the Hebrews, and the Woman Clothed with the Sun" (item 1079)
Martin Butlin, "Blake, Varley, and the Graphic Tele-scope" (item 791)
Raymond Lister, "References to Blake in Samuel Palmer's Letters" (item 715)
Suzanne R. Hoover, "William Blake in the Wilderness: A Closer Look at His Reputation, 1827-1863" (item 380)
G.E. Bentley, Jr., "Geoffrey Keynes's Work on Blake: *Fons et Origo*, and a Checklist of Writings on Blake by Geoffrey Keynes, 1910-1972" (item 18a)

Robert N. Essick, "The Altering Eye: Blake's Vision in the *Tiriel* Designs" (item 1652)
F.R. Leavis, "Justifying One's Valuation of Blake" (item 384)
Josephine Miles, "Blake's Frame of Language" (item 617)

241.   Faulkner, Dewey. (rev., *William Blake: Essays in Honour of Sir Geoffrey Keynes*). *Yale Review*, LXIII (1974), 590-599.

"The results are mixed in value."

242.   Gleckner, Robert F. (rev., *William Blake: Essays in Honour of Sir Geoffrey Keynes*). *Philological Quarterly*, LIII (1974), 651-653.

"... the energy evidenced in this volume is certainly commendable if not always delightful-- whether it is commensurate with Sir Geoffrey's achievement remains perhaps inevitably in doubt."

243.   Grant, John E. (rev., *William Blake: Essays in Honour of Sir Geoffrey Keynes*). *Blake Studies*, VII (1975), 85-96.

Only one essay is likely to achieve classic status in Blake studies: "Reading the Illumina- tions of Blake's *Marriage of Heaven and Hell*" by Erdman, Dargan and Deverell-Van Meter.

244.   Trawick, Leonard M. (rev., *William Blake: Essays in Honour of Sir Geoffrey Keynes*). *Studies in Burke and His Time*, XVII (1976), 156-159.

"Some essays will be of value primarily to Blake specialists, others will interest the more general student of Burke and his time."

245.   Phillips, Michael, ed. *Interpreting Blake*. Cambridge: Cambridge University Press, 1978.

Frank M. Parisi, "Emblems of Melancholy *for Children: The Gates of Paradise*" (item 1370)
Harald A. Kittel, "*The Book of Urizen* and *An Essay Concerning Human Understanding*" (item 1318)
John Beer, "Influence and Independence in Blake" (item 962)
Heather Glen, "Blake's Criticism of Moral Thinking in *Songs of Innocence and of Experience*" (item 1571)

Peter Butler, "*Milton*: The Final Plates" (item 1458)
James Ferguson, "Prefaces to *Jerusalem*" (item 1388)
E.P. Thompson, "London" (item 1639)

246. Pinto, Vivian de Sola. "William Blake: The Visionary
      Man." *Journal of the Royal Society of Arts*, CVI (1958),
      74-89.

      Typical of a great number of introductions which very
      broadly sketch the lineaments of Blake's work without
      touching the heart.

247. Price, Martin. "The Standard of Energy." *To the Palace
      of Wisdom: Studies in Order and Energy from Dryden
      to Blake*. Garden City, N.Y.: Doubleday, 1964. See item
      527.

      Argues that Blake is primarily distinguished from the
      Augustans in regard to his shift from moral judgment to
      a standard of energy. Blake's divine vision is one based
      on energy. The virtue of Price's entire volume is in
      its presentation of energy as a continuous undercurrent
      in the eighteenth century.

      248. Dorris, George. "The Alone Distinction." (rev.,
            To the Palace of Wisdom). *Sewanee Review*, LXXIII
            (1965), 529-531.

            Price's final chapter is on Blake, who leaves
            behind order and espouses energy.

249. Raine, Kathleen. *William Blake*. New York and Washington,
      D.C.: Praeger, 1970. 216pp.

      This brief, undocumented introduction with many plates,
      some colored, is too permeated with Raine's Neoplatonic
      view of Blake to stand as an introduction to Blake for
      the unwary reader. Raine states immediately in her in-
      troduction that Blake's is a Platonic view of art, a
      highly debatable view.

      250. Grant, John E. (rev., *William Blake*). *Philological
            Quarterly*, L (1971), 409-410.

            "The chief value of this volume is that it
            makes available by far the largest collection
            of Blake's art to be had at a reasonable price."

      251. Tolley, Michael J. (rev., *William Blake*). *Blake
            Newsletter*, VI (1972), 30-31.

> "... the publishers made an inappropriate
> choice of author for their text...." "Raine's
> derivative in her art opinions, prejudiced in
> regard to Blake's literary influences, her 'value'
> judgments are ... perverse ... her style is bad ...
> her text painful reading."

252. Wackrill, H.R. (rev., *William Blake*). *Blake Studies*,
     IV (1971), 110-113.

     > Raine's role is "that of austere interpreter
     > of Blake's mystical philosophy."

253. Rawson, Wyatt. "William Blake--Psychic, Visionary, and
     Prophet." *Light*, XC (1970), 188-194.

     A representative essay written by one who does not
     objectively study Blake but believes in his vision.

254. Reubart, A., ed. *Blake Through Student Eyes*. Oakland,
     Calif.: Mills College, Roussel Sargent, 1971.

     Variety of papers and poems on Blake by college stu-
     dents.

255. Rodway, Allan. "Blake." *The Romantic Conflict*. London:
     Chatto and Windus, 1963, 115-139.

     Blake's poetry is not great because of its metaphysic
     or goal of a larger harmony but because of "the pungent
     revelations of life as it actually was, and is, in a time
     of terrors and horrors."

256. Rosenfeld, Alvin H., ed. *William Blake: Essays for S.
     Foster Damon*. Providence, R.I.: Brown University
     Press, 1969.

     Hazard Adams, "Blake and the Postmodern" (item 648)
     Harold Bloom, "The Visionary Cinema of Romantic Poetry"
     (item 586)
     Harold Fisch, "Blake's Miltonic Moment" (item 1002)
     Geoffrey Hartman, "Blake and the 'Progress of Poesy'"
     (item 1510)
     Daniel Hughes, "Blake and Shelley: Beyond the Uroboros"
     (item 1044)
     Vivian de Sola Pinto, "William Blake and D.H. Lawrence"
     (item 1256)
     Martin Butlin, "The Evolution of Blake's Large Color
     Prints of 1795" (item 790)

Anne T. Kostelanetz, "Blake's 1795 Color Prints: An Interpretation" (item 1676)

George M. Harper, "The Divine Tetrad in Blake's *Jerusalem*" (item 1391)

Paul Miner, "Visions in the Darksom Air: Aspects of Blake's Biblical Symbolism" (item 509)

Piloo Nanavutty, "*Materia Prima* in a Page of Blake's *Vala*" (item 1356)

Martin K. Nurmi, "Negative Sources in Blake" (item 1077)

Robert Gleckner, "Blake's Verbal Technique" (item 601)

John E. Grant, "Two Flowers in the Garden of Experience" (item 1574)

Jean H. Hagstrum, "The Fly" (item 1674)

Kathleen Raine, "A Note on Blake's 'Unfettered Verse'" (item 634)

Morton Paley, "Blake's *Night Thoughts*: An Exploration of the Fallen World" (item 896)

Albert S. Roe, "'The Thunder of Egypt': 'Israel deliver'd from Egypt, is Art deliver'd from Nature and Imitation'" (item 531)

Asloob Ahmad Ansari, "Blake and the Kabbalah" (item 952)

Northrop Frye, "Blake's Reading of the Book of Job" (item 824)

David V. Erdman, "A Temporary Report on Texts of William Blake" (item 40)

257. Bottrall, M. (rev., *William Blake: Essays for S. Foster Damon*). *Critical Quarterly*, XII (1970), 286-287.

A worthy festschrift.

258. Malekin, P. (rev., *William Blake: Essays for S. Foster Damon*; *Blake and Tradition* [item 1096]). *Review of English Studies*, XXII (1971), 93-95.

Rosenfeld--"It is much to the credit of the editor that he has contrived to make the volume a whole containing within it the pleasures of diversity." Raine--Her perceptions regarding physical sexuality and the body are "nearer to Blake's thinking than some of the extremely permissive" interpretations.

259. Schulz, Max F. (rev., *William Blake: Essays for S. Foster Damon*). *Eighteenth Century Studies*, IV (1971), 223-229.

An article which not only reviews the festschrift favorably, but also provides an interesting look at the course of Blake criticism.

260. Stevenson, W.H. (rev., *William Blake: Essays for
S. Foster Damon*). *Blake Studies*, II (1969), 91-
97.

Two critical approaches: "... those who con-
centrate on the ascertainment of fact, and those
who seek to interpret the works...." "There is
very little dead wood in this volume."

261. Sankey, Benjamin. "A Preface to Blake." *Spectrum*, IV
(1960), 108-112.

The reader of Blake needs a description of what Blake
did.

262. Weathers, Winston, ed. *William Blake: The Tyger*. Columbus,
Ohio: Charles E. Merrill, 1969.

Includes excerpts from Damon's *William Blake: His
Philosophy and Symbols*; Roy Basler's *Sex, Symbolism and
Psychology in Literature*; Stanley Gardner's *Infinity
on the Anvil* (item 166); Hazard Adams's *William Blake:
A Reading of the Shorter Poems* (item 66); and E.D.
Hirsch, Jr.'s *Innocence and Experience* (item 1582).
Jesse Bier, "A Study of Blake's 'The Tyger'"
Martin K. Nurmi, "Blake's Revisions of 'The Tyger'"
(item 1680)
Philip Hobsbaum, "A Rhetorical Question Answered:
Blake's Tyger and Its Critics" (item 1591)
Morton D. Paley, "Tyger of Wrath" (item 1613)
Rodney M. Baine, "Blake's 'Tyger': The Nature of the
Beast" (item 1529)
Kay P. Long, "William Blake and the Smiling Tyger"

263. Wittreich, Joseph A., ed. *Nineteenth Century Accounts
of William Blake*. Gainesville, Fla.: Scholars Facsimiles, 1970.

Facsimile copies of essays by Malkin, Crabb Robinson,
John Thomas Smith, Allan Cunningham, Tatham and Yeats.

264. Wolfe, Thomas P. "The Blakean Intellect." *Hudson Review*,
XX (1967-68), 610-614.

Argues that the failure of the poetry is the failure
of the intellect to achieve the task it has set for
itself.

CHAPTER THREE

BLAKE'S LIFE AND CONTEMPORARIES

Two of the basic biographical reference works--Gilchrist (item 309) and Bentley's *Blake Records* (item 10)--have been cited in Chapter One; a third, Wilson (item 351), is cited in this chapter. Jack Lindsay's *William Blake: His Life and Work* (item 204), H.M. Margoliouth's *William Blake* (item 213) and Raymond Lister's *William Blake* (item 206) are more modern biographies, but in none of these does the commentary on Blake's work reach a satisfactory level.

Lindsay refers to *Blake Records* in his Foreword and frequently in his notes. He feels that putting his study "in biographical form" makes it more accessible than Bentley's *Blake Records*, and this is probably true. However, the demands of a consecutive, coherent narrative in which the biographer is assumed to have a comprehensive understanding of "the full interaction of a writer or artist with his world, while at the same time doing [his] best to define [the artist's] specific contribution in all its personal and aesthetic aspects" (Lindsay, xii) amount only to presumption on the part of the biographer and naiveté on the part of the reader. Lindsay's is a very readable account, but his Blake is a Millenarian and Antinomian while Margoliouth's is an orthodox Christian. Lister's work contains no footnotes; his comments on individual works and on influences are slight. Since Lister is an artist, one finds the comments on artistic technique most interesting.

Bindman's *Blake as an Artist* (item 96) and Todd's *William Blake, the Artist* (item 923) focus on Blake the working artist. Todd's book is a chronological account of Blake's active life as an artist. The historical Blake can be found in Erdman's *Blake: Prophet Against Empire* (item 130) while June Singer attempts a Jungian work-up of Blake the man in *The Unholy Bible* (item 1111), a very reductivist work-up indeed.

Both *Blake Records* and Erdman's *Blake: Prophet Against Empire* present Blake's contemporaries in the context in which

we are interested in them. While Bentley is recording facts,
Erdman is promoting the idea that to a great extent Blake is
comprehensible within his own time, a man among men, a man
affected by his contemporaries. All of Crabb Robinson's accounts of Blake are reprinted in *Blake Records*. *William Blake
in the Art of His Time* (item 933) is much more than an exhibi-
tion catalogue. Its thesis is that "Blake's contemporaries--
Henry Fuseli, John Flaxman, Alexander Runciman, James Mortimer,
James Barry and even in some periods of their careers the
paintings of George Romney, Thomas Lawrence and Benjamin West ...
share many characteristics with William Blake in both style
and content" (10). Brief biographies of these contemporaries
are presented on pp. 95-100 and a bibliography entitled "Blake
and His World" appears on p. 100 of item 933. *Blake: An
Illustrated Quarterly* in 1979 expanded its annual bibliography
to include "Blake and His Circle."

265.   Adams, Hazard. "Revisiting Reynolds's *Discourses* and
       Blake's Annotations." *Blake in His Time* (item 149),
       128-144.

       Feels that Blake wasn't fair to Reynolds and that
       later discourses might have redeemed Reynolds in Blake's
       eyes.

266.   Adlard, John. "Blake Enters Beulah." *Neuphilologische
       Mitteilungen*, LXXVIII (1977), 62-64.

       Beulah Hill is a place in the vale of the River Effra,
       beneath the Surrey Hills.

267.   Anon. "T.V. Program on William Blake." *London Times*,
       Feb. 7, 1969, 9.

       A popular version of Blake's life.

268.   Ashton, Dore. "Fuseli and Blake: Two Against the Grain."
       Art Digest, XXVIII (1954), 8-9.

       Notes for a Fuseli-Blake exhibit.

269.   Bennett, Shelley M. "Thomas Stothard, R.A." *DAI*, XXXVIII
       (1977), 2380A (UCLA).

       Blake, Flaxman and Stothard exploited "the expressive
       potential of line."

270.   Bentley, G.E., Jr. "Blake's Trial Documents." *Blake:*
       An Illustrated Quarterly, XIV (1980), 37–39.

       Adds court documents from the East Sussex Record
       Office in Lewes, thus supplementing his account of the
       trial in *Blake Records* (item 10).

271.   Bentley, Gerald E., Jr. "William Blake as a Private
       Publisher." *Bulletin of the New York Public Library*,
       LXI (1957), 539–560.

       Essentially an account of Hayley's attempts to sell
       Blake's work.

272.   Bentley, Gerald E., Jr. "Additions to Blake's Library."
       Bulletin of the New York Public Library, LXIV (1960),
       595–605.

       Adds 17 works to Keynes's list. See item 197.

273.   Bentley, Gerald E., Jr. "A Footnote to Blake's Treason
       Trial." *Notes & Queries*, CC (1955), 118–119.

       Hayley paid Samuel Rose to defend Blake.

274.   Bentley, Gerald E., Jr. "Thomas Butts, White Collar
       Maecenas." *PMLA*, LXXI (1956), 1052–1066.

       Butts was really just a clerk and his support of Blake
       was a big part of Blake's income.

275.   Bentley, G.E., Jr. "William Blake, Samuel Palmer, and
       George Richmond." *Blake Studies*, II (1970), 43–50.

       Richmond and Palmer were two of Blake's ardent dis-
       ciples, and attendants at his deathbed.

276.   Bentley, G.E., Jr. "A Collection of Prosaic William
       Blakes." *Notes & Queries*, N.S. XII (1965), 172–178.

       There were 24 other William Blakes in England during
       the William Blake's lifetime.

277.   Bentley, G.E., Jr. "A Different Face: William Blake and
       Mary Wollstonecraft." *Wordsworth Circle*, X (1979),
       349–350.

       The "different face" of the original of "Mary" is
       Mary Wollstonecraft's creation Maria in *The Wrongs of*
       Woman.

278.   Bentley, G.E., Jr. "Almost Blake." *Blake: An Illustrated
       Quarterly*, XIII (1979), 109.

       Three examples of items by other William Blakes.

279.   Bentley, Gerald E., Jr. "Blake's Engravings and His
       Friendship with Flaxman." *Studies in Bibliography*,
       XXII (1959), 161-188.

       Traces Blake's relationship with Flaxman and Hayley
       and their intercessions on behalf of Blake.

280.   Bentley, Gerald E., Jr. "William Blake and 'Johnny of
       Norfolk.'" *Studies in Philology*, LIII (1956), 60-74.

       Traces reference to Blake in the Johnson-Hayley letters.

281.   Bentley, Gerald E., Jr. "Blake, Hayley and Lady Hesketh."
       Review of English Studies, VII (1956), 264-286.

       Attempts to correct the view that Lady Hesketh whole-
       heartedly disapproved of Blake.

282.   Bentley, Gerald E., Jr. "Blake and Young." *Notes &
       Queries*, CXCIX (1954), 529-530.

       Notes a verbal echo in Blake's *Gates of Paradise* and
       Young's *Night Thoughts*. Concludes that this illustrates
       that "Blake was thoroughly grounded in the poetry and
       thought of the 18th century and used both in his poetry."

283.   Bentley, Gerald E., Jr. "A.S. Mathew, Patron of Blake
       and Flaxman." *Notes & Queries*, CCIII (1958), 168-178.

       A biographical sketch of a man Bentley feels was of
       "considerable importance in the lives of Blake and
       Flaxman."

284.   Bentley, G.E., Jr. "John Flaxman and Thomas Taylor."
       Notes & Queries, N.S. XVI (1969), 354-355.

       If Flaxman knew Taylor well, then Taylor probably
       knew Blake.

285.   Bentley, G.E., Jr. "Ozias Humphry, William Upcott, and
       William Blake." *Humanities Association Review*, XXVI
       (1975), 116-122.

       Ozias Humphry and his natural son, William Upcott,
       knew William Blake.

286. Bentley, G.E. "Blake and Cromek: The Wheat and the Tares." *Modern Philology*, LXXI (1974), 366-379.

    "Some facts which have recently come to light make possible a fuller understanding of the relationship between the two men, suggest that Blake was more patient and tolerant than appeared formerly ... and indicate that there was a surprising breadth of aesthetic and intellectual sympathy between Blake and Cromek, at least for a time."

287. Betz, Paul F. "Wordsworth's First Acquaintance with Blake's Poetry." *Blake Newsletter*, III (1970), 84-89.

    "... the question of when the poems were read and transcribed into the Commonplace Book still remains to be settled."

288. Bidney, Martin. "*Cain* and *The Ghost of Abel*: Context for Understanding Blake's Response to Byron." *Blake Studies*, VIII (1979), 145-165.

    In *The Ghost of Abel* Blake attempted to show "how the dilemmas of Cain in Generation, like those of Lucifer in 'Ulro' and Adam in 'Beulah' might be transcended through the fourfold vision of a restored and reorganized imaginative Eden or 'Eternity.'"

289. Bogen, Nancy. "William Blake, the Pars Brothers and James Basire." *Notes & Queries*, N.S. XVIII (1970), 313-314.

    The Pars brothers may have recommended Basire to Blake.

290. Butlin, Martin. "The Rediscovery of an Artist: James Jefferys 1751-1784." *Blake Newsletter* X (1977), 123-124.

    Jefferys can be added to "the circle of artists whose work lies behind the proto-Romantic Neo-Classicism of much of Blake's work."

291. Crown, Patricia D. "Edward P. Burney: An Historical Study in English Romantic Art." *DAI*, XXXVIII (1977), 4414A (UCLA).

    States that Burney was a contemporary of such well-known artists as Rowlandson, Blake and Stothard.

292. Curtis, F.B. "Blake and the Booksellers." *Blake Studies*,
      VI (1976), 167-178.

      Blake may have heard a good number of conversations
      at Joseph Johnson's and at other London booksellers of
      the day.

293. Davis, Michael. *William Blake: A New Kind of Man*.
      Berkeley and Los Angeles: University of California
      Press, 1977. 181pp.

      There are no footnotes in this biography, not even
      references to Gilchrist (item 309) or Bentley's *Blake
      Records* (item 10). Davis holds the view that Blake has
      no aesthetic control in his later books, although this
      work exudes total conviction. One is certainly advised
      to read Gilchrist or the updated Wilson biography (item
      351).

      294. Anon. (rev., *William Blake: A New Kind of Man*).
            Times Literary Supplement, May 20, 1977, 622.

            No documentation. "There is, indeed, a case
            almost equally strong for calling him a very
            old kind of man; the Old Testament is full of
            such."

295. Deck, Raymond H., Jr. "Mr. Rudall, the Flautist: An
      Authentic Blake Anecdote." *Blake: An Illustrated
      Quarterly*, XI (1977), 123.

      Blake was living near Clare Market but he told Rudall
      that he really lived in a palace.

296. Deck, Raymond H., Jr. "New Light on C.A. Tulk, Blake's
      Nineteenth Century Patron." *Studies in Romanticism*,
      XVI (1977), 217-236.

      Argues that Tulk touted Blake's Swedenborgianism,
      argued publicly in 1830 that Blake's works were sane
      and was indirectly responsible for Carlyle's and Emer-
      son's and Henry James, Sr's interest in Blake.

297. Dorfman, Deborah. "Blake in 1863 and 1880: The Gilchrist
      Life." *Bulletin of the New York Public Library*, LXXI
      (1969), 216-238.

      Study of the changes between the 1863 and 1880 edi-
      tions of Gilchrist's *Life of Blake* (item 309).

298. Dörrbecker, Detlef W. "Jean Paul Friedrich Richter and Blake's *Night Thoughts*." *Blake: An Illustrated Quarterly*, XI (1977), 124-125.

    1801 copy of Young's *Night Thoughts* illustrated with Blake's engravings was given to Jean Paul.

299. Erdman, David V. "Blake's 'Nest of Villains.'" *Keats-Shelley Journal*, II (1953), 61-71.

    Tells the stories of Blake's involvement with an abandoned review, his relations with Phillips of the *Monthly*, with Hoare of *Artist*, and his battle with the *Examiner*.

300. Erdman, David V. "William Blake's Exactness in Dates." *Philological Quarterly*, XXVIII (1949), 465-470.

    Blake's dates are historically accurate, even in regard to the chronology of the prophetic books.

301. Erdman, David V. "Desire Under the Oak." *Bulletin of the New York Public Library*, LXIV (1960), 565-566.

    Anecdote about Blake and his wife's thumbing through Bysshe's *Art of English Poetry*.

302. Erdman, David V. "'Blake' Entries in Godwin's *Diary*." *Notes & Queries*, CXCVIII (1953), 354-356.

    Thirteen entries refer to the name "Blake." Concludes that no one named Blake loomed very large in Godwin's acquaintance.

303. Erdman, David V. "Blake and Godwin." *Notes & Queries*, CXCIX (1954), 66-67.

    Blake loaned Godwin £40 but Godwin never mentioned it in his diary.

304. Erdman, David V. "Blake's Landlord." *Bulletin of the New York Public Library*, LXIII (1959), 61.

    Thomas Taylor of 23 Green St. was a tailor.

305. Essick, Robert N. "William Blake and Sir Thomas Lawrence." *Notes & Queries*, N.S. XXV (1978), 211-213.

    Sir Thomas was interested in Blake from 1822 to 1827 and assisted him financially.

306. Fawcus, Arnold. "William Blake, Republican and Anti-
       Imperialist." *Connoisseur*, CLXXII (1969), 78-80.

       Follows Erdman's view that Blake concealed his radi-
       calism behind a complex array of symbols.

307. Folkenflik, Robert. "Macpherson, Chatterton, Blake and
       the Great Age of Literary Forgery." *The Centennial
       Review*, XVIII (1974), 378-391.

       Blake wasn't a forger, and forgers achieved success
       and he didn't. "Staggering problems often require radi-
       cal solutions; getting out from under the burden of
       Atlas may take some undignified trickery."

308. Fulbright, James. "William Blake and the Emancipation
       of Woman." *DAI*, XXXIV (1974), 7132A (University of
       Missouri, Columbia).

       Discussion of Blake and his friends and their associa-
       tion with eighteenth-century woman's emancipation. Harriet
       Mathew, James Barry, Mary Wollstonecraft, Henry Fuseli.

309. Gilchrist, Alexander. *Life of William Blake, "Pictor
       Ignotus."* 1863; London: J.M. Dent, 1942, Ruthven Todd,
       editor.

       Bentley writes, "Intrinsically, the merit of the book
       is such that it can never be outdated" (*Blake Books*
       [item 5], 816).

310. Hall, Carol L. "Henry Fuseli and the Aesthetics of
       William Blake: Fuseli as Transmitter of J.J. Winckel-
       mann, J.J. Rousseau and J.C. Lavater." *DAI*, XL (1979),
       2651A (University of Maryland).

       Argues that Fuseli's role as "intellectual mediator
       of ideas to Blake" has been underestimated.

311. Henning, C.M. "Blake's Baptismal Font." *Blake: An
       Illustrated Quarterly*, XI (1977), 38.

       A modern tablet commemorates Blake's baptism at St.
       James Church, Piccadilly.

312. Heppner, Christopher. "Notes on Some Items in the Blake
       Collection at McGill with a Few Speculations Around
       William Roscoe." *Blake Newsletter*, X (1977), 100-108.

       Discussion of two apparent plagiarisms and of Blake's
       contemporary Roscoe.

313. Heppner, Christopher. "Blake and the *Seaman's Recorder*:
     The Letter and the Spirit in a Problem of Attribution."
     Blake: An Illustrated Quarterly, XII (1978), 15-17.

     An E. Blake was probably responsible for the six
     plates of *The Seaman's Recorder*.

314. Hilles, Frederick W. "Reynolds Among the Romantics."
     Literary Theory and Structure. Edited by F. Brady,
     et al. New Haven: Yale University Press, 1973.

     Blake overstated his objections; Hazlitt was amused;
     Haydon was straightforward.

315. Hunsberger, Bruce. "Kit Smart's *Howl*." *Wisconsin Studies
     in Contemporary Literature*, VI (1965), 34-44.

     Smart has had just as much influence on Beat poetry
     as Blake.

316. Hunt, Albert. "The Jerusalem Show: 'Tyger.'" *New Society*,
     XXIX (1971), 203.

     Review of Adrian Mitchell's play *Tyger*.

316a. Johnson-Grant, Mary Lynn. "Mapping Blake's London."
     Blake Newsletter, X (1977), 117-122.

     Reproduces maps of Blake's Britain, Blake's Holy Land
     and Blake's London.

317. Kennedy, Wilma. "A Mystic's Conception: By William
     Blake." *The English Heritage of Coleridge of Bristol
     1798*. New Haven: Yale University Press, 1947.

     Blake put into effect all Coleridge's claims for the
     creative imagination, and Blake's poetry exemplified
     an idealism which was part of Coleridge's canon for
     more than 30 years.

318. Keynes, Geoffrey. "William Blake and John Gabriel
     Stedman." *Times Literary Supplement*, May 20, 1965,
     400.

     An exhaustive account of the Blake-Stedman relation-
     ship. Blake engraved 16 plates for Stedman's *Narrative*,
     1796. "Clearly Blake's house in Lambeth was always ready
     to receive Stedman as a guest."

319. Keynes, Geoffrey. "Some Uncollected Authors XLIV: George
     Cumberland 1754-1848." *The Book Collector*, XXX (1970),
     31-65.

Gathered from the Cumberland papers in the British Museum.

320. King, James. "Charlotte Smith, William Cowper, and William Blake: Some New Documents." *Blake: An Illustrated Quarterly*, XIII (1979), 100-101.

The author cites three Charlotte Smith letters at McMaster University and suggests they are of interest because she refers to Blake and Cowper.

321. Kroeber, Karl. "The Relevance and Irrelevance of Romanticism." *Studies in Romanticism*, IX (1970), 297-306.

Summarizes certain themes and aspects of Blake's work and concludes that Blake is not a Romantic.

322. Lister, Raymond. "Blake's Appearance in a Textbook on Insanity." *Blake Newsletter*, IX (1976), 120-121.

Reproduces a section on Blake from L. Forbes Winslow's *Mad Humanity: Its Forms Apparent and Obscure*.

323. See item 316a.

324. Mabbott, Thomas O. "The Hour of Blake's Birth." *Notes & Queries*, CXCIII (1948), 7.

Cited in J.T. Hacket's *The Student Assistant in Astronomy and Astrology*, 1836.

325. Macmillan, Malcolm K. "Dialogue Between Blake and Wordsworth: Written in Rome Before 17 April 1889 and Left Unfinished." *Blake Newsletter*, VIII (1974), 38-41.

Imaginary dialogue by an antecedent of the Macmillan publishing family, who disappeared on Mount Olympus. A strange piece.

326. Margoliouth, Herschel M. "The Marriage of Blake's Parents." *Notes & Queries*, CXCII (1947), 380-381.

They were married in St. George Chapel on Oct. 15, 1752.

327. Margoliouth, Herschel M. "William Blake's Family." *Notes & Queries*, CXCIII (1948), 296-298.

Tries to lay to rest the contention that Blake was of Irish ancestry.

328. Margoliouth, Herschel M. "Blake's Mr. Mathew." *Notes & Queries*, CXCVI (1951), 162-163.

Biography of Mathew, who promoted the reputation of Blake.

329. Margoliouth, Herschel. "Blake's 'Sons of Albion.'" *Notes & Queries*, CXCIV (1949), 94-95.

Traces the 12 sons to contemporaries of Blake.

330. Miner, Paul. "William Blake's London Residences." *Bulletin of the New York Public Library*, LXII (1958), 535-550.

Revises the chronology of Blake's residences and lists all the addresses of Blake.

331. Montgomery, John. "Felpham and the Poets." *Sussex County Magazine*, XXI (1947), 124-126.

The Hayley-Blake connection is discussed. Both cottages are extant.

332. Murray, E.B. "A Suggested Redating of a Blake Letter to Thomas Butts." *Blake: An Illustrated Quarterly*, XIII (1979-80), 148-151.

10 January 1802 should be 10 January 1803 based on internal evidence.

333. Murray, Roger. "Working Sir Joshua: Blake's Marginalia in Reynolds." *British Journal of Aesthetics*, XVII (1977), 82-91.

Argues that Reynolds "presented a very special and formidable problem to Blake, one that required not merely more artistic achievement on his part, along with careful study of the *Discourses* ... but also the fullest possible understanding of the philosophical and even the political dimensions of Reynolds's aesthetics."

334. Ower, John. "The Epic Mythologies of Shelley and Keats." *Wascana Review*, IV (1969), 61-72.

Ower does mention that Blake has his own system; Shelley and Keats continue the epic tradition based on Milton and the Bible.

335. Paley, Morton D. "Cowper as Blake's Spectre." *Eighteenth Century Studies*, I (1968), 236-252.

      The Spectre's speech was probably inspired by Blake's knowledge of and compassion for Cowper.

336. Parris, Leslie. "William Blake's Mr. Thomas." *Times Literary Supplement*, Dec. 5, 1968, 1390.

      "Joseph Thomas, 1765-1811, friend of artists and occasional purchaser of Blake's work." First owner of *Comus* and *Paradise Lost* drawings now in Huntington Library.

337. Paulson, Ronald. "The Spectres of Blake and Rowlandson." *Listener*, XC (1973), 140-142.

      "If Bacon was Shakespeare, might not Blake be Rowlandson?"

338. Phillips, Michael. "William Blake and the 'Unincreasable Club': The Printing of *Poetical Sketches*." *Bulletin of the New York Public Library*, LXXX (1976), 6-18.

      Could Blake have been informally "tutored" by the scholars of the Unincreasable Club? The mastery of *Poetical Sketches* points to this.

339. Piper, J. "English Painting at the Tate." *Burlington Magazine*, LXXXIX (1947), 285.

      Blake, Hogarth, Constable and Turner. Very complimentary to Blake.

340. Read, Dennis M. "George Frederick Cooke: Another *Grave* Subscriber Heard From." *Blake: An Illustrated Quarterly*, XI (1977), 37-38.

      Cooke, a well-known actor, was a subscriber to *The Grave*.

341. Reed, Mark. "Blake, Wordsworth, Lamb, etc.: Further Information from Henry Crabb Robinson." *Blake Newsletter*, III (1970), 76-84.

      Not included in *Blake Records* (item 10).

342. Shroyer, Richard J. "The 1788 Publication Date of Lavater's *Aphorisms on Man*." *Blake: An Illustrated Quarterly*, XI (1977), 23-26.

Argues that the 1788 publication date of Lavater's *Aphorisms* is fairly secure.

343. Stevenson, W.H. "Blake's 'From Cratetos': A Source and a Correction." *Notes & Queries*, N.S. XV (1968), 21.

On Blake's knowledge of Greek.

344. Tayler, Irene. "Blake Meets Byron on April Fool's." *English Language Notes*, XVI (1978), 85-93.

Blake's *The Ghost of Abel* is directed at the conversion of Byron.

345. Todd, Ruthven. "A Recollection of George Richmond by His Grandson." *Blake Newsletter*, VI (1972), 24.

George Richmond closed Blake's eyes at death saying, "to keep the vision in."

346. Todd, Ruthven. "The Rev. Dr. John Trusler (1735-1820)." *Blake Newsletter*, VI (1972), 71.

Trusler and Blake would have gotten along if not for the drawing "Malevolence."

347. Tyson, G.P. "An Early Allusion to Blake." *Blake Newsletter*, IX (1975), 43.

A Thomas Henry letter to Joseph Johnson.

348. Wardle, Judith. "'Satan Not Having the Science of Wrath, but only of Pity.'" *Studies in Romanticism*, XIII (1974), 147-154.

Corrects Wittreich's views on the relationship of Hayley's critical ideas as expressed in his *Essay on Epic Poetry* and Blake's views.

349. Warner, Janet A. "James Vine." *Blake Newsletter*, IV (1971), 106-107.

James Vine, the man who commissioned *Milton*, is mentioned in the 1843 Bohn catalogue, but he is not mentioned in *Blake Records* (item 10).

350. Welch, Dennis M. "In the Throes of Eros: Blake's Early Career." *Mosaic*, II (1978), 101-113.

Argues that "Blake's attitudes toward energy and desire in the first half of his career are extremely ambiguous."

351. Wilson, Mona. *The Life of William Blake*. Ed. and ex-
          panded by Geoffrey Keynes. New York: Oxford University
          Press, 1971.

          Originally published in 1927. Keynes has supplied some
          footnotes. The biography to be read by all Blake students
          along with the Gilchrist biography (item 309), which
          was last printed in 1945.

CHAPTER FOUR

BLAKE'S REPUTATION

This chapter contains items in three categories: excerpts of comments on Blake, surveys of Blake's reputation and present-day essays on Blake's reputation.

Bentley's *William Blake: The Critical Heritage* (item 92) is a reworking of *Blake Records* (item 10). It contains excerpts from Blake's contemporaries regarding his work, mostly the pictorial work since *Poetical Sketches*, the *Songs* and the *Descriptive Catalogue* (1809) were Blake's only "published" poetry and prose. Bentley's "Introduction," pp. 1-26, includes sections on "Blake's Critical Reputation" and "Blake Studies." The comments here are the comments of his "Blake's Reputation and Interpreters," pp. 15-51 of *Blake Books* (item 5). O'Neill's *Critics on Blake* (item 223) does not have a cut-off date of 1863 but extends to 1964. Complete essays by Schorer, Frye, Erdman and Gleckner among others are included. Wittreich's *Nineteenth Century Accounts of William Blake* (item 263) contains facsimiles of material by Malkin, Crabb Robinson, Smith, Cunningham, Tatham and Yeats.

Deborah Dorfman's *Blake and the Nineteenth Century* (item 363) is a well-documented, thorough survey of Blake's reputation from his own day up to the Ellis-Yeats edition of Blake's work, 1893.

Present-day estimations of Blake are not unanimously favorable. While a coterie of energetic Blake scholars and critics approach Blake's work with the assumption that that work is inexhaustibly rich and capable of bearing any degree of imaginative and profound exegesis, the non-Blakean literary scholar maintains a position in regard to Blake not much different from T.S. Eliot's in 1920. Eliot reported at that time that he found confusion rather than neatly wrapped objective correlatives in the work of Blake. Blake, according to Eliot, had left both Poetry and The Tradition behind and was spelunking in his own world of ideas.

I have most often found an Eliot-like view in the reviews of Blake commentary. What, the specially selected non-

Blakean-though-erudite reviewer asks, is the purpose of delv-
ing time and again into work which is muddled? Blake's omis-
sion from the 1957 MLA Romantics Bibliography indicates a
fairly recent low estimation of Blake. Thus, while the energetic
Blakeans are laboring mightily to establish Blake, there yet
remains an aura of bewilderment and skepticism on the part
of others.

     However, Blake was held in great esteem by the generation
of the 1960's in America, by Ginsberg, N.O. Brown, Theodore
Roszak and R.D. Laing. That alone is sufficient to relegate
Blake back to the abyss of irrationality in the view of a New
Right America. The ferment of the 1960's provided an accommo-
dating ground for an acceptance and recognition of Blake's
genius. The American critical machine saw in Blake a fitting
challenge to its relentless exegetical expertise. Both generated the Age of Blake. And while the critical machine would
most likely prefer to do its work without a surrounding ferment, the Blake who was inspired prophet, who sought to reach
his fellow man, would certainly not welcome a reduction in
status to literary artifact. Hazard Adams predicts a rebuilt
continental critical machine operating on Blake in the near
future:

> We shall have to defend Blake criticism from the trendy.
> Soon the hanger-ons of the generation influenced by the
> continental criticism of our time will try to grind
> poor Blake exceeding fine. It is too bad that some of
> the first generation didn't do the job and get it over
> with. They would have done better.

352.   Allentuck, Marcia. "William Blake and William Bell Scott:
       Unpublished References to Blake's Late Nineteenth
       Century Reputation." *Blake Studies*, II (1970), 55-56.

       Scott (1811-1890) was influential along with the
       Rossettis and Swinburne in the Blake revival.

353.   Auden, W.H. "'A Mental Prince.'" *Observer*, XVII (Nov.
       17, 1957), 12; (Nov. 24, 1957), 23; (Dec. 1, 1957),
       6.

       Auden responds to Kathleen Raine's charge that he
       was ignorant of Blake's work when he wrote his bicen-
       tenary tribute to Blake.'

354.   Balakian, Anna. "The Literary Fortune of William Blake
       in France." *Modern Language Quarterly*, XVII (1956),
       261-272.

Reviews Blake's literary fortune in France in regard
to reputation, influence and scholarship.

355. Barach, Frances K., ed. "William Blake 1757-1827." *The
Critical Temper*. Edited by Martin Tucker. New York:
Ungar, 1969, II, 271-295.

Collection of quotations from various commentators
on Blake from Gilchrist to Bloom, 1963.

356. Bentley, G.E., Jr. "The Vicissitudes of Vision: The
First Account of William Blake in Russian." *Blake
Newsletter*, X (1977), 112-114.

Detected an 1834 article on Blake in Russian.

357. Bodgener, J. Henry. "Blake's Vision and Imagination:
A Bicentenary Appreciation." *London Quarterly and
Holborn Review*, CLXXXII (1957), 292-298.

Intended as a guide as well as an appreciation.

358. Butlin, Martin. "The Very William Blake of Living Landscape and Painters." *Blake Newsletter*, X (1976),
33-34.

J.M.W. Turner cited thus in the *Illustrated London
News*, May 10, 1845.

359. Cross, Colin. "Blake Revealed." *Observer*, XXI (Nov. 21,
1971), 19.

In the galleries and the exhibitions, not in the
criticism.

360. Dearnaley, G. "Editorial: William Blake and Modern
Technology." *Physics in Technology*, II (1974), 73-78.

Blake anticipates microelectronics.

361. Deck, Raymond. "Blake's *Poetical Sketches* Finally Arrive
in America." *Review of English Studies*, XXXI (1980),
183-192.

Nine poems from *Poetical Sketches* published in the
Harbinger, 1848.

362. Dorfman, Deborah. "The Development of William Blake's
Reputation as a Poet in the Nineteenth Century."
Dissertation, Yale University, 1964. See item 363.

363. Dorfman, Deborah. *Blake in the Nineteenth Century: His Reputation as a Poet from Gilchrist to Yeats*. New Haven: Yale University Press, 1969.

The discovery of Blake following the publication of Gilchrist's *Life* (item 309) up to Yeats, and the opinions accrued along the way. Documentation is literally overflowing.

364. Anon. "Some Anglo-American Divergencies in the Appraisal of William Blake." (rev., *Blake in the Nineteenth Century*; *William Blake: Essays for S. Foster Damon* [item 256]; *Blake and Tradition* [item 1096]). *Times Literary Supplement*, Dec. 25, 1969, 1461-1463.

Dorfman's book is a convenient and useful guide; the Rosenfeld collection is obscure on the subject of Blake's own ideas; Raine's attempt at caging Blake within her system fails.

365. Bostetter, Edward E. (rev., *Blake in the Nineteenth Century*). *Modern Philology*, LXVIII (1971), 385-388.

Poor organization of copious material; story is interesting but she has erred on the side of Urizen.

366. Freiberg, S.K. (rev., *Blake in the Nineteenth Century*; *William Blake: An Introduction to the Man and His Work* [item 206]). *Dalhousie Review*, XLIX (1969), 430-431.

Dorfman's book is "carefully and comprehensively documented...." Lister's book has far too many purposes. He succeeds in defining the significance of Blake's paintings and engravings.

367. Grant, John E. (rev., *Blake in the Nineteenth Century*). *Philological Quarterly*, XLIX (1970), 328-329.

Focused mostly on Blake's reputation as a poet but overall a well-documented, temperate account.

368. Harper, George M. (rev., *Blake in the Nineteenth Century*). *Blake Studies*, II (1970), 103-104.

> Genuinely useful study. But Harper reacts to
> the disparagement of the "infamous Ellis-Yeats
> edition" blurb on the jacket. "Miss Dorfman's
> reminder of the remarkable affinity between
> these two seminal nineteenth century poets may
> be the most suggestive if not the most important
> feature of her study."

369. Johnson, Mary Lynn. (rev., *Blake in the Nineteenth Century*). *Journal of English and Germanic Philology*, LXIX (1970), 525-528.

> "... the presence of so many trivial problems
> in *Blake in the Nineteenth Century* means that
> the book is self-defeating. The constant in-
> trusion of some petty obscurity necessarily blots
> out whatever real merits the book has ... it is
> like a marvellously complex subway system which
> was never designed for real riders...."

370. McSweeney, Kerry. (rev., *Blake in the Nineteenth Century*; *William Blake: An Introduction to the Man and His Work* [item 206]). *Queen's Quarterly*, LXXVI (1969), 731-733.

> Dorfman: "she has not taken the time thorough-
> ly to digest her material." Lister: "as a brief
> introduction to Blake's life and work, this is
> a well-proportioned and useful book."

371. Ostriker, Alicia. (rev., *Blake in the Nineteenth Century*). *Victorian Studies*, XIV (1970), 113-114.

> Summary of the book without evaluative comment.

372. Eaves, Morris. "Postscript: Blake's Abnormal Psychology." *Blake Newsletter*, IX (1976), 121-122.

In the 1972 text *Abnormal Psychology: Current Perspectives* Blake is described as an unfortunate lunatic, obviously a paranoid schizophrenic.

373. Fawcus, Arnold. "The Work of the 'Insane' Genius." *Picture Post*, LXIX, no. XIII (Dec. 24, 1955), 30-31.

Popular but energetic account.

374. Fletcher, Ian, ed. "John Todhunter's Lectures on Blake, 1872-1874." *Blake Newsletter*, VIII (1974), 4-14.

Lectures given as a part of a cycle on the English
poets delivered at Alexandria College, Dublin. Todhunter
stresses Blake's psychological ideas. "He is probably
the most intensely subjective of all our poets."

375. Fletcher, Ian. "The Ellis-Yeats-Blake Manuscript Cluster."
      Book Collector, XXI (1972), 72-94.

      "The image of Blake presented by Ellis and Yeats,
      aesthetic but mystical too, flattens Swinburne's heroic
      Blake into one devoid of all revolutionary and political
      impulse. But to Yeats' and Ellis' attempts to penetrate
      Blake's opaque 'system,' something heroic clings also."

376. Gleckner, Robert F. "Blake and Fuseli in a Student's
      Letter Home." *Blake Newsletter*, VI (1972), 71.

      Passage from the anonymous *Letters from an Irish
      Student in England to his Father in Ireland* (1809), in
      the "English Painters" chapter: "Mr. W. Blake, a miserable
      engraver, and one of the most eccentric men of the age."

377. Goyder, George. "An Unpublished Poem about Blake by
      William Bell Scott." *Blake Newsletter*, X (1977), 125.

      Found in an 1808 quarto edition of Blair's *Grave*.

378. Grunfield, Frederic V. "Quotations from Chairman Blake."
      Horizon, XIV (1972), 106-111.

      A smug, condescending bit about the "applicability of
      Blake's thought in the present."

379. Hoover, Suzanne. "William Blake in the Wilderness: The
      Early History of His Reputation." *DAI*, XXXI (1970),
      1231A (Columbia University). See item 380.

      "This is a narrative and analysis of Blake's repu-
      tation from the earliest notices through the 1860's...."
      Contains about 25 items not mentioned previously.

380. Hoover, Suzanne R. "William Blake in the Wilderness:
      A Closer Look at His Reputation, 1827-1863." *William
      Blake: Essays in Honour of Sir Geoffrey Keynes* (item
      240), 310-368.

      "The present study of Blake's reputation takes up
      the narrative after his personal battles with the public
      were closed by his death."

381. Hoover, Suzanne. "The Public Reception of Gilchrist's
      Life of Blake." *Blake Newsletter*, VIII (1974), 26-31.

      The *Life* "served greatly to widen the knowledge of
      Blake and his works beyond the limited circle of his
      admirers." Includes a list of reviews and articles on
      Gilchrist's *Life* (item 309).

382. Keynes, Geoffrey. "Blake in the Provinces." *Blake News-
      letter*, IX (1975), 41-42.

      Blake mentioned in *Birmingham Gazette* as inventor of
      Grave designs.

383. Larrabee, Stephen A. "Some Additional American References
      to Blake 1830-1863." *Bulletin of the New York Public
      Library*, LXI (1957), 561-563.

      Includes 16 references.

384. Leavis, F.R. "Justifying One's Valuation of Blake."
      William Blake: Essays in Honour of Sir Geoffrey Keynes
      (item 240), 66-85.

      "There isn't any book one can recommend as a guide,
      either on Blake in general, or even on *Songs of Inno-
      cence and of Experience*. In fact, it is one's responsi-
      bility to warn the student against being hopeful of
      light and profit to be got from the Blake authorities
      and the Blake literature. More than that, he should be
      told unequivocally that none of the elaborated prophetic
      works is a successful work of art."

385. Malmquist, N.G.D. "Blake in China." *Blake: An Illustrated
      Quarterly*, XIII (1979), 24-28.

      Traces views which hold Blake as a mystic, a Taoist,
      and those which hold that Blake used allegorical terms
      to express ideas which were inimical to the reactionary
      English Establishment.

386. Nelson, J. Walter. "Blake Anthologies." *Blake Newsletter*,
      X (1976), 32.

      Blake is now among the most commonly anthologized
      poets in English, and there is more scholarly interest
      in him than in any other eighteenth-century British
      author.

387.   Raine, Kathleen, et al. "Kidnapping Blake." *Spectator*,
       CXCIX (Dec. 13, 20 and 27, 1957); CC (Jan. 3 and 10,
       1958).

       A record of Blake critics in "urizenic" frenzy.

388.   Ransom, John C. "Blake Triumphant." *New York Review of
       Books*, Oct. 23, 1969, 4-5.

       This is ostensibly a review of Raine's *Blake and Tra-
       dition* (item 1096), but it is really a rather interest-
       ing, disjointed series of comments. Ransom even sum-
       marizes Blake's myth for a reader he seems sure has
       probably not considered Blake more seriously than he
       himself has.

389.   Reiman, Donald H. "A Significant Early Review of Blake."
       Blake Newsletter, VI (1973), 94-95.

       A brief notice favorable to Blake the artist, 1802.

390.   Sankey, Benjamin. "A Preface to Blake." *Spectrum*, IV
       (1960), 108-112.

       Blake's poetry isn't worth the trouble critics take
       with it.

391.   Stevens, L. Robert. "The Exorcism of England's Gothic
       Demon." *Midwest Quarterly*, XIV (1973), 151-164.

       Suggests that except for Emily Brontë, Hardy, Blake,
       Hawthorne and Melville, England and America are free
       of the Gothic temper and secure in reason and order.

392.   Taylor, James B. "The Case of William Blake: Creation,
       Regression and Pathology." *Psychoanalytic Review*, L
       (1963), 139-154.

       Taylor believes he is refuting Ernst Kris's theory
       that creativity involves conscious deliberative regres-
       sion on the part of the ego by presenting Blake as an
       example of pathologically motivated regression which is
       conducive to creativity. It means that Taylor, in 1963,
       thinks Blake mad.

393.   Taylor, Walter. "The Mysticism of William Blake." *Aryan
       Path*, XXXV (1964), 63-67.

       The date 1864 might possibly vindicate this essay.

394. Tener, Robert H. "The Authorship of the *Spectator* Review of Gilchrist." *Blake: An Illustrated Quarterly*, XIII (1979), 33-35.

     Contends that the review was written by Richard Holt Hutton, literary editor of the *Spectator*.

395. Ussher, Arland. "The Thought of Blake." *Dublin Magazine*, XXIII (1948), 23-32.

     "I can think of no other men of genius with an equal range, except perhaps (in their different ways) Leonardo da Vinci and Goethe."

396. Warner, Janet. "A Contemporary Reference to Blake." *Blake Newsletter*, IX (1976), 122.

     Blake is praised as an engraver in Ackermann's *Repository* for June 1810.

397. Watson, J.R. "The Romantics." *Critical Quarterly*, XXI (1979), 3-15.

     "... currently Blakean fundamentalism is being replaced, as a centre of interest, by an appreciation of the other major poets in the romantic movement."

398. White, Wayne. "William Blake: Mystic or Visionary?" *College Language Association Journal*, IX (1966), 284-288.

     A distinction that Frye made in 1947 is here announced.

399. Wieland-Burston, Joanne B. "Blake in France: The Poet and Painter as Seen by French Critics in the Nineteenth and Twentieth Centuries." *DAI*, XXXIX (1978), 914A (Vanderbilt University).

     Traces a reaction ranging from complete ignorance to curiosity to rabid interest.

400. Wild, David W. "The Emergence of Literacy: 1780-1860." *DAI*, XXXIII (1972), 2349A (University of Washington).

     "A chronological study of his [Blake's] major poems in this period [1770-1794] ... shows Blake adapting the polite, literary forms with the language, forms and republican fervor of the new urban culture." Blake, like Cobbett and Dickens, is a product of the new mass literacy.

401.   See item 263.

402.   See item 264.

CHAPTER FIVE

BLAKE'S SYMBOLS AND THEMES

Yeats in 1893 interpreted Blake's "Symbolic System" by
referring to the mixture of esoteric lore he himself had been
exposed to: Blavatsky, the Cabbala and the Rosicrucians. In
"Blake's Treatment of the Archetype" (item 162), Frye refers
to Blake's work as "one of the hottest poetic crucibles of
modern times." Frank Lentricchia in *After the New Criticism*,
1980, writes,

> ... readers of his [Frye's] study of Blake, *Fearful*
> *Symmetry* (1947), know that that book had forecast the
> whole of his literary theory as well as the furious
> rebirth of interest in a problematic writer. Its general
> critical claims aside, the *Anatomy* gave the Blake re-
> vivalists their proper poetics, the renewal of interest
> in Jung their proper psychology. (4)

Blake in Frye's view is rich in the kind of archetypal patterns
which inhere in literature, which, for Frye, form a basic
anatomy of a critical approach. Yeats may have sought the
source of Blake's symbols in theosophy and the Cabbala but
Frye's source is literature itself. Frye's view is that Blake's
symbols are "controlled by a small number of abiding literary
universals, 'four narrative pregeneric' categories which are
'logically prior' to the usual literary genres ..." (Lentricchia, 8).

In Chapter II, "Blake's Archetypes," of *William Blake:*
A Reading of the Shorter Poems (item 66), Hazard Adams constructs a theory of vision from which archetypes and their
symbols emerge. The inner or mental world determines what
we see in the outer or material world and therefore every
object, from Blake's tiger to his rose, must be seen as refer-
ential to that inner world. Since "all men are ultimately one
Man or God" (33), symbols register equally with all of us.
Rather than a common tradition, Christian, Neoplatonic,
Theosophist or Cabbalistic, serving as a source of symbols,

the Frye-Adams archetypal view posits one mind as the common
source. Adams maintains that Blake probably first recognized
the archetypes in the Bible and then theorized regarding their
origin and potency.

Although neither Frye nor Adams refers to Jung's psychology, perhaps true to the notion that the "gigantic palace of
art contains all life within" (Lentricchia, 23), the Jungian
notion of a common unconscious, a collective unconscious,
seems to be very much the basis of Frye's *Anatomy*. The archetypes which reside in literature are not archetypes by virtue
of that fact but because they elicit a common response. They
exist, for both Blake and Jung, not on an ethereal plane,
to be understood gnostically or mystically, but on a mental
plane. Therefore, Jung's discussion of symbol and archetype
becomes extremely relevant in a study of Blake.

Rose in "Blake's Fourfold Art" (item 541) argues for an
interrelatedness of symbolism in Blake's work, but Johnson
in "Emblem and Symbol in Blake" (item 485) argues that Blake
worked with both symbol and allegory. The prophecies therefore
have an allegorical side, one in which characters have fixed
referents and play out Blake's myth. The self-constructed
myth is, however, to some degree archetypal (Frye's Orc cycle,
for instance), and therefore characters and objects that
appear simply allegorical may, to the degree they are also
archetypal, be symbolical.

Frye's "hottest poetic crucible" is symbol-rich and not
allegory-rich. Interesting questions arise regarding the degree
to which Blake's myth is archetypal and the degree to which
Blake is determined by the archetype. Also, if the Bible and
Milton were fruitful sources of archetypes expressed in
commonly apprehended symbols, why was Blake moved to rewrite
both? If, as Frye suggests, literature glosses literature,
then why is Blake's work not so glossed? If Blake's misreadings of Ezekiel gloss "London," then who, Ezekiel or Blake,
is the rightful purveyor of the archetype? To what extent
are Blake's symbols personally apprehended symbols that do
not strike a uniform note in his reader? And even though
there are archetypes symbolically manifested in Blake's work,
is there not also a more pervasive vision which is personally
Blake's, which is overriding, which indeed urged him to
create his own system?

The task of pointing out a coherent symbolism in Blake's
work might involve the archetypal symbolism, the symbolism
Raine, Hirst and Harper (items 1096, 1036, 1025) believe
Blake takes from a Neoplatonic tradition, reworked Christianity, Cabbalistic and Theosophist symbolism, and a personal
symbolism understood only in terms of Blake's own work. Rather

than believe that Blake's symbolism is determined either by archetypes, esoteric, Christian or radical Christian traditions, meaningful only in those contexts, one hopes that Blake's symbolism is effective within the boundaries of his own work.

The best summary of this entire problem is presented in Kiralis's "A Guide to the Intellectual Symbolism of William Blake's Later Prophetic Writings" (item 495). Gardner in his chapter "Blake's Poetic Symbolism" in *Blake* (item 163) also argues for a personal symbolism in Blake, one in which Blake appended fresh associations to traditional symbols. "And since it is essential that a symbol be instinctively recognized, he could only do this by repetition." It seems that regardless of the foundation of Blake's symbols or the degree to which that source is determining, Blake's symbols must be artistically effective. We cannot begin to consider their artistic effectiveness unless they are first both comprehensible and noncontradicting.

Whitehead (item 577) points out that Blake is explicable in social-economic terms and argues that Frye has led us into a consideration of Blake which ignores the political Blake. Erdman (item 129) points to the existence of an historical approach to Blake which clarifies Blake in terms of the political-cultural-philosophic events of his day.

In the final analysis the breadth of symbolism in Blake's work is the breadth of interests in Blake the man. Is Blake more religious than political? more philosophical than aesthetic? more psychological than visionary? The breadth of symbolism in Blake's work is also the breadth of interests in Blake's reader.

Items in this chapter on various themes are really about Blake's symbolism. Or in Kiralis's words, they are really about Blake's "intellectual symbolism."

403. Abrams, Lois. "William Blake: The Lineaments of History." *DAI*, XXXIV (1974), 4223A (Brandeis University).

   Blake felt that history had failed, that neither doctrinaire theology or science had defined the future for man. Through the power of visionary art he sought the reintegration of man into the Bosom of the Divine Image.

404. Adams, Hazard. "Blake and the Philosophy of Literary Symbolism." *New Literary History*, V (1973), 135-146.

"Blake may be treated as a more complete symbolist than those who have gone under the 'symboliste' banner, if one means by symbolist a poet who regards literature as a 'symbolic form' of experience, in the sense that has become common since Cassirer."

405. Adams, Hazard. "The Blakean Aesthetic." *Journal of Aesthetics and Art Criticism*, XIII (1954), 233-248.

Blake's aesthetic was not based on nature or some abstraction from it but on a pattern of symbolism.

406. Adlard, John. "Bawdy Blake." *English Studies*, LVI (1975), 320-321.

Blake is for the most part frank in sexual matters but he sometimes used traditional bawdy images like the tulip.

407. Adlard, John. "Fields from Islington to Mary-bone." *Blake Newsletter*, IX (1976), 120.

Once owned by the Order of St. John of Jerusalem.

408. Adlard, John. "Blake and the Wild Thyme." *Folklore*, LXXXVII (1976), 219.

Thyme and rejuvenation and Los.

409. Aers, D. "William Blake and the Dialectics of Sex." *ELH*, XLIV (1977), 500-514.

Argues that Blake's work, especially *Visions of the Daughters of Albion* and *Europe* "is the evolution of an original and profound understanding of the dialectics of sexual conflict."

410. Ault, Donald D. "Incommensurability and Interconnection in Blake's Anti-Newtonian Text." *Studies in Romanticism*, XVI (1977), 277-303.

Blake used "incommensurability" to point out contradictions in the nature of explanation. He emphasizes "interconnections" of characters and events by "highlighting the very 'facts' of incommensurability on which the narrative insists." Blake is anti-Newton because Newton's view of a coherent world left out much of human experience.

411. Baine, Mary R. "Satan and the Satan Figure in the Poetry of William Blake." *DAI*, XXXV (1975), 5335A (University of Georgia).

     Discusses all versions of Satan and evil in Blake's work and points out the distinctions between these and the orthodox conception of good and evil.

412. Baine, Rodney M., and Mary Baine. "Blake's Inflammable Gass." *Blake Newsletter*, X (1976), 51-52.

     Gass is probably William Nicholson (1753-1815).

413. Baker, Carlos H. "William Blake--Soldier of Christ." *Theology Today*, XIV (1957), 80-88.

     Blake is seen as "a special kind of dissenter ... joyfully aggressive, an exponent of doctrinal heterodoxy." He is a representative of the transcendentalist heresy.

414. Banta, Martha. "Adonais and the Angel: Light, Color, and the Occult Sublime." *Wordsworth Circle*, VIII (1977), 113-120.

     Argues that Blake denies the sublime, that he represents the anti-sublime, since he does not accept inferiority, obedience to a superior power and impenetrable mystery.

415. Bloom, Harold. "To Reason with a Later Reason: Romanticism and the Rational." *Midway*, XI (1970), 96-112.

     An important essay marking pertinent distinctions.

416. Bottrall, Margaret. "Blake and the Coming of the Kingdom." *The Wind and the Rain*, VI (1949), 26-42.

     On Blake as a Christian.

417. Bowman, Marcia B. "William Blake: A Study of His Doctrine of Art." *Journal of Aesthetics and Art Criticism*, X (1951), 53-66.

     For Blake, the chief function of art is to free the imagination and expose spiritual reality.

418. Brisman, Leslie. "Re: Generation in Blake." *Romantic Origins*. Ithaca, N.Y.: Cornell University Press, 1978, 224-275.

     Argues that in his successive retellings of the story of generation moving to generation, Blake finally, in *Jerusalem*, puts aside "the story of remembered origins."

419. Brisman, Leslie. "Blake and the Eternals' Time." *Milton's Poetry of Choice and Its Romantic Heirs*. Ithaca, N.Y.: Cornell University Press, 1973.

Blake denies historical time as well as narrative time.

420. Chayes, Irene H. "The Circle and the Stair: Patterns of Romantic Theme and Form in the Poetry of Blake, Wordsworth, Coleridge, Shelley, and Keats." Dissertation, Johns Hopkins University, 1960.

421. Chillag, Robert C. "Image and Meaning in William Blake's Poetry." *DA*, XIV (1954), 2343 (Northwestern University).

Traces Blake's poetic imagery from the *Poetical Sketches* to *Jerusalem*.

422. Christian, Diane. "Inversion and the Erotic: The Case of William Blake." *The Reversible World: Symbolic Inversion in Art and Society*. Ithaca, N.Y.: Cornell University Press, 1977, 117-128.

Blake's startling inversions of the erotic tradition.

423. Conner, William F. "Satan as Negative Consciousness in Milton, Blake and Shelley." *DAI*, XL (1980), 4604A (University of Missouri, Columbia).

Argues that Blake's Satan is negative consciousness, which stems from Urizen.

424. Cooke, Michael G. *The Romantic Will*. New Haven: Yale University Press, 1976.

The will is "the concept which for the romantics consummately expresses the metaphysics of engagement...." The Romantic consciousness is engaged, is intentional. *Jerusalem* is uncompromisingly geared to the satisfaction of the will of Los.

425. Corrigan, Matthew. "Metaphor in William Blake: A Negative View." *Journal of Aesthetics and Art Criticism*, XXVIII (1969), 188-199.

Corrigan fails to recognize Blake's use of symbol
rather than metaphor; thus Blake is condemned by foreign
laws.

426. Cox, Stephen D. "'The Stranger Within Thee': The Self
     in British Literature of the Later Eighteenth Century."
     DAI, XXXVII (1976), 2193A (UCLA).

     Believes that Blake did not solve questions of personal
     identity and significance nor did he formulate a fully
     consistent theory of the self.

427. Curry, H. Wilson. "William Blake: Poet of Divine Forgive-
     ness." *Expository Times* (Edinburgh), LXXX (1969), 371-
     374.

     Forgiveness and its generator, love, are the bases of
     self-annihilation--the cornerstone of Blake's vision.

428. Dargan, Tom. "Blake's Idea of Brotherhood." *PMLA*, XCIV
     (1979), 146-147.

     "Is it possible, in the catastrophe of *Jerusalem*,
     that Blake in his intensity, or Los in his victory,
     abandons male supremacy?"

429. Davis, John L. "Blake and the Rhetoric of Humor." *DAI*,
     XXXV (1974), 2936A (University of Texas, Austin).

     Blake's humor is didactic, satiric and ironic.

430. DeGroot, H.B. "The Ouroboros and the Romantic Poets:
     A Renaissance Emblem in Blake, Coleridge, and Shelley."
     English Studies, L (1969), 553-564.

     Significance in Blake of the archetypal image of the
     ouroboric snake, a common Renaissance emblem. In Blake
     it refers to the temporal process which Eternity tran-
     scends.

431. DeLuca, V.A. "The Lost Traveller's Dream: Blake and the
     Seductions of Continuity." *Ariel*, XI (1980), 49-69.

     We are all travellers stuck in mid-journey and seeking
     routes that promise continuity.

432. DeLuca, V.A. "Proper Names in the Structural Design of
     Blake's Myth-Making." *Blake Studies*, VIII (1978), 5-22.

     Proposes that Blake's naming patterns are largely in-
     dependent of thematic arguments, that they are made up

of syllables of related names and that these clusters of
names are related positively or negatively on the levels
of phonetics and categorization.

433. Derderian, Nancy C. "Against the Patriarchal Pomp: A
      Study of the Feminine Principle in the Poetry of
      William Blake." *DAI*, XXXV (1975), 4425A (SUNY, Buffalo).

      Blake was a rebel from the "classical" attitude in
      regard to his radical affirmation of the feminine in
      his work.

434. DiSalvo, Jackie. "William Blake on the Unholy Alliance:
      Satanic Freedom and Godly Repression in Liberal Society."
      Wordsworth Circle, III (1972), 212-222.

      Struggle between Urizen and Luvah each for dominion
      suppresses the freedom of communal man. Some contemporary
      notions here regarding "communal man."

435. Domke, Charlotte F.T. "Progeny of Fire: A Study of Blake's
      Satanic Images." *DAI*, XXXII (1971), 4733A (University
      of Texas, Austin).

      Blake's conception of the person of the Devil and of
      evil, which he holds as relative to particular societies.

436. Donaghue, Denis. "The Peremptory Imagination." *Thieves
      of Fire*. New York: Oxford University Press, 1973, 61-
      86.

      A discussion of the importance of the imagination to
      Blake, who presents the struggle of Prometheus and Zeus
      as that of Orc and Urizen.

437. Duerksen, Roland A. "The Life of Love: Blake's Oothoon."
      Colby Library Quarterly, XIII (1977), 186-194.

      Oothoon is free but isolated from others. Her freedom
      and sense of what might be shared enable her to pursue
      the awakening of others.

438. Durstine, Jean M. "William Blake's Theory of Art and
      Its Application to His Poetry." *DA*, XXVI (1965),
      2748 (Indiana University).

      "The chaotic form of the prophecies is not failure
      but application of the principle that form follows con-
      tent. Chaotic form represents the disunity of fallen
      Albion."

439.   Ferber, Michael. "Blake's Idea of Brotherhood." *PMLA*,
        XCIII (1978), 438-447.

        Blake is the chief poet and prophet of an eternal spirit
        of brotherhood most recently presented in protest move-
        ments of the late 1960's.

440.   Fisher, Peter F. "Blake's Attacks on the Classical Tra-
        dition." *Philological Quarterly*, XL (1961), 1-18.

        Blake countered the classical conception of culture
        and community based on reason, nature and common sense
        with his own conception of the eternal community of the
        human spirit in the form of Albion.

441.   Flatto, Elie. "The Social and Political Ideas of William
        Blake." *DA*, XXVII (1967), 3870A (New York University).

        "... Blake's social and political philosophy is
        animated by an idealistic spirit that is in strong con-
        trast to the materialistic views of his age."

442.   Folsom, L. Edwin. "'Nobodaddy': Through the Bottomless
        Pit Darkly." *Blake Newsletter*, IX (1975), 45-46.

        Nobodaddy could be a character, Abaddon, who appears
        in Job and Revelation.

443.   Fox, Susan. "The Female as Metaphor in William Blake's
        Poetry." *Critical Inquiry*, III (1976-77), 507-519.

        Blake held a theory of mutuality of the sexes, but
        this theory was undermined by certain recurrent stereo-
        types which he used in his early work and could not re-
        dress in his later work.

444.   Freiberg, S.K. "The Fleece-Lined Clock: Time, Space,
        and the Artistic Experience in William Blake." *Dal-
        housie Review*, XLIX (1969), 404-415.

        Time and Space are simultaneously "realities of the
        senses and conceptualizations of the visionary experi-
        ence."

445.   Freiberg, Stanley K. "The Artist's Year: A Study of
        the Meaning of Time in the Life and Works of William
        Blake." *DA*, XVII (1957), 848 (University of Wisconsin).

        Studies time in relation to the contraries, circle
        of destiny and the eternal now.

446.   Frosch, Thomas R. *The Awakening of Albion: The Renova-
       tion of the Body in the Poetry of William Blake.*
       Ithaca, N.Y.: Cornell University Press, 1974.

   Study of Blake's concepts of "Ratio," "Vision," "Imagination," "Eden," "sensual enjoyment," "Vortex," "Center
   and circumference" and "Horizon" in relation to the Fall
   and Resurrection of the human body. And Blake's idea of
   sensuality and sexuality is at once visionary and anti-
   mystical. An excellent work which takes a non-theist
   position in regard to Blake's view of regeneration.

   447.   Adams, Hazard. (rev., *The Awakening of Albion*).
          ELN, XII (1974), 152-153.

         "Oddly enough the book has also the virtue
         of being a readable introduction to the whole
         of Blake's poetry."

   448.   See item 450.

   449.   Erdman, D.V. (rev., *The Awakening of Albion*). *ELN*,
          XII (1974), 32-33.

         "This is a very fine book, so clear (and sound)
         in its explanation of difficult concepts (spectre
         and emanation, Blake's idea of line, Blake's
         auditory style) and hard passages...."

   450.   Faulkner, Dewey. (rev., *The Awakening of Albion*).
          Yale Review, LXIII (1974), 590-599.

         Faulkner is disturbed by Frosch's assumptions.

   451.   Minnick, Thomas L. (rev., *The Awakening of Albion*).
          Blake Studies, VI (1976), 192-194.

         Frosch relies on the terms of modern epistemo-
         logical perspectivism. A genuine contribution
         because "it shows that the poet who was once
         dismissed as mad may be placed among the most
         serious modern philosophers and emerge as grand."

   452.   Nurmi, Martin K. (rev., *The Awakening of Albion*).
          Philological Quarterly, LIV (1975), 904-905.

         "All in all, this is an illuminating piece of
         work, which any serious study of Blake should
         take into account."

453. Frye, Northrop. "The Keys to the Gates." *Some British
      Romantics: A Collection of Essays*. Edited by James V.
      Logan, et al. Columbus: Ohio State University Press,
      1966, 3-40.

      "The cyclical movement of history is summarized by
      Blake in four stages." Frye's Orc Cycle: revolution,
      oppression, objectification, and collapse.

454. Galbraith, Thomas W. "A 'Fresher Morning': Blake Labors
      to Awaken Man." *DAI*, XXXVI (1976), 984A (University
      of Washington).

      Believes that Blake finally advocated self-examination
      and not political action or historical process.

455. George, Diana. "Is She Also the Divine Image? Feminine
      Form in the Art of William Blake." *Centennial Review*,
      XXIII (1979), 129-140. See item 689.

      Blake held that both men and women reduced the feminine
      to object status. However, his notion of Female Will is
      too abstract to cover all aspects of the feminine plight.

456. Glausser, Wayne E. "Blake and the Daughters of Memory."
      DAI, XL (1979), 267A (Yale University).

      Delves into the later prophecies to define Blake's
      rejection of memory as a visionary resource. Argues that
      Blake and Wordsworth hold antithetical views of imagina-
      tion and memory.

457. Gleckner, Robert. "Blake's Religion of the Imagination."
      Journal of Aesthetics and Art Criticism, XIV (1956),
      359-369.

      Seeks to derive a sense of Blake's theory of the ima-
      gination from studying his imaginative products.

458. Gleckner, Robert F. "Blake and the Senses." *Studies in
      Romanticism*, V (1965), 1-15.

      Relationship between the senses and the imagination,
      "a relationship which constitutes the core of Blake's
      theory of vision."

459. Goldberg, Jerome. "William Blake: A Study in the Human
      Sciences." *DAI*, XXXIX (1979), 4271A (University of
      Toronto).

Defends the thesis that Blake's poetry presents "an ontology in psychological terms" and not a Cartesian ontology.

460. Grant, John E. "The Fate of Blake's Sun-Flower: A Forecast and Some Conclusions." *Blake Studies*, V (1973), 7-64.

Discusses the symbol of the sunflower as traditionally represented, gives a close reading of the poem and considers the design.

461. Greenberg, Alvin. "The Real World of Blake's Manuscript Lyric." *Bucknell Review*, XII (1964), 26-46.

Poems in the Rossetti and Pickering Mss. are more in the "real world" than the later books, but less so than the *Songs*.

462. Greenberg, Mark. "Blake's Vortex." *Colby Library Quarterly*, XIV (1978), 198-212.

Vortex generally refers to a jealous, consuming selfhood. "And it represents an individual's existence within mental states, as well as passage through thresholds of consciousness."

463. Gretton, Francis. "Images of Color in the Poetry of William Blake." *DAI*, XXXV (1974), 3740A (Columbia University).

"Blake humanized color, reaffirming a mythology rather than a science of color." Color symbolism suggested.

464. Grimes, Ronald L. "The Dynamics of Vision in the Major Prophetic Works of William Blake." *DAI*, XXXIII (1973), 5816A (Columbia University). See item 466.

465. Grimes, Ronald L. "Time and Space in Blake's Major Prophecies." *Blake's Sublime Allegory* (item 118), 59-81.

Time in Blake's eschatology.

466. Grimes, Ronald L. *The Divine Imagination: William Blake's Major Prophetic Visions*. Metuchen, N.J.: Scarecrow Press, 1972.

"My own training and interests are in philosophy of religion and specifically in the phenomenological school which is concerned with mythic language and symbolic forms. I mention the matter only so the reader will be relieved of the question, What is this, as he reads my book about Blake's what-is-this. This is a work in the area sometimes called 'religion and literature studies,' and it owes more to the phenomenology of religion than to either literary criticism or theology." Includes a very fine bibliography.

467. Rieger, James. (rev., *The Divine Imagination*). *Blake Studies*, VI (1976), 194-196.

This is an eschatological approach to Blake.

468. Hagstrum, Jean H. "Babylon Revisited, or the Story of Luvah and Vala." *Blake's Sublime Allegory* (item 118), 101-118.

Blake "probes the psychological, social, and political dimensions of love and embodies the combined excellencies of Richardson, D.H. Lawrence and Freud."

469. Hagstrum, Jean H. "'The Wrath of the Lamb': A Study of William Blake's Conversions." *From Sensibility to Romanticism*. Edited by F.W. Hilles and Harold Bloom. New York: Oxford University Press, 1965.

Tyger and lamb represent Blake's polarities of Pity and Wrath.

470. Hagstrum, Jean H. "Blake's Blake." *Essays in History and Literature Presented by Fellows of the Newberry Library to Stanley Pargellis*. Edited by Heinz Bluhm. Chicago: Newberry Library, 1965.

Blake is a "dramatis persona" in his own works.

471. Hamilton, Kenneth M. "William Blake and the Religion of Art." *Dalhousie Review*, XXIX (1949), 167-181.

Feels that Blake is a true romantic because he withdrew into the realm of art and paid no attention to the objective world, a world in which art has no validity.

472. Hampton, Nigel. "William Blake's 'Art of Poetry': A Critical Supplement to Five Minor Prophecies." *DAI*, XXXI (1971), 5185A (University of Connecticut).

"Blake's poetics stresses the supremacy of the imagination, or 'the divine vision,' and in the so-called minor prophecies the role and function of the imagination is

stated, developed, modified and finally established as
a perceptual power superior to reason."

473.   Harding, D.W. "Experience and Symbol in Blake." *Experience
       into Words*. New York: Horizon Press, 1963.

       An attack on Blake commentators. "The commentators'
       extended but limiting interpretation sacrifices Blake's
       combination of a very general, complex meaning with a
       vivid-phrase embodied symbol." However, the author sub-
       scribes to a "great passages" approach to the reading
       of Blake and doubts the rewards of "wrestling" with the
       later books.

474.   Hareswape, G. "The Poet's Active and Passive Attributes."
       English Studies in Africa, V (1962), 166-170.

       Dichotomy between male creativity and female passivity,
       which may be based specifically on mythic associations
       related to African mythology. Blake among others is cate-
       gorized.

475.   Harper, George M. "The Neo-Platonic Concept of Time in
       Blake's Prophetic Books." *PMLA*, LXIX (1954), 142-155.

       Time and space are evil in themselves, although they
       are the means by which fallen man achieves salvation.

476.   Hartley, William J. "The Golden String: William Blake's
       Epistemology." *DAI*, XXXIV (1974), 5102A (Vanderbilt
       University).

       "... Blake's development of a theory of knowing which
       would permit man to see past his fallen state on to the
       state of the Eternals."

477.   Hazen, James. "Blake's Tyger and Milton's Beasts."
       Blake Studies, III (1971), 163-170.

       Satan assumes the mask of the tiger in *Paradise Lost*.

478.   Heinzelman, Kurt. "William Blake and the Economics of
       the Imagination." *Modern Language Quarterly*, XXXIX
       (1978), 99-120.

       A poem's business is to secure a human economy without
       economic "valorization."

479.   Hess, M. Whitcomb. "William Blake: 1757-1957." *Christian
       Century*, LXXIV (1957), 1376-1377.

Distinguishes the true and false elements in his teaching, Christianly speaking.

480. Hobsbaum, Philip. "The Romantic Dichotomy." *British
Journal of Aesthetics*, XVI (1976), 32-45.

"Blake is the archetypal Romantic who let go of a
lyric gift in favor of didacticism and pseudo-prophecy."
Blake is long-winded and arbitrary. The dichotomy is
between mind and body, education and emotion, knowledge
and intuition.

481. Humma, John B. "Poe's 'Ligeia': Glanville's Will or
Blake's Will?" *Mississippi Quarterly*, XXVI (1973),
55-62.

Feels that Poe is actually moving in two directions
in regard to the will, Blake's and Glanville's.

482. James, William L. "The Black Man in English Romantic
Literature, 1772-1833." *DAI*, XXXVIII (1977), 2808A
(UCLA).

Blake is portrayed as a champion of justice for Blacks.

483. Jewkes, W.T. "Blake's Creation Myths as Archetypes of
Art." *Directions in Literary Criticism*. Edited by
S. Weintraub and P. Young. University Park: Pennsyl-
vania University Press, 1973, 127-140.

"In the process of recreating a myth of creation to
satisfy himself, Blake discovered what was missing from
the ancient stories of creation, and by a great burst
of imaginative power, he was able to produce the first
truly archetypal myth of art."

484. John, Brian. "William Blake's 'Hereford, Ancient Guardian
of Wales.'" *Blake Studies*, IV (1971), 33-41.

Hereford identified as John Davies of Hereford (ca.
1565-1618) and not Inigo Jones as Damon suggested.
Davies's chief work was *Microcosmos* (1603).

485. Johnson, Mary Lynn. "Emblem and Symbol in Blake."
Huntington Library Quarterly, XXXVII (1974), 151-170.

Blake worked in both the symbolic, as defined by
Coleridge, and the emblem tradition, a tradition lean-
ing toward allegory.

486.   Johnston, Kenneth R. "Blake's Cities: Romantic Forms of
       Urban Renewal." *Blake's Visionary Forms Dramatic* (item
       139), 413-442.

       "Like Blake, perceptive modern city planners go beyond
       city plans to plans for regions; Blake went further, to
       plan for nations, or worlds. Granted, somewhere in these
       progressive enlargements of focus, 'plan' becomes an in-
       adequate word, and must be replaced by 'vision,' but
       that is as Blake would have it. From city to nation to
       world, even to the revolution of history and conscious-
       ness. Thus Blake's urban symbolism fits into the story
       of the fall and regeneration which provides the basic
       plot for most of his major work."

487.   Jones, William P. "The Idea of the Limitations of
       Science from Prior to Blake." *Studies in English
       Literature*, I (1961), 97-114.

       Blake fought the mechanistic spirit of experiment be-
       cause he felt it crushed the imagination.

488.   See item 1595.

489.   Kauvar, Elaine M. "Landscape of the Mind: Blake's Garden
       Symbolism." *Blake Studies*, IX (1980), 57-73.

       "An understanding of Blake's triumphant conception of
       an urban paradise surrounded by a fertile garden repre-
       sentative of Higher Innocence demands an understanding
       of the garden images in the early *Poetical Sketches* as
       well as those occurring with increasing complexity
       through *Jerusalem*."

490.   Kauvar, Elaine M. "Blake's Botanical Imagery." *DAI*,
       XXXII (1972), 3255A (Northwestern University).

       "Blake, imbued in the emblem tradition and keenly
       aware of the botanists, Erasmus Darwin and Thornton,
       found ample sources for natural imagery in emblems,
       the Bible, alchemy, and in the 'botony' of such philo-
       sophers as Boehme, Paracelsus, and Swedenborg."

491.   Kauvar, Elaine. "Los's Messenger to Eden: Blake's Wild
       Thyme." *Blake Newsletter*, X (1976), 82-84.

       Sources of Blake's use of wild thyme in *Milton* could
       have come from Paracelsus or from Robert John Thornton's
       Herbal. Thyme is a symbol of sex and creation and pre-
       sents Blake's view that sexuality must replace the hypoc-
       risy of chastity if paradise is to be achieved.

492. Keene, Michael L. "The Expansive Vision: Visual Percep-
      tion and Romantic Poetry." *DAI*, XXXVII (1977), 5143A
      (University of Texas, Austin).

      Blake and others described both the process of expan-
      sive vision and also relayed their view of human vision.

493. Kemper, F. Claudette. "Blake, Wickstead and the Wicked
      Swan." *Notes & Queries*, N.S. VII (1960), 100-101.

      The swan is an alchemical source rather than a harlot
      swan. Jung pointed out that the swan spits out the ar-
      senic of the philosophers.

494. Keynes, Geoffrey. "Blake's *Spectre*." *Book Collector*,
      XXVIII (1979), 60-66.

      Spectre as Vampire Bat of Surinam.

495. Kiralis, Karl. "A Guide to the Intellectual Symbolism
      in Blake's Later Prophetic Writings." *Discussions of
      William Blake* (item 182), 102-114.

      Focuses on *Jerusalem* and discusses Blake's combination
      of personal and Biblical symbols and his reason for
      establishing his own set of symbols.

496. Kline, Alfred A. "The English Romantics and the American
      Republic: An Analysis of the Concept of America in
      the Work of Blake, Burns, Wordsworth, Coleridge, Byron
      and Shelley." *DA*, XIV (1954), 112 (Columbia University).

      For Blake, the American Revolution was the first
      break in the mind-forged manacles which bound humanity.

497. Larson, Gary D. "The Role of God in Blake's Later Vision:
      The Fall and the Apocalypse." *DAI*, XXVIII (1968),
      5059A (Emory University).

      Argues that Blake believes that God and man are pro-
      gressing toward a common goal.

498. Livingston, Judith H. "The Impact of Africa upon Major
      British Literary Figures, 1787-1902." *DAI*, XXXVIII
      (1977), 4847A (University of Wisconsin, Madison).

      Africa had an impact on Blake's work.

499. Lowery, Margaret R. "William Blake and the 'Divine
      Imagination.'" *Northwest Missouri State College
      Studies*, XIV (1950), 105-131.

      Superficial introduction to Blake.

500. See item 507a.

501. Malmquist, Goran. "The Dean of Morocco--George Cumberland?"
      Blake: An Illustrated Quarterly, XIII (1979), 109.

      Figure appearing in *An Island in the Moon*.

502. Mandell, Robert. "The Emergence of Los within Blake's
      Archetypal Dialectic." *DAI*, XXXIII (1973), 4354A
      (University of Wisconsin, Madison).

      The history of Los, his importance in the Blakean myth,
      his roles, his development.

503. Marken, Ronald. "'Eternity in an Hour'--Blake and Time."
      Discourse, IX (1966), 167-183.

      Two central themes in Blake in relation to the con-
      cept of time "are, first, the Poet-Prophet-Artist who
      in vision and imagination is enabled to apprehend Eternity
      in a moment, and, second, the 'Divine Analogy' which
      makes clear the relationship Blake creates between Time
      and Eternity."

504. Marks, M. "Renovation of Form: Time as Hero in Blake's
      Major Prophecies." *Studies in Eighteenth Century Cul-
      ture*, V. Madison: University of Wisconsin Press,
      1976, 55-66.

      Blake wasn't a mystic concerned with eternity but
      had interesting ideas regarding time and space.

505. Masterson, Donald J. "The Method of Openness and the
      Theme of Love in the Early Poetry of William Blake."
      DAI, XXXVI (1975), 6117A (University of Illinois,
      Urbana-Champaign).

      The theme of sexual love unifies Blake's early poetry.

506. Mathews, Lawrence M. "The Stems of Generation: The Figure
      of the Victim in the Poetry of William Blake." *DAI*,
      XXXVIII (1977), 285A (University of British Columbia).

      The victim appears in all Blake's work, from a victim
      of memory in *Songs of Innocence* and a victim of experi-
      ence in *Songs of Experience* to the major prophecies
      where Blake attempts to bring into existence a world
      in which victims do not exist.

507. Matteson, Lynn R. "Apocalyptic Themes in British Romantic
      Landscape Painting." *DAI*, XXXVII (1976), 5A (University
      of California, Berkeley).

      Blake's art is not considered. His poetry is said to
      represent an eighteenth-century distaste of city life.

507a. Middleman, Louis I. "William Blake and the Form of
      Error: Satiric Craft in the Engraved Minor Prophecies."
      DAI, XXXV (1974), 2947A (University of Pittsburgh).

      "The purpose of this study is to demonstrate that the
      formulation of error, so far from being merely doctrinal,
      provides in fact the underlying poetic technique...."

508. Mills, Alice. "The Spectral Bat in Blake's Illustrations
      to *Jerusalem*." *Blake Studies*, IX (1980), 74-86.

      Ignores earlier discussions of the bat.

509. Miner, Paul. "Visions in the Darksom Air: Aspects of
      Blake's Biblical Symbolism." *William Blake: Essays
      for S. Foster Damon* (item 256), 256-292.

      Traces specifically the Bible's influence on Blake's
      work.

510. Morkan, Joel. "Blake's 'Ancient Forests of Europe.'"
      Blake Newsletter, VI (1973), 93.

      Blake's epithet for the nobility. "They represent the
      old world of privilege and dominance that maintains the
      world of Nature over the human world."

511. Murray, Roger. "Blake and the Ideal of Simplicity."
      Studies in Romanticism, XIII (1974), 89-104.

      Argues that the later books can only be rightly judged
      if we acknowledge Blake as an exponent of sublime sim-
      plicity. Particularity is an important aspect of Blake's
      Edenic simplicity.

512. Nathan, Norman. "Blake and Nontheism." *PMLA*, LXXV (1960),
      147.

      Attacks Bloom's view that Blake is a non-theist.
      Blake, Nathan argues, denies a transcendental God but
      accepts an immanent one.

513. Nathan, Norman. "Blake's 'Head Downwards.'" *Notes &
      Queries*, CXCV (1950), 302-303.

Christ had his teachings so mutilated that he was
treated as a criminal of a scorned religion.

514. Neubauer, John. "The Sick Rose as an Aesthetic Idea:
      Kant, Blake, and Symbol in Literature." *Studies in
      Eighteenth Century Culture*, V. 2. *Irrationalism in
      the Eighteenth Century*. Edited by Harold E. Pagliaro.
      Cleveland: Press of the Case Western Reserve University,
      1972, 167-179.

      "Though the poem embodies a Kantian esthetic idea,
      the re-mythologization of nature runs counter to the
      aims of Kant's philosophy."

515. Nicolson, Marjorie H. "The Poetic Damnation of Newton."
      Newton Demands the Muse. Princeton: Princeton Univer-
      sity Press, 1946, 165-174.

      Summarizes Blake's attack on Bacon, Locke and especially
      Newton.

516. Nurmi, Martin K. "Blake's Doctrine of Contraries: A
      Study in Visionary Metaphysics." *DA*, XIV (1954), 977-
      978 (University of Minnesota). See item 1440.

517. O'Hare, Susan C. "Going Wonder-Ways: Sacrality and Skep-
      ticism in British Romantic Poetry." *DAI*, XXXVII (1976),
      2203A (Rice University).

      Blake discovers a concrete religion, as defined by
      Mircea Eliade, which expresses a dialectic between pure
      wonder and systematization. This wonder or imagination
      is identified in Blake with "Being" itself.

518. Oras, Ants. "Kathleen Raine, the Ancient Springs, and
      Blake." *Sewanee Review*, LXXX (1972), 200-211.

      Upholds Raine's view that Blake's symbolic language
      was traditional and collective rather than personal.

519. Ordonez, E.A. "William Blake's Theory of the Imagination."
      Diliman Review, IX (1961), 250-264.

      A good introductory-level discussion.

520. Ott, Judith. "The Bird-Man of William Blake's *Jerusalem*."
      Blake Newsletter, X (1976), 48-51.

      The Bird-Man signifies Los, the melancholy artist and
      St. John of Patmos--all at once.

521. Paley, Morton D. "Energy and the Imagination: A Study
      of the Development of Blake's Thought." *DA*, XXVIII
      (1967), 689A (Columbia University). See item 229.

522. Paley, Morton D. "The Figure of the Garment in *The Four
      Zoas*, *Milton*, and *Jerusalem*." *Blake's Sublime Allegory*
      (item 118), 119-139.

      The garment is a mediator between "humanity and forces
      within and without."

523. Peckham, Morse. "On Romanticism: Introduction." *Studies
      in Romanticism*, IX (1970), 217-224.

      Has a very specialized sense of Romanticism, one which
      excludes the achievement of unity through apocalypse.
      Thus Blake is "anti-Romantic."

524. Pederson, Glenn M. "The Religion of William Blake: In-
      terpreted from the Fall and Regeneration of Albion,
      Divine Man in the Myth of Blake." *DA*, XIV (1954), 830
      (University of Washington).

      Mentions among other things Jung's four psychological
      functions in relation to *The Four Zoas*.

525. Pedrini, Lura N. "Serpent Imagery and Symbolism in the
      Major English Romantic Poets: Blake, Wordsworth,
      Coleridge, Byron, Shelley, Keats." *DA*, XX (1959),
      2277 (University of Texas, Austin).

      "One of the most highly symbolic entities in the
      physical world is the serpent, and an animal which the
      Romantics found interesting and useful in their attempt
      to reconcile the spiritual and the physical worlds."

526. Pollard, Arthur. "Five Poets on Religion 2. Cowper and
      Blake." *Church Quarterly Review*, CLX (1959), 436-445.

      Blake is an "enthusiast" in the tradition of Wesley.
      Pollard finds in Blake "morality in the highest Christian
      pattern."

527. Price, Martin. *To the Palace of Wisdom: Studies in Order
      and Energy from Dryden to Blake*. Garden City, N.Y.:
      Doubleday, 1964. See item 247.

      Chapter on Blake, "Standard of Energy," also reprinted
      in Bloom's collection, *Romanticism and Consciousness*.
      "What primarily distinguishes Blake as satirist from the

Augustans is the shift from moral judgment to a standard
of energy. It is not the evil man so much as the soulless
and dead man that Blake disdains. In fact, of course, any
standard of vitality tends to transform itself into one
of morality...."

528. Punter, David. "Blake: Creative and Uncreative Labor."
      Studies in Romanticism, XVI (1977), 535-561.

      Bronowski advocated a mystical interpretation of
      Blake, though for Blake "there is no gap between social
      and metaphysical contradiction...." Erdman does not re-
      gard "the economic level of comment primary." Sabri-
      Tabrizi's work is worth mentioning only because it
      attempts to provide a Marxist view of Blake.

529. Quasha, George. "Orc as a Fiery Paradigm of Poetic
      Torsion." *Blake's Visionary Forms Dramatic* (item 139),
      263-284.

      Orc is primitive power released as formative power.
      He must be combined with poetic prophecy.

530. Roberts, Mark. "Blake and the Damnation of Reason."
      The Tradition of Romantic Morality. New York: Barnes &
      Noble, 1973, 82-122.

      Argues that Blake represents "the ne plus ultra" of
      Romantic thinking and that in Blake one can observe the
      clearest rejection of the eighteenth century.

531. Roe, Albert S. "'The Thunder of Egypt': 'Israel deliver'd
      from Egypt, is Art deliver'd from Nature and Imitation.'"
      William Blake: Essays for S. Foster Damon (item 256),
      158-195.

      All things Egyptian are for Blake symbols of the
      fallen world and of spiritual annihilation.

532. Rollins, Mark E. "The Necessity of Art: A Study of
      William Blake." *DAI*, XXXV (1975), 6156A (University
      of Massachusetts).

      Argues that Blake did not support violent revolution
      but advocated a change in values.

533. Rose, Edward J. "Mental Forms Creating: Fourfold Vision
      and the Poet as Prophet in Blake's Designs and Verse."
      Journal of Aesthetics and Art Criticism, XXII (1964),
      173-183. See item 534.

534. Rose, Edward J. "Mental Forms Creating: A Study of
      Blake's Thoughts and Symbols." *DA*, XXV (1965), 1923
      (University of Toronto). See item 533.

      Blake's symbols, metaphors and images related to the
      creative process. His poetry itself dramatizes his view
      of art.

535. Rose, Edward J. "Blake's Human Insect: Symbol, Theory,
      and Design." *Texas Studies in Literature and Language*,
      X (1968), 215-232.

      Fly and worm are symbols for man.

536. Rose, Edward J. "Good-bye to Orc and All That." *Blake
      Studies*, IV (1972), 135-151.

      Orc is a symbol of thwarted creativity and thus repre-
      sents an aspect of Blake's theory of art.

537. Rose, Edward J. "Blake's Metaphorical States." *Blake
      Studies*, IV (1971), 9-31.

      "State" itself is a symbol which gains clarity from
      juxtaposition with its contrary. It is the product of
      imaginative perception.

538. Rose, Edward J. "'Forms Eternal Exist For-ever': The
      Covenant of the Harvest in Blake's Prophetic Poems."
      Blake's Visionary Forms Dramatic (item 139), 443-462.

      The seasonal cycle as a symbol of both a final harvest
      and an eternal spring. "Every particular Form becomes
      the Form of the Divine Vision."

539. Rose, Edward J. "Blake's Human Root: Symbol, Myth, and
      Design." *Studies in English Literature*, XX (1980),
      575-590.

      "As root and insect, man falls into the vegetative world
      and then rises from it. The process describes, there-
      fore, not only a physical metamorphosis but a spiritual
      or mental one."

540. Rose, Edward J. "The Spirit of the Bounding Line: Blake's
      Los." *Criticism*, XIII (1971), 54-76.

      Los, the imagination, draws the line which distinguishes
      art from non-art, vision from fallen, contrary from
      spectre.

541. Rose, Edward J. "Blake's Fourfold Art." *Philological Quarterly*, LXIX (1970), 400-423.

      The interrelatedness of Blake's symbolism.

542. Rose, Edward J. "'A Most Outrageous Demon': Blake's Case Against Rubens." *Bucknell Review*, XVII (1969), 35-54.

      Rubens was remiss in his political, social and aesthetic practices.

543. Rose, Edward J. "Los, Pilgrim of Eternity." *Blake's Sublime Allegory* (item 118), 83-99.

      Los is the embodiment of Blake's ideas regarding art and perception. Rose discusses Time and uses as a gloss Tillich's notion of "kairos."

544. Rose, Edward J. "The Shape of Blake's Vision." *Literature and History*. Edited by Harry R. Garvin. Lewisburg, Pa.: Bucknell University Press, 1977.

      Studies eye symbolism to reveal Blake's view of perception and its relation to creativity.

545. Rose, Edward J. "The Gate of Los: Vision and Symbol in Blake." *Texas Studies in Literature and Language*, XX (1978), 1-14.

      Contains an interesting comparison of Blake and Whitman in regard to their views of the minute and the simple. "The Gate of Los is to be found in the infinitesimal particular in space, time, and act, of which the grain of sand, the moment in each day that Satan cannot find, are symbols."

546. Rose, Edward J. "Blake and the Double: The Spectre as Doppelganger." *Colby Library Quarterly*, XIII (1977), 127-139.

      Surveys the Romantic interest in the double, the Romantics' sense of the existence of two worlds, and argues that much of Blake's work can be traced to the theme of the double.

547. Sachs, Myron. "The Development of Blake's Extended Myth." *DAI*, XXXIII (1972), 2903A (Tufts University).

      "Tiriel, Thel, Visions; *Marriage* and the *Songs*; *French Revolution* and *America*; the Lambeth Books; the *Four Zoas*; *Milton*; *Jerusalem*: seven steps in the development of an extended myth."

548. See item 745.

549. Sanzo, Eileen. "Blake's Beulah and Beulah Hill, Surrey."
      Blake Newsletter, IX (1975), 46.

      Believes that the mystical Beulah may have a parallel
      "in Blake's concrete experience of the suburbs and bor-
      dering countryside of the city he lived in."

550. See item 744.

551. Sanzo, Eileen. "Blake and the Symbolism of the New Iron
      Age." *The Evidence of the Imagination*. Edited by Donald
      H. Reiman, Michael C. Jaye and Betty T. Bennett. New
      York: New York University Press, 1978, 1-11.

      According to Blake, the Iron Age will give way to an
      age of love and brotherhood.

552. Schorer, Mark. "Blake as a Religious Poet." *Sewanee
      Review*, LIV (1946), 241-249.

      Blake sought from the works of independent religious
      thinkers symbols which could express his political and
      social views.

553. Sherry, P.M. "The 'Predicament' of the Autograph:
      'William Blake.'" *Glyph 4: Johns Hopkins Textual
      Studies*. Edited by S. Weber and H. Sussman. Baltimore:
      Johns Hopkins University Press, 1978, 131-155.

      "Clearly the autograph exemplifies a tension between
      text and body, verbal and visual signifiers, in which
      each both supplements and displaces the other in a power-
      ful pulsation of enclosure or contraction and opening
      or expansion, reflected in the curling progress of the
      framing outline itself."

554. Spinks, Cary W. "The Valley of Vision: A Study of Los
      in Blake's Prophecies." *DAI*, XXXI (1971), 4136A
      (University of Nebraska, Lincoln).

      Los the symbol traced from minor to major prophecies,
      exploring his role as a redeeming creative imagination.

555. Steiner, Henry Y. "The Emanation and Its Spectre: William
      Blake's Theory of Poetry." *DA*, XXIV (1963), 4684
      (University of Oregon).

Asserts that symbol, allegory and myth are all based
on an abstract concept of object and referent and that
Blake did not abide by abstractions.

556. Stepto, Michele L. "Blake, Urizen, and the Feminine:
      The Development of a Poetic Logic." *DAI*, XXXIX (1978),
      2960A (University of Massachusetts).

      Presents the thesis that Urizen remains the central
      idea in all Blake's work and exists in the later prophe-
      cies as a "highly reductive and limiting sexual" symbol.

557. Stevenson, W.H. "On the Nature of Blake's Symbolism."
      Texas Studies in Literature and Language, XV (1973),
      445-460.

      Blake was a symbolist because he could express himself
      in no other way. Consistency of personal emotions and
      literary habits he developed generate consistent sym-
      bolism.

558. Sutherland, John. "Blake: A Crisis of Love and Jealousy."
      PMLA, LXXXVII (1972), 424-432.

      Blake's view of sexual love shifted from sex as po-
      tentially liberating to sex as a power which ties people
      to a fallen universe.

559. Sutherland, John. "Blake and Urizen." *Blake's Visionary
      Forms Dramatic* (item 139), 244-262.

      Blake's psychology supersedes "both direct and sym-
      bolic references to outward events." Blake was very
      ambivalent regarding mental activity.

560. Szenczi, Nicholas J. "Reality and the English Romantics."
      Huntington Library Quarterly, XXXI (1968), 179-198.

      Symbolic interpretation of reality, observable in
      Blake and Shelley, does not mean a departure from reality,
      nor is it a less meaningful interpretation than that
      of the scientist.

561. Taylor, Clyde R. "William Blake and the Ideology of
      Art." *DAI*, XXIX (1968), 277A (Wayne State University).

      "William Blake is the exemplary figure of the ideology
      of art, which is that romanticism of art, or esthetic
      humanism, that arose as a reaction to the threat of de-
      humanization posed by the industrial revolution...."

562. Tolley, Michael J. "Blake's Songs of Spring." *William Blake: Essays in Honour of Sir Geoffrey Keynes* (item 240), 96-128.

     Analysis of the song at the end of *Jerusalem* 77, "To Spring," "The Ecchoing Green," "Spring," "The School Boy," *The Book of Thel*, *Visions of the Daughters of Albion*, *The Four Zoas* VIII, IX, and *Milton* 31. These songs of spring are very expressive of the joyful Blake.

563. Trent, Robert J. "The Case Against Death: Transformation of 'Generation' in the Writings of William Blake." *DAI*, XXXVII (1976), 1573A (New York University).

     Maintains that Blake's battle against physical death is discernible in the various ways "generation" is presented in his work.

564. Twitchell, James B. "'The Mental Traveller,' Infinity and the 'Arlington Court Picture.'" *Criticism*, XVII (1975), 1-14.

     Argues that the symbol of infinity is a major poetic icon of Blake's and can be used to crack "The Mental Traveller" and the Arlington Court picture.

565. Viereck, Peter. "The Muse and the Machine." *Etudes Anglaises*, XX (1967), 38-66.

     Blake among many others is on the side of the muse.

566. Viscoli, Lois K. "The Promethean Archetype." *DAI*, XXXV (1975), 6114A (University of New Mexico).

     Argues that Blake found that through suffering man achieves brotherhood while Shelley's Prometheus strives to overcome suffering.

567. Ward, Aileen. "The Forging of Orc: Blake and the Idea of Revolution." *Literature in Revolution*. Edited by G.A. White and C. Newman. New York: Holt, 1972.

     Blake's revolutionary zeal is too often equated only with the Orc cycle.

568. Wardle, Judith. "William Blake's Iconography of Joy: Angels, Birds, Butterflies, and Related Motifs from *Poetical Sketches* to the Pickering Ms." *Blake Studies*, IX (1980), 5-44.

Blake utilized both Christian and classical symbols to "develop part of his personal iconography expressing the joys of earthly and spiritual life and some of the dangers which beset them."

569.   Wardle, Judith. "Blake and Iconography: Analogues of Urizen and Vala." *Colby Library Quarterly*, XIV (1978), 125-165.

Blake's development of an iconographic shorthand began in 1788.

570.   Warner, Janet A. "Blake's Use of Gesture." *Blake's Visionary Forms Dramatic* (item 139), 174-195.

Argues for the existence of archetypes of gestures in Blake's art.

571.   Warner, Nicholas O. "Blake's Moon-Ark Symbolism." *Blake: An Illustrated Quarterly*, XIV (1980), 44-59.

Argues that "if we study the moon-boat in relation to its sources in art and myth, modified by Blake into a motif compatible with his own iconography, we will discern its value as a vehicle of transition from a lower to a higher state of spiritual perception, and as a symbol of redemptive power." This symbol appears in only one line in *Milton*, four pictures in *Jerusalem* and a design from the Dante illustrations.

572.   Warner, Nicholas O. "Blake's Iconic Mode: Tradition and Transformation in the Works of William Blake." *DAI*, XXXIX (1978), 877A (University of California, Berkeley).

Describes Blake's "iconic mode" in which Blake fused his own symbols out of traditional elements. These symbols represent several themes and are constructed through an examination of Blake's composite art.

573.   Weiskel, Thomas. "Darkning Man: Blake's Critique of Transcendence." *The Romantic Sublime*. Baltimore: Johns Hopkins University Press, 1976.

Blake couldn't stomach the sublime but the author attempts "to uncover something of Urizen's felt predicament in the moment of his fall, for it seems ... a version of the sublime moment."

574. Weitzman, Arthur J. "Eighteenth Century London: Urban
     Paradise or Fallen City?" *Journal of the History of
     Ideas*, XXXVI (1975), 469-480.

     "... the archetypal antagonism pointed up in the mythic
     cities of Jerusalem and Babylon, as juxtaposed by Blake,
     is an eternal conflict in the way men regard the urban
     environment."

575. Welch, Dennis M. "Center, Circumference, and Vegetation
     Symbolism in the Writings of William Blake." *Studies
     in Philology*, LXXV (1978), 223-242.

     Argues that Blake's vision of unity and the whole is
     expressed in his center and circumference symbolism and
     is a reaction to Locke's mechanistic understanding which
     holds things disparate.

576. White, Mary E. "Woman's Triumph: A Study of the Changing
     Symbolic Values of the Female in the Works of William
     Blake." *DAI*, XXXIII (1972), 2348A (University of Wash-
     ington).

     Both angry and peaceful.

577. Whitehead, Frederick A. "Studies in the Structure of
     European History in Blake's Epics." *DAI*, XXXV (1975),
     7927A (Columbia University).

     Blake's prophecies represent the entire history of
     European man.

578. Whitehead, Fred. "William Blake and the Radical Tradi-
     tion." *Weapons of Criticism: Marxism in America and
     the Literary Tradition*. Edited by Norman Rudich. Palo
     Alto, Calif.: Ramparts Press, 1976, 191-214.

     Allies himself with the social-economic critics of
     Blake, although he contends that people like Frye provide
     fine psychological insight, although their idealism is
     a limitation. Derides "overly mentalized and psycholo-
     gized" views. Considers labor as a theme in Blake and
     points out its affinities to contemporary Mexican and
     Soviet art. Blake's apocalypse marks an end to the
     world of stock exchanges.

579. Williams, Raymond. "Literature and the City." *Listener*,
     LXVIII (1967), 653-656.

     Interesting view of the city and the crowd as a symbol
     in Blake, among others.

580. Wilner, Eleanor. "The Eye of the Storm: An Inquiry into
      the Role of Imagination in Maintaining Human Order and
      Mediating Social and Personal Change." *DAI*, XXXIV
      (1973), 3362A (Johns Hopkins University).

      Imagination maintains human order in a period of social
      and personal change.

581. Wilner, Eleanor. "The Uncommon Eye: Vision in the Poetry
      of Blake, Beddoes, and Yeats." *Gathering the Winds:
      Visionary Imagination and Radical Transformation of
      Self and Society*. Baltimore: Johns Hopkins University
      Press, 1975.

      Blake perceived the malaise around him by means of his
      own personal perception of the laws of the imagination.

582. Wiltshire, John. "Blake's Simplicity." *Cambridge Quarter-
      ly*, V (1971), 211-222.

      Blake is simple--at least the early Blake, the *Songs*
      and the *Marriage*. And Eliot was right about simplicity
      and abstraction in Blake. "... the poems in *Songs of
      Innocence and Experience* are quite various, they do not
      (in my experience at least) help each other to grow,
      become a landscape or a world."

583. Wittreich, Joseph A. "The 'Satanism' of Blake and Shelley
      Reconsidered." *Studies in Philology*, LXV (1968), 816-
      833.

      Attempted clarification of Blake's and Shelley's
      attitudes toward *Paradise Lost*.

584. Wooster, Margaret, and Arthur Efron. "On Blake's 'Streams
      of Gore': An Exchange." *Paunch*, XL (1975), 152-165.

      Wooster feels that Blake's unprecedented affirmation
      of women in *Visions* vindicates Blake against charges of
      hostility toward women.

585. Ziegelman, Lois A. "William Blake: The Lineaments of
      History." *DAI*, XXXIV (1974), 4223A (Brandeis Univer-
      sity).

      Blake's meaning of history and its divergence from
      the thought of Blake's time.

CHAPTER SIX
STYLE AND FORM

Gleckner's "Most Holy Forms of Thought" (item 602) asks
provocatively how the prophet Blake can redeem the one Word by
a recourse to a fallen language which must itself be redeemed?
He discusses "Blake's conception of the language of Eternity,"
Blake's presentation of "fallen" language, and Blake's conception of the redemption of language. Ostriker's study of
Blake's prosody (item 621) is too much devoted to the prosody
at the expense of the vision; Blake is perhaps the worst
choice for a study such as this. Mellor's book-length study
(item 610) uncovers what she believes to be a contradiction
between Blake's rejection of reason and the body and his
acceptance of definite outline in art. This contradiction exists
only if one believes as Mellor does that Blake rejected the
human body and the necessity of giving form to the moral
world--two very questionable assumptions.

In *Poetic Form in Blake's Milton* (item 595), Fox argues
for a poetic structure in *Milton* as profound as its thematic
structure. This hypothesis may be questionable, though certainly not as questionable as Mellor's, but it does not re-
strict Fox's discussion of *Milton* in the way Mellor's hypothesis restricts her discussion. Unfortunately, there is some
irony in Fox's approach since she argues for some two hundred
pages of close exegeses on behalf of a suprarational order
in *Milton*.

I would recommend discussions of style, language and form
which are not the paramount concerns of the critic but which
are incorporated within a total exegesis. Gleckner's *The Piper
and the Bard* (item 180) and Gillham's *Blake's Contrary States*
(item 168) are sensitive to language in their discussion of
the *Songs*. Bloom's "Dialectic in *The Marriage of Heaven and
Hell*" (item 1424) is sensitive to form, as is his "The Visionary Cinema of Romantic Poetry" (item 586).

586. Bloom, Harold. "The Visionary Cinema of Romantic Poetry."
      William Blake: Essays for S. Foster Damon (item 256),
      18-35.

      The cinematic quality of Blake's visionary world leads
      to a "defeat of sight," an attack on the bounded ear
      and eye. Blake is "poised between the phantasmagoria
      of the surrealists and the massive and detailed vision-
      ary realism of Milton."

587. Brooke-Rose, Christine. *A Grammar of Metaphor*. London:
      Secker & Warburg, 1958.

      "Blake really lets himself go with genitive links...."

588. Carner, Frank. "Four Contexts for the Study of the Re-
      lationship of Text and Design in the Illuminated Books
      of William Blake." *DAI*, XXXVIII (1978), 6138A (Uni-
      versity of Toronto).

      Generic, archetypal, canonical and specific contexts.
      Blake is fruitfully studied from all approaches.

589. Christian, Diane. "'The Eternal Body': A Study of the
      Structural Metaphor in the Work of William Blake."
      DAI, XXXIV (1974), 7183A (Johns Hopkins University).

590. Cook, Albert. "Blake's *Milton*." *Costerus*, VI (1972),
      27-33.

      Description of the verse form.

591. Daeley, Carol A. "Image of Infinite: William Blake's
      Language of Poetry." *DAI*, XXXVI (1975), 2215A (Uni-
      versity of California, Riverside).

      Believes that through a study of Blake's language,
      the reader can understand Blake's entire cosmology.

592. DeLuca, Vincent. "Ariston's Immortal Palace: Icon and
      Allegory in Blake's Prophecies." *Criticism*, XII
      (1970), 1-19.

      Iconic poetry distinguished from allegorical poetry.

593. Eaves, Morris. "Blake and the Artistic Machine: An
      Essay in Decorum and Technology." *PMLA*, XCII (1977),
      903-927.

      Blake criticized the transformation of artistic
      technique and practice into basic artistic principles.

He advocated a relationship between conception and execution, means and end. The artistic machine is society's preference for a single technique.

594. Epstein, E.L. "The Self-Reflexive Artefact: The Function of Mimesis in an Approach to a Theory of Value for Literature." *Style and Structure in Literature: Essays in the New Stylistics*. Edited by Roger Fowler. Ithaca, N.Y.: Cornell University Press, 1975.

"The Tyger" presents an extremely complex emotional situation, which is revealed to the reader through close analysis of the "mimetic schemata."

595. Fox, Susan. *Poetic Form in Blake's Milton*. Princeton: Princeton University Press, 1976.

An in-depth study of the rhetorical structure of *Milton* undertaken to prove that this structure is, in the later prophecies, as profound as the themes which it presents.

596. Brisman, Leslie. (rev., *Poetic Form in Blake's Milton*). *Studies in Romanticism*, XVI (1977), 260-267.

"It may be hard to isolate great visionary moments in this book, but the cumulative effect is to make Blake's visionary moments seem not so far away."

597. Chayes, Irene. (rev., *Poetic Form in Blake's Milton*). *ELN*, XV (1977), 46.

"... her study tends to be over-conceptualizing and over-rationalizing, with a drive toward the abstract and the doctrinal beyond the demands of the text."

598. Freiberg, Stanley K. (rev., *Poetic Form in Blake's Milton*). *Ariel*, VIII (1977), 97-99.

"The initiated Blake student will find most of the interpretations rather worn; nonetheless, he can expect to be enlightened as to the structural density of the work and with its high degree of parallelism."

599. Wesling, Donald. (rev., *Poetic Form in Blake's Milton*). *Wordsworth Circle*, VIII (1977), 233-236.

"Professor Fox ... has shown the moral reach
and intellectual coherence and power of narrative structures in *Milton*...."

600. Gleckner, Robert F. "Blake and Satire." *Wordsworth
Circle*, VIII (1977), 311-326.

Models for Blake's satire may have been Butler, Swift,
Byron, Henry Carey, Prior, Churchill, Fielding and
Sterne.

601. Gleckner, Robert F. "Blake's Verbal Technique." *William
Blake: Essays for S. Foster Damon* (item 256), 321-332.

"I propose to examine some of the poetry to see to
what extent 'Every word' seems to have been 'studied
and put into its fit place,' and to what extent and
how (and perhaps) all are necessary to each other."

602. Gleckner, Robert F. "Most Holy Forms of Thought: Some
Observations on Blake and Language." *ELH Essays for
Earl R. Wasserman*. Baltimore: Johns Hopkins Univer-
sity Press, 1976, 262-284.

"How then is the poet to regenerate or redeem the
word via the use of the fallen elements that 'signal
their complicity with that which makes the [word] un-
realizable,' and that therefore require regeneration
and redemption themselves?"

603. Heppner, Christopher A.E. "The Problem of Form in Blake's
Prophecies." *DAI*, XXXII (1971), 433A (University of
Toronto).

"This dissertation uses as its basic structure the
four-level model of interpretation used by, among others,
medieval allegorists, Blake himself, and Northrop Frye.
The intention is to show that a single level view of
form is incomplete, and that a view of form must consider the changing nature of a reader's participation
in a work."

604. Herrstrom, David S. "Mythopoeia and Blake's Major
Prophecies." *DAI*, XXXVI (1975), 3652A (New York
University).

Blake displays mythical cognition in his work because
he perceives the perceptual unity of subject and object,
of perceiver and the world perceived.

605. Hilton, Howard N. "Revelation in the Literal Expression:

Blake's Polysemous Words." *DAI*, XL (1979), 2073A
(University of California, Santa Cruz).

Various words are examined in the hope of proving
that they represent more than images or arbitrary sig-
nifications. "They are 'ideographs' whose polysemous
meanings are literally accessible."

606. Hollander, John. "Blake and the Metrical Contract."
      *From Sensibility to Romanticism: Essays Presented to
      Frederick A. Pottle*. Edited by R.W. Hilles and H.
      Bloom. New York: Oxford University Press, 1965.

      The "whole Augustan tradition of the two couplet epi-
      gram is undermined by the unyielding hammered insistence
      of the repeated line and the ironic absence of wit...."

607. Jakobson, Roman. "On the Verbal Art of William Blake and
      Other Poet-Painters." *Linguistic Inquiry*, I (1970), 3-23.

      The other painters discussed are Henri Rousseau and
      Paul Klee. A discussion of the way in which Blake's
      composite art works.

607a. Kroeber, Karl. *Romantic Narrative Art*. Madison: Uni-
      versity of Wisconsin Press, 1960.

      Blake is representative of Romantics in his progres-
      sion from "relatively naturalistic narrative to thorough-
      ly imaginative narrative of a mythical kind." Truths
      of intuitive art surpass the findings of science.

608. Kumbier, William. "Blake's Epic Meter." *Studies in
      Romanticism*, XVII (1978), 163-192.

      Argues that there is deliberation behind Blake's epic
      meter and that Blake realized the claims he made for
      his versification in the preface to *Jerusalem*.

609. McClellan, Jane. "Dramatic Movement as a Structuring
      Device in Blake's *Jerusalem*." *Colby Library Quarterly*,
      XIII (1977), 195-208.

      Los's actions are the dramatic structure of the poem.

610. Mellor, Anne K. *Blake's Human Form Divine*. Berkeley:
      University of California Press, 1974.

      Discusses the growth of form in Blake's work in regard
      to theme and style. A number of questionable points: com-
      position of design means more than symbol; Innocence is a
      complete, ideal state; Blake rejects the human body; the
      Songs were complete in vision and the later books were a
      chaos. Finally, terms Blake's art "romantic classicism."

611.   See item 613.

612.   Chayes, Irene. (rev., *Blake's Human Form Divine*).
       ELN, XIII (1975), 32.

         "Unfortunately, like an increasing number of
         her predecessors in recent years, the author is
         committed to a factitious thesis, one which in
         her case involves what other Blakeists may con-
         sider a false problem--the supposed contradic-
         tion between Blake's graphic style and his early
         views of both the human body and human systems
         of thought--and an illusory solution, summed
         up in the phrase used as her title."

613.   Faulkner, Dewey. (rev., *Blake's Human Form Divine*).
       Yale Review, LXIII (1974), 590-599.

         "The book's ultimate value is probably as an
         introductory work, and as such can be recommended."

614.   Marks, Mollyanne. (rev., *Blake's Human Form Divine*).
       Philological Quarterly, LIV (1975), 908-909.

         "... emphasizes what has lately emerged as
         the central problem in Blake studies--the rela-
         tion of form to idea, image to word, and illustra-
         tion to text. In her investigation of this
         problem, Mellor argues strongly for a chrono-
         logical development in Blake's ideas and style."

615.   Metcalf, Francis W. "Reason and 'Urizen': The Pronunci-
       ation of Blakean Names." *Blake Newsletter*, VI (1972),
       17-18.

       "Whether Blake usually spoke 'Urizen' as a pure dactyl
       or with a secondary final stress--as 'Benjamin' or as
       'Benjamite'--is not finally deducible from the metrics,
       and raises the forbidding problem of vowel quality."

616.   Miles, Josephine. "The Sublimity of William Blake."
       Eras and Modes in English Poetry. Berkeley and Los
       Angeles: University of California Press, 1957.

       Civic and cosmic--that is the sublimity of William
       Blake. Blake "seems to have participated congenially in
       usages which were changing as gradually as in other
       centuries and carried as much weight of tradition. This
       participation in basic practice encourages us to study

him not only as different but as similar, not only as
odd but as representative of poetic community, first in
his choice of major poetic language and then in the context of his use of it."

617. Miles, Josephine. "Blake's Frame of Language." *William
Blake: Essays in Honour of Sir Geoffrey Keynes* (item
240), 86-95.

Discusses the results and significance of Erdman's
Concordance (item 35) and the basic rightness of her
own earlier sampling. "... Blake's most traditional
materials provide words of sense and feeling and per-
ceiving, moving away from such classical generalities
as *nature*, *youth*, *fate*, *virtue*, *thought*, toward the
nineteenth century's *little*, *child*, *daughter*, *death*,
earth, *weep*...."

618. Mitchell, W.J.T. "Style as Epistemology: Blake and the
Movement Toward Abstraction in Romantic Art." *Studies
in Romanticism*, XVI (1977), 145-164.

There is a basic vocabulary of "linear pattern" at
the foundation of Blake's style that reveals the cog-
nitive process itself. Blake's paintings are therefore
an exploration of perception.

619. Nelson, J. Walter. "Blake's Diction--An Amendatory Note."
Blake Studies, VII (1975), 167-175.

Argues that Blake coined a number of words, and was
very innovative in his diction.

620. Ostriker, Alicia. "William Blake: A Study in Poetic
Technique." *DA*, XXIV (1964), 3754 (University of
Wisconsin). See item 621.

621. Ostriker, Alicia. *Vision and Verse in William Blake*.
Madison: University of Wisconsin Press, 1965.

A study of Blake's prosody. Basically an attempt to
reduce vision to the level of the minor technical laws
of prosody, since she supposes the latter can explain
the former.

622. Adams, Hazard. (rev., *Vision and Verse in William
Blake*). *Journal of Aesthetics and Art Criticism*,
XXV (1966), 107-109.

"In general, Ostriker's flights into critical
interpretation are as unsteady as her theoretical
confusions."

623.   Bentley, G.E., Jr. (rev., *Vision and Verse in
        William Blake*). *Modern Language Review*, LXI
        (1966), 684-685.

        "Mrs. Ostriker is to be congratulated on a
        stimulating piece of work."

624.   Benziger, James. (rev., *Vision and Verse in William
        Blake*). *Criticism*, VIII (1966), 289-293.

        "Blake's contemporary Hegel may have sought
        to develop all his topics--history, religion,
        art, and so forth--within the structure of one
        metaphysical scheme, but at least he developed
        them separately. Blake, as Mrs. Ostriker and
        others have noted, often seeks to develop them
        all at once."

625.   Cooper, Danielle C. (rev., *Vision and Verse in
        William Blake*). *Books Abroad*, XL (1966), 343-344.

        Prosody is an austere subject, but Ostriker
        is refreshing.

626.   Grant, John E. (rev., *Vision and Verse in William
        Blake*). *Philological Quarterly*, XLV (1966), 536-
        537.

        "Mrs. Ostriker is always suggestive when she
        is working closely with a text but her summary
        statements are occasionally inspired more by a
        desire to write neatly than to be perfectly
        accurate."

627.   Harding, D.W. (rev., *Vision and Verse in William
        Blake*). *Notes & Queries*, N.S. XIII (1966), 235-
        236.

        "... one can still doubt whether it really
        is prosody that provides the illumination. The
        alternative view is that knowledge of English
        as a spoken language shows Mrs. Ostriker how
        to read Blake rhythmically, scansion marks allow
        her to communicate her reading, and prosodic
        analysis adds only a superimposed and often un-
        convincing description of what she has done."

628. Harper, George M. (rev., *Vision and Verse in William Blake*). *South Atlantic Quarterly*, LXV (1966), 410-411.

> Some criticism of her work (not for all readers), but generally considers the book a good piece of scholarship.

629. Nurmi, Martin K. (rev., *Vision and Verse in William Blake*). *Journal of English and Germanic Philology*, LXVI (1967), 461-463.

> Response to Ostriker's claim that prosody reveals meaning on a substantial level. Nurmi points to Ostriker's interpretation of "The Tyger," where almost every word is knit up through sound with every other word.

630. Nurmi, Martin K. (rev., *Vision and Verse in William Blake*). *ELN*, IV (1966), 23-24.

> "A metrical study of Blake would be most welcome, but it should be made with a more subtle analytical scheme than one which points out iambs and trochees and does little more, and it should be made with a firmer grasp of Blake's meaning."

631. Shook, Margaret L. (rev., *Vision and Verse in William Blake*). *Modern Philology*, LXV (1967), 79-81.

> "'The Mental Traveller' is a metrical bore-- does that really matter? Perhaps for Mrs. Ostriker driven by her concern for prosody."

632. Pananides, Dean N. "Vision and Form in William Blake's Illuminated Poetry." *DAI*, XXXVII (1977), 7765A (University of California, Santa Barbara).

> Myth solves the problem of conveying Blake's own vision of the universe. *Jerusalem* resolves the problem of vision and form.

633. Peterson, Jane E. "Metric and Syntactic Experimentation in Blake's Prophecies of 1788-95." *DAI*, XXXVI (1975), 3661A (University of Arkansas).

> Blake's metric and syntactic experimentation reveal many of the qualities he possessed as an artist.

634. Raine, Kathleen. "A Note on Blake's 'Unfettered Verse.'"
      William Blake: Essays in Honor of S. Foster Damon
      (item 256), 383-392.

      A poet's comments on Blake's verse. Raine also suggests
      that Chapman may have been a source for Blake's "un-
      fettered verse."

635. Rawson, W.J. "'Ida's Shady Brow': Parallels to Blake."
      Notes & Queries, N.S. XII (1965), 183.

      These three words appear elsewhere in literature--
      Parnell, Dryden, Pope and Milton.

636. Rhodes, Jack L. "A Study in the Vocabulary of English
      Romanticism: 'Joy' in the Poetry of Blake, Wordsworth,
      Coleridge, Shelley, Keats, and Byron." *DA*, XXVII
      (1967), 3434A (University of Texas, Austin).

      The use of the word "joy"--context and symbolization.
      Blake's use "of joy as power, force, energy, a symbol
      of the spiritual rebirth of the fallen world...."

637. Scott, Janis M. "The Stubborn Structure of the Language:
      A Study of the Syntax of William Blake." *DAI*, XXXIV
      (1974), 5148A (University of Mississippi).

      "A descriptive analysis of the syntax of William
      Blake provides a critical apparatus with which his
      poetry can be more effectively studied."

638. Shroyer, Richard. "Studies in the Chronology and Con-
      texts of William Blake's Early Poems: The First Decade,
      1783-1793." *DAI*, XXXVII (1977), 6513A (University of
      Toronto).

      Urges that the title-page date must stand without
      "overwhelming proof of the contrary."

639. Singh, Gurbhagat. "Meditations on William Blake: An
      Experiential Approach to His Poetry." *DAI*, XXXVI
      (1975), 286A (University of California, Santa Cruz).

      Blake not only discussed the "Edenic" body but also
      used it as the basis of his poetry. Poems must be read
      "bodily."

640. Speirs, John. "Blake, Coleridge, Keats and Shakespeare."
      Poetry Toward Novel. London: Faber & Faber, 1971,
      11-48.

Blake used language not in the characteristic eighteenth-century fashion but in an imaginative, creative,
Shakespearean way, and influenced nineteenth-century
fiction.

641. Taylor, Anya. "Blake's Moving Words and the Dread of
      Embodiment." *Cithara*, XV (1976), 75-85.

Blake rejects the occult notion that language is
magical. "When words create they cruelly bind; when
they bring imaginary things into being, they doom them
to fixity."

642. Taylor, Ronald C. "The Semantics of Time in the Later
      Poetry of William Blake: A Stylistic Study." *DAI*,
      XXXVII (1977), 5857A (University of California,
      Berkeley).

Extends the work of Josephine Miles and others to
include "the broader applications of temporal semantics."

643. Tolley, Michael J. "Blake's 'Eden's Flood' Again."
      Notes & Queries, N.S. XV (1968), 11-19.

A reconsideration of lines 12-20 of "The Everlasting
Gospel." See item 1126.

644. Wang, Alfred S. "The Imagery of Blake's Minor Prophecies."
      DAI, XXVIII (1968), 3652A (Tulane University).

Imagery in *Thel*, *Tiriel*, *Visions*, *Marriage* and "The
Mental Traveller."

645. Ward, Marney. "Text and Design in Blake's Developing
      Myth." *DAI*, XXXV (1974), 3704A (University of British
      Columbia).

Examines the interrelationship of text and design
in *Songs of Innocence and of Experience*, *Urizen* and
Jerusalem.

646. Wittreich, Joseph A. "Painted Prophecies: The Tradition
      of Blake's Illuminated Books." *Blake in His Time*
      (item 149), 101-115.

Blake observes prophetic tradition literally by
marrying pictures with words.

CHAPTER SEVEN

BLAKE'S INFLUENCE

The periodic rediscovery of Blake in the nineteenth cen-
tury by various individuals--Gilchrist, Swinburne, Rossetti,
Yeats--is something very different from Blake's total effect
on the twentieth century. Certainly, there is the rediscovery
by various writers who remodel Blake just as he remodeled
Milton--Joyce, Hart Crane, Joyce Cary, D.H. Lawrence, André
Gide, Patrick White, Thomas Merton, J.R.R. Tolkien, Theodore
Roethke, Gary Snyder, Allen Ginsberg, Colin Wilson. But
Blake's visibility in our own time combined with an energetic
Blake critical industry has discovered Blake's influence on
lesser lights--James Hogg, Shaw Neilson, Samuel Menashe, Peter
Carter, George MacDonald, Ralph Chubb, Anna Wickham. Each
of these may be fortunate enough to someday find a Gilchrist.

While Robert Bly (item 666) looked forward to more Blakean
imagination in contemporary American poetry, Dudek (item 680)
hailed Blake as one of the forerunners of a new Romantic poetry.
McGann (item 718) discovered Blake as a forerunner of Ginsberg's "wildmen" school of poetry, and Bartlett (item 661)
found this "new romanticism" with Blakean undertones decadent.
And, indeed, a relatively short time after Blake became top-
grade grist for the scholarly mills, he became also an influential force outside of academe, within a subculture that
was finding spokesmen in Allen Ginsberg, N.O. Brown, Theodore
Roszak, Charles Reich and Gary Snyder among others.

This generation of the 1960's was, in John Humma's words,
descendental romantics, romantics who achieved "consummation
directly by way of the senses, through 'blood-knowledge'"
(item 700). They became what Beaty (item 662) called the new
moralists, moralists who found their inspiration in Blake's
equation of body and soul. Brown (item 670) referred to it
as a "spritual body," the regenerated body which Blake had
envisioned. Only an unrepressed sexuality could create this
body, a body which was love's body as opposed to a mind which
was reason's mind.

Although neither Ginsberg nor Brown acknowledged Blake's
contraries and the dialectic of energy based on equally accepted
contraries of reason and energy, Blake's work did express a
decided rhetorical preference for energy and imagination, for
an exuberant display of bodily energies. In the 1960's, Blake
found his first popular audience. The "new consciousness,"
doomed to burn out very shortly, created a receptive environ-
ment for Blake's vision, and was in turn molded by that vision.
Michael Ferber (item 439) has taken the optimistic view that
the Blake who was a spirit of fraternity in the 1960's remains
a spirit of fraternity today.

Blake has been referred to in a number of contexts that
either directly or indirectly relate to the "new romanticism"
of the 1960's. Shain (item 746) looks to Blake's work as a
model for estrangement. Ketters (item 705) and Suvin (item 751)
refer to Blake as an influence on science fiction. Ketters ties
Blake to apocalyptic literature and Suvin to repressed subcultures. Sutherland (item 750) sees Blake as an advocate of
nonviolence. Raine (item 735) sees Blake as a model for the
assertion of imagination in education. Thomas Altizer (item 651)
looks to Blake as a source for his own "Death of God" movement,
one in which man turns from Nobodaddy and seeks to affirm his
own role in salvation. Stevenson (item 749) refers to Blake's
similarity with Berdyaev. Theirs is a mutual concern for an eschatology of immanence and of redemption based on creativity
and perception.

Blake takes a stand in the twentieth century against
"objectification" which is "the ejection of man into the
external ... an exteriozation [sic] of him ... the sub-
jection of him to the conditions of space, time, causality,
and rationalization" (Berdyaev, *The Beginning and the End*).
Blake is a twentieth-century existentialist. On the other
hand, according to Raine in "Blake's Last Judgment" (item
733), Blake's work has been the most effective source of the
perennial wisdom of the present day.

Blake has also had an effect upon contemporary critical
theory. Thorslev (item 753) terms this a dialectic criticism
which is at heart opposed to logical discourse. Though poetry
is not equated with logical discourse "it must in some sense
also be that" (Thorslev, 68). Thorslev's intention is to
ferret out the "other culture," the culture which has "not
been deeply affected by philosophical analysis or by the
mathematical ordering of scientific method." Blake is chosen
as the "most consistently and explicitly dialectic of all
the English Romantics...." Hazard Adams in "Blake and the
Postmodern" (item 648) applauds Blake's effect on a criticism
based on dialectic. "The most viable Blakean criticism insists that poetry and the mode of science stand contrary,

that neither can quite afford the luxury of the autonomy it
must nevertheless insistently profess, that neither can quite
devour its opposite. To sustain a proper intellectual struggle
between these forms of knowing is to provide ourselves with
what cultural and spiritual harmony we can, as symbolizing
animals, achieve" (17).

Blake has doubtless been influential in twentieth-century
psychology. N.O. Brown's extension of Freudian theory to include an equal dialectic of Reality and Pleasure Principles
is heavily indebted to Blake. Jung cites Blake directly as
an example of a visionary artist, an artist whose symbols
emerge from archetypes of the collective unconscious. Phenomenological psychology, which focuses upon consciousness and
perception determined by individual intentions, is a rephras-
ing of Blake's views in regard to perception. Deborah Austin
(item 74) focuses on Blake's intentions in an attempt to
generate in the reader "an awareness of the wholeness of these
great poems ..." (80).

The variety of the influence points to the variety of
Blake. In the dialectic between Blake and the twentieth century, Blake has found much deserved recognition, and the
twentieth century has heeded a voice which had already done
much to shape the century. The pendulum in the last quarter
of this century seems, however, to be swinging back toward
Bacon, Newton and Locke.

647. Adams, Hazard. "Blake, Jerusalem and Symbolic Form."
        Blake Studies, VII (1975), 143-166.

        Argues that Blake "made the most complete utterance
        of a philosophy of literary symbolism in his time."
        Blake follows Cassirer here in holding that we have no
        direct access to the world and its objects in a one-
        on-one fashion but in actuality create it. The poetic
        form of apprehension is in Blake's view a holistic
        rather than a limited view, fourfold rather than single.

648. Adams, Hazard. "Blake and the Postmodern." *William
        Blake: Essays for S. Foster Damon* (item 256), 3-17.

        "Postmodern" is the work of Frye, criticism based on
        dialectic, Husserl's phenomenology, and existentialism.
        Adams opposes Wimsatt's attacks on criticism based on
        Blake and Yeats and insists that the "conjunction of
        Blake and Cassirer enables postmodern criticism to re-
        constitute or broaden the modernist critical ideas of
        paradox, tension, drama, and irony."

649. Allen, Orphia. "William Blake's Criticism of the English
      Poets." *DAI*, XL (1979), 2068A (University of Oklahoma).

      Argues that Blake has left us significant criticism
      of various English poets, a criticism which is based
      on Blake's own system of progression to fourfold vision.

650. Altizer, Thomas J. "William Blake and the Role of Myth
      in the Radical Christian Vision." *Centennial Review*,
      IX (1965), 461–482.

      Blake's myth foreshadows the contemporary theme of
      the death of God.

651. Altizer, Thomas J. *The New Apocalypse: The Radical
      Christian Vision of William Blake*. East Lansing:
      Michigan State University Press, 1967.

      A thought-provoking work which preceded Altizer's
      "Death-of-God" studies and was the impetus of those
      studies. It goes far toward describing Blake's connec-
      tions with contemporary religious thought. There are
      surprising connections between Altizer, N.O. Brown,
      T. Roszak, N. Berdyaev and others in regard to the
      Blakean notions of the resurrected or spiritual body.

      652. Merton, Thomas. "Blake and the New Theology"
            (rev., *The New Apocalypse*). *Sewanee Review*,
            LXXVI (1968), 673–682.

            Merton finds Altizer's work generally fine
            but believes him wrong regarding Blake's connec-
            tion with Hegel and Blake's conjectured admira-
            tion for the Satan of institutionalized Chris-
            tianity.

      653. Wilson, Francis. (rev., *The New Apocalypse*).
            Modern Age XI (1967), 419–421.

            "Hegel, it would seem to me, merely makes
            Blake less understandable than before."

      654. Woolley, Mary L. (rev., *The New Apocalypse*).
            Journal of English and Germanic Philology,
            LXVIII (1969), 186–191.

            Many Blake students "have suspected that an
            understanding of Blake's affinity with Kirke-
            gaard, Bultmann, Bonhoeffer, Buber, and Tillich
            illuminates his poetry even more than an in-
            vestigation of his debts to Swedenborg and Boehme."

655. Anon. "Symposium on Violence." *Twentieth Century* (Winter 1964-65).

Blake quoted *passim*.

656. Arber, Agnes. *The Mind and the Eye*. Cambridge: Cambridge University Press, 1964.

In the course of her argument, this biologist refers to Blake on the expression of ideas (ideas exist as words), on seeing with the mind (looking through not with the eye), and on truth (truth and expression).

657. Archibald, Douglas N. "Yeats's Encounters: Observations on Literary Influence and Literary History." *New Literary History*, I (1970), 439-469.

Blake mentioned as an important influence.

658. Averitt, Margie. "And Three's a Crowd: A Study of Joyce Cary's First Trilogy." *DA*, XXIV (1964), 5405 (University of Texas, Austin).

"The Blakean myth structure supports and gives coherence to the symbolic roles of Cary's personages." The trilogy includes *Herself Surprised*, *To Be a Pilgrim*, and *The Horse's Mouth*.

659. Baird, Sister Mary Julian. "Blake, Hopkins and Thomas Merton." *Catholic World*, CLXXXIII (1956), 46-49.

Merton was influenced by Blake and by Hopkins.

660. Ballin, Michael G. "D.H. Lawrence and William Blake: A Critical Study in Influence and Analogy." *DAI*, XXXIV (1974), 5154A (University of Toronto).

The following are discussed: religious tradition, theory of knowledge, theory of integration, the sexual metaphysics and science.

661. Bartlett, Norman. "'The Hairy Image': Underground in London." *Meanjin Quarterly*, XXIX (1970), 381-393.

Reviews views of Alex Comfort (*Guardian*, March 21, 1970) and Arthur Koestler (*Encounter*, May 1970) concerning the "new romanticism," the one with decidedly Blakean undertones. Roszak's *The Making of a Counterculture* was the impetus. The final verdict: decadence.

662.   Beaty, F.L. "The New Moralists." *Light from Heaven*.
        DeKalb: Northern Illinois University Press, 1971,
        109-131.

        A very fine discussion of Blake's views of love and
        sexuality, referring to Blake's equation of body and
        soul.

663.   Bentley, E.B. "Vision in Fiction: Two Novels About
        William Blake." *Blake: An Illustrated Quarterly*,
        XII (1978), 209-210.

        Peter Carter's *The Gates of Paradise*, 1974, and Rev.
        W.E. Heygate, *William Blake*, 1848.

664.   Blackstone, Bernard. "*Poetical Sketches* and 'Hyperion.'"
        Cambridge Journal, VI (1952), 160-168.

        Argues that Keats knew *Poetical Sketches* and was
        influenced by it.

665.   Bloxham, Laura J. "William Blake and Visionary Poetry
        in the Twentieth Century." *DAI*, XXXVI (1975), 5275A
        (Washington State University).

        Blake has influenced Roethke, Snyder and Ginsberg,
        and has inspired a consciousness school of criticism
        in the twentieth century.

666.   Bly, Robert. "Looking for Dragon Smoke." *Stand*, VIII
        (1967), 10-12.

        There is a need for more Blakean imagination in con-
        temporary American poetry and less "Urizenic technique."
        Vision is dragon smoke.

667.   Bonham, Ronald A. "Hart Crane's 'Mystical Empirical'
        Poetry and Its Relation to Nineteenth Century Tradi-
        tions." *DAI*, XXXVII (1976), 4350A (University of
        British Columbia).

        Blake is discussed among others in an attempt to
        define Crane's relationship to English Romanticism.

668.   Brantlinger, Patrick M. "Classic and Romantic: An Augury
        of Innocence." *College English*, XXXIII (1972), 702-
        711.

        A short story about a professor teaching Blake who
        encounters a student, Sweat, whose visions he doubts.
        "He who shall teach the Child to Doubt/ The rotting
        Grave shall ne'er get out."

669. Brown, Norman O. *Love's Body*. New York: Random House,
      1966.

      Brown here uses Blake as a persistent voice echoing
      his own belief based in the body, imagination, the un-
      conscious, dreams and vision. Brown perceives only
      Blake's rhetorical stance in the *Marriage* and not his
      dialectic of Reason and Energy.

670. Brown, Norman O. *Life Against Death: The Psychoanalytic
      Meaning of History*. Middletown, Conn.: Wesleyan Uni-
      versity Press, 1959.

      The boundaries of superego and conscious rational
      ego are in the service of a society no man could want,
      a society which could not possibly aid man in accepting
      his mortality, or permit him the rewards of life based
      on an acceptance of the body. Brown quotes Blake here
      but much more extensively in *Love's Body* (item 669),
      where Blake is something of a parallel voice. Energy,
      imagination, the body, which contains both spiritual
      and physical affinities--the Spiritual Body of Boehme,
      Blake and St. Paul--would have to intrude into the
      acceptable precincts of conscious ego control, sublima-
      tion and repression, so that the new expanded conscious-
      ness, Blake's integrated man, could be formed.

671. Burke, Herbert C. "The Man of Letters." *Continuum*,
      VII (1969), 274-285.

      Thomas Merton's interests included Blake, Camus,
      Pasternak, among others. Merton cites the importance
      of the Blake tie in *Seven Storey Mountain*.

672. Carey, Frances A. "James Smetham (1821-1889) and Gil-
      christ's *Life of Blake*." *Blake Newsletter*, VIII
      (1974), 17-25.

      Smetham did an 1869 review of Gilchrist's *Life of
      Blake* (item 309). Smetham had an imaginative life which
      the author traces through his marginal illustrations
      to Gilchrist's *Life*.

673. Cohen, Paul N. "Words Alone Are Certain Good: Yeats
      and the Unity of the Arts." *DAI*, XXXVIII (1977),
      2801A (Rutgers, New Brunswick).

      Believes that Blake, as well as Morris and Rossetti,
      was a model for Yeats's attempt to work in more than
      one medium.

674. Colbert, Alison. "A Talk with Allen Ginsberg." *Partisan Review*, XXXVIII (1971), 289-309.

      Interesting insofar as Ginsberg discusses Thomas Taylor and gnosticism as well as Blake.

675. Curran, Stuart. "Detecting the Existential Blake." *Blake Studies*, II (1969), 67-76.

      Nonacademic response to Blake, such as Colin Wilson's *The Glass Cage*, merits consideration. Wilson in this detective story casts light upon and continues the Radical Christian vision of Blake.

676. Custance, John. *Wisdom, Madness and Folly*. London: Victor Gollancz, 1951.

      Custance, a confined "madman," presents an account of his "experiences" which provide an amazing parallel to Blake's vision, especially in regard to the themes of the *Marriage*.

677. Davie, Donald. "The Poetry of Samuel Menashe." *Iowa Review*, I (1970), 107-115.

      Connection between Menashe and Blake, whom Menashe is supposedly indebted to.

678. DeGroot, H.B. "R.H. Horne, Mary Howitt, and a Mid-Victorian Version of 'The Ecchoing Green.'" *Blake Studies*, IV (1971), 81-88.

      In the 1854 *Pictorial Calendar of the Seasons* by Mary Howitt, Blake's "Ecchoing Green," stanzas 2 and 3, are reproduced as "A Summer Evening on a Village Green."

679. DeGruson, Eugene. "Bentley and Nurmi Addendum: Haldeman-Julius's Blake." *Blake Studies*, I (1969), 203-205.

      Haldeman-Julius of Kansas in 1919 published a five-cent anthology of Blake for the working classes.

680. Dudek, Louis. "Poetry as a Way of Life." *English Quarterly*, II (1969), 71-80.

      Blake, Whitman, Lawrence and Williams are the forerunners of Rock poetry, a new Romantic poetry foreign to the Eliot-Academic tradition.

681. Dörrbecker, Detlef. "Query: *Gates of Paradise* and Quarles' *Emblems*." *Blake Newsletter*, IX (1976), 120.

    Charles H. Bennett and W. Harry Rogers did woodcuts for the 1839 Quarles. They may have been influenced by Blake.

682. Fairchild, Bertram H. "'Such Holy Song': Music as Idea, Form and Image in the Poetry of William Blake." *DAI*, XXXVI (1975), 900A (University of Tulsa). See item 151.

    Argues that "cavern'd man" was vegetable and thus bounded by the senses, but was also enlarged by sensory windows through which poetry, painting and music came to man.

683. Fischer, Michael. "The Legacy of English Romanticism: Northrop Frye and William Blake." *Blake: An Illustrated Quarterly*, XI (1978), 276-283.

    Reviews of *The Secular Scripture* and *Spiritus Mundi* and a general survey of Frye's work since *Fearful Symmetry*.

684. Fite, Monte D. "Yeats as an Editor of Blake: Interpretation and Emendation in *The Works of William Blake, Poetic, Symbolic and Critical*." *DAI*, XXXI (1971), 355A.

    Yeats's view of Blake via his editing and his commentary.

685. Frye, Northrop. "The Keys to the Gates." *Romanticism and Consciousness*. Edited by Harold Bloom. New York: W.W. Norton, 1970, 233-254.

    Blake is a good introduction to the nature and structure of poetic thought; the keys to poetic thought are in him. "He was ... the first English poet to work out the revolutionary structure of imagery that continues through Romantic poetry and thought to our own time."

686. Gandelman, Claude. "Joyce, Pre-Raphaelism, Art Nouveau: Pictorial Influences on *Finnegans Wake*." *Orbis Litterarum*, XXX, 4 (1975), 277-285.

    Blake was a predecessor of Art Nouveau, and his drawings influenced Joyce.

687. Gandolfo, Anita M. "Every Man's Wisdom: Literary Affiliation Among Blake, Yeats and Joyce." *DAI*, XXXVIII (1977), 1408A (City University of New York).

Applies Bloom's views of literary influence in order
to recreate "Yeats's Blake" and "Joyce's Blake." Such
recreations enable the critic to gloss the work of Yeats
and Joyce more effectively.

688. George, Diana H. "Malignant Fires and the Chain of
      Jealousy: Blake's Treatment of Oedipal Conflict."
      University of Hartford Studies in Literature, XI
      (1979), 197-211.

      "Blake knew what Freud knew."

689. George, Diana. "Is She Also the Divine Image? Values
      for the Feminine in Blake, Milton and Freud." *DAI*,
      XXXIX (1979), 7356A (SUNY, Buffalo). See item 455.

      Argues that Blake anticipated Freud, especially in
      his view of feminine psychology.

690. Gleckner, Robert F. "'The Lamb' and 'The Tyger'--How
      Far with Blake?" *English Journal*, LI (1962), 536-543.

      Blake should be taught in the high schools since he
      is sure to jar students out of their lethargy.

691. Goldman, Arnold. "Blake and the Roscoes." *Notes & Queries*,
      N.S. XII (1965), 178-182.

      A Roscoe imitated a Blake poem in 1834.

692. Greenberg, Mark. "Dante Gabriel Rossetti and William
      Blake." *DAI*, XXXIX (1979), 6141A (University of
      Michigan).

      Argues that "Blake provided a visionary alternative
      to Pre-Raphaelitism's naturalism, stressed the Image's
      renovating power and offered Rossetti a capacious well-
      spring of images and poetic structures which Rossetti
      appropriated throughout his life."

693. Haddow, A. "Sir Ernest Laurence Kennaway FRS, 1881-
      1958: Chemical Causation of Cancer Then and Today."
      Perspectives in Biology and Medicine, XVII (1974),
      543.

      Blake mentioned as one of those influential in al-
      leviating the condition of chimney sweeps. They suffered
      from cancer of the scrotum.

694. Harper, George M. "Blake's *Nebuchadnezzar* in 'The City
       of Dreadful Night.'" *Studies in Philology*, L (1953),
       68-80.

       James Thomson, who admired Blake, probably had Blake's
       color print *Nebuchadnezzar* in mind when he wrote Canto
       XVIII of "The City...."

695. Heffernan, J.A. "Politics and Freedom: Refractions of
       Blake in Joyce Cary and Allen Ginsberg." *Romantic and
       Modern*. Edited by G. Bornstein. Pittsburgh, Pa.:
       University of Pittsburgh Press, 1977, 177-195.

       Cary sees Blake as an embodiment of artistic inde-
       pendence while Ginsberg sees him as a champion of poli-
       tical independence. "The British novelist and the Ameri-
       can poet share with Blake a redemptive purpose, a yearn-
       ing to liberate man from the categories of time."

696. Helms, Randel. "Blake at Felpham: A Study in the Psychol-
       ogy of Vision." *Literature and Psychology*, XXII (1972),
       57-66.

       Comparison of Blake's union with Los and Milton, and
       studies by Freud and Anton Boisen. Freud's study is on
       paranoia.

697. Henn, T.R. *The Apple and the Spectroscope*. London:
       Methuen, 1951.

       Blake here becomes a small part--a lecture on symbols--
       of literature lectures for Cambridge Science undergradu-
       ates. Blake's "The Sick Rose" is discussed.

698. Hill, Charles G. "Andre Gide and Blake's *Marriage of
       Heaven and Hell*." *Comparative Literature Studies*, III
       (1966), 21-32.

       Gide's notions of creativity, art and the devil issue
       from Blake.

699. Hoffman, E. "Some Sources for Munch's Symbolism."
       Apollo, LXXXI (1965), 93.

       Blake's small floating figures, especially those in
       his illustrations to the Book of Job, are very like
       figures in Klinger. And Klinger influenced Munch.

700. Humma, John B. "From Transcendental to Descendental:
       The Romantic Thought of Blake, Nietzsche, Lawrence."
       DAI, XXX (1970), 4454A (Southern Illinois University).

Distinction between "transcendental" and "descendental."
"... in contradistinction of the transcendental Romantic's conception of consummation as a state of spiritual
ascendance that is removed from the realm of sensory
experience, the descendental Romantic achieves consummation *directly* by way of the senses, through 'blood-
knowledge.' ..."

701. Ironside, Robin. "The Followers of William Blake."
     Magazine of Art, XL (1947), 309-314.

     They represent the climax in the evolution of English
     Romanticism.

702. James, Carl. "Eldridge Builds Art at Golgonooza: Blakean
     Spirit Motivates." *The Messenger*, XXV (1973), C-1.

     Aethelred Eldridge and his Church of the Blake Recital
     in Ohio.

703. James, G.I. "The New Criticism and the New Morality."
     Christian Scholar, XLVIII (1965), 279-279.

     Strange amalgam of relativistic critical and moral
     standards, and a tradition supporting these "new" per-
     ceptions--Blake, Forster, Lawrence and Leavis.

704. John, Brian. "Yeats and Carlyle." *Notes & Queries*,
     N.S. XVII (1970), 455.

     Although Yeats didn't admire many qualities of Carlyle,
     he agreed with his "espousal of Blakean energy."

705. Ketters, David. "New Worlds for Old: The Apocalyptic
     Imagination, Science Fiction and American Literature."
     Mosaic, V (1971), 37-57.

     Blake, among others, is referred to in this attempt
     to bring science fiction into the realm of apocalyptic
     literature.

706. Killinger, John. "The Death of God in American Litera-
     ture." *Southern Humanities Review*, II (1968), 149-172.

     Suggests American antecedents for Altizer's radical
     theology. Altizer focused primarily on Europeans, in-
     cluding Blake.

707. Kiralis, Karl. "James Hogg and William Blake." *Notes &
     Queries*, CCIV (1959), 12-14.

References to Blake in Hogg's novel *The Private Memoirs and Confessions of a Justified Sinner*, 1824.

708. Kogan, Pauline. *Northrop Frye: The High Priest of Clerical Obscurantism*. Montreal: Progressive Books, 1969.

"Frye distorts Blake by making a thorough idealist and a clerical obscurantist out of him. The Blake who has been the centre of so much idealistic criticism since 1947 is Frye's Blake, the poet of visionary imagination and a guide to Christian interpretations of literature. Frye's Blake has so little to do with the world in which he lived and is so other worldly that one cannot help wondering whatever happened to the politically and socially active poet...."

709. Kreiter, Carmen S. "Evolution and William Blake." *Studies in Romanticism*, IV (1965), 110-118.

Darwinian theory represented in *Urizen*'s Orc.

710. Laing, Ronald D. *The Divided Self*. London: Tavistock; Penguin, 1960.

"The best description of any such condition [chaotic nonentity] I have been able to find in literature is in the Prophetic Books of William Blake.... These books require prolonged study, not to elucidate Blake's psychopathology, but in order to learn from him what somehow, he knew about in a more intimate fashion, while remaining sane...."

711. Leary, D.J. "Shaw's Blakean Vision: A Dialectic Approach to *Heartbreak House*." *Modern Drama*, XV (1972), 89-103.

"... I make use of the writings of William Blake not so much to show the direct influence of the Romantic poet on Shaw as to suggest Shaw's connection with the whole mythopoetic content of English art."

712. Leavis, F.R. "Introductory: Life Is a Necessary Word." *Nor Shall My Sword*. New York: Barnes & Noble, 1972, 11-37.

Leavis attempts to explain why he has invoked Blake in the title of his collection of essays. His goal is not to build Jerusalem but to create a university. "The need is to find a way to save cultural continuity, that continuous, collaborative renewal which keeps the 'heritage' of perception, judgment, responsibility and spiri-

tual awareness alive...." Somehow this Arnoldian cultural continuity that Leavis envisions seems like the
bones of Urizen's conventional world.

713. Lechay, Daniel T. "The Escape from the Lonely Dell:
      Studies in Spenser, Shakespeare, Wordsworth and Blake."
      DAI, XXXVI (1975), 2220A (University of Iowa).

      Applies three statements by Blake to various poets
      in an attempt to demonstrate their critical usefulness.

714. Lister, Raymond. "Samuel Palmer's Milton Watercolours."
      Connoisseur, CXCIV (1977), 16-19.

      Discusses Blake's influence, especially on "The Lonely
      Tower."

715. Lister, Raymond. "References to Blake in Samuel Palmer's
      Letters." *William Blake: Essays in Honour of Sir
      Geoffrey Keynes* (item 240), 305-309.

      Palmer's later letters indicate Blake's waning influ-
      ence on him, Edward Calvert and George Richmond.

716. Lister, Raymond. "'The Ancients' and 'The Classics.'"
      Studies in Romanticism, XV (1976), 395-404.

      Blake's Virgil illustrations influenced "The Ancients":
      Samuel Palmer, Edward Calvert, Francis Finch and George
      Richmond. They introduced a classical note into English
      Romanticism.

717. McAuley, James. "Shaw Neilson's Poetry." *Australian
      Literary Studies*, II (1966), 235-253.

      Neilson is rather like Blake in his concern for child-
      hood innocence, in his religious iconoclasm, in his
      depiction of experience and in his criticism of societal
      ills.

718. McGann, Jerome J. "Blake and a Tradition." *Poetry*,
      CXVII (1970), 45-49.

      The tradition is the "wildmen" school of poetry--
      Ginsberg and company.

719. Mackenzie, Manfred. "Patrick White's Later Novels: A
      Generic Reading." *Southern Review* (Adelaide), I
      (1965), 5-18.

The progression on an allegorical level from innocence to experience to hell to paradise in *The Aunt's Story*, *The Tree of Man*, *Voss*, and *Riders in the Chariot* follows Blake's four-stage progression from innocence to paradise.

720. Majdiak, Daniel, and Brian Wilkie. "Blake and Freud: Poetry and Depth Psychology." *Journal of Aesthetic Education*, VI (1972), 87-98.

    William Blake anticipated psychoanalytic theory. Refers specifically to *The Book of Urizen* and the Oedipus complex.

721. Medawar, Peter. "Science and Literature." *Perspectives in Biology and Medicine*, XII (1969), 529.

    Discussion of the character and interaction of imagination and critical reasoning in literature and science. Medawar states that Blake's use of the two is antithetical.

722. Meltzer, Helen L. "The Ancients: Samuel Palmer, Edward Calvert, George Richmond and Francis Finch." *DAI*, XXXVIII (1977), 3776A (Columbia University).

    The Ancients owed a debt to Blake's simple style, to Blake's belief "that outline was the principal means for defining ideal forms."

723. Mercier, Vivian. "Blake Echoes in Victorian Dublin." *Blake: An Illustrated Quarterly*, XI (1977), 32-34.

    John Todhunter's two imitations of Blake, whom he considered a master of song.

724. Moore, Virginia. "Religion and William Butler Yeats." *DA*, XII (1952), 427 (Columbia University).

    Chapter IV deals with Blake's influence on Yeats.

725. Moore, Virginia. "Blake as a Major Doctrinal Influence." *The Unicorn: William Butler Yeats' Search for Reality*. New York: Macmillan, 1954, 84-102.

    Discusses Blake's doctrine of correspondence, his views of God and Man. Not a reliable discussion.

726. Newlin, Margaret. "Anna Wickham: 'The Sexless Part Which Is My Mind.'" *Southern Review* (Adelaide), XIV (1978), 281-302.

Interesting comparison of this little-known poet who possessed a very Blakean vision, especially in regard to the mutuality of female and male wisdom.

727.   Novak, Jane. "Verisimilitude and Vision: Defoe and Blake as Influences on Joyce's Molly Bloom." *The Carrell*, VIII (1967), 7-20.

"Although not his only spiritual masters, Defoe and Blake acted in the same way upon Joyce's creative imagination. And the contrast between their influences is the essence of Molly Bloom's success...."

728.   Paley, Morton D. "The Critical Reception of *A Critical Essay*." *Blake Newsletter*, XVIII (1974), 32-37.

Reviews of Swinburne's essay on Blake.

729.   Parisi, Frank M. "Review of 'The Mental Traveller,' a Dance-Drama Based on the Ballad by William Blake." *Blake Newsletter*, IX (1976), 128-132.

Reviews the ballet in terms of Blake's postures and gestures as revealed in his designs.

730.   Perry, Donna Marie. "From Innocence Through Experience: A Study of the Romantic Child in Five Nineteenth Century Novels." *DAI*, XXXVII (1976), 3599A (Marquette University).

Wordsworth and Blake created a romantic archetype of the child which was imitated in Victorian fiction.

731.   Pinto, Vivian de Sola. "In Our Era of Chaos William Blake Points the Way." *Aryan Path*, XXVIII (1957), 488-495.

Blake is a deterrent to inhuman Communism.

732.   Pirie, N.W. "The Size of Small Organisms." *Publications of the Royal Society Bulletin*, CLX (1964), 149-160.

Swedenborg took Leeuwenhoek's veneration for the six-fold subdivision seriously. Blake's opinion of Swedenborg is quoted from the *Marriage*.

733.   Raine, Kathleen. "Blake's Last Judgment." *The Ampleforth Journal*, LXXVI (1971), 70-84.

"The art of the present time testifies not to knowledge of, but ignorance of this wisdom [the perennial

wisdom], by which all great ages have lived and died
and which a new generation is now, it seems, beginning
to rediscover; with singularly little help from Church
or University, but much from William Blake."

734. Raine, Kathleen. "Yeats's Debt to William Blake." *Texas
Quarterly*, VIII (1965), 165-181.

Similar views of the gyre-like aspect of history and
the sacredness of art. Yeats and Blake shared traditional symbols, symbols that Raine feels the Neoplatonic
tradition interprets.

735. Raine, Kathleen. "Blake and the Education of Childhood."
Southern Review (Adelaide), VIII (1972), 253-272.

Raine believes that spontaneity, free self-expression
and imagination have their place in education.

736. Rao, Valli. "Vivie Warren in the Blakean World of
Experience." *Shaw Review*, XXII (1979), 123-134.

Uses Blake's archetypal concepts of innocence and
experience to analyze Vivie Warren.

737. Ray, William E. "William Blake and the Critical Development of William Butler Yeats." *DAI*, XXXII (1971),
2652A (University of North Carolina, Chapel Hill).

What and how Yeats learned about poetry from Blake.

738. Read, Herbert. *The Contrary Experience*. London: Faber
and Faber, 1963.

"... there is no poet with whom today I would more
readily identify the poetic essence. For me, Blake is
absolute. Shakespeare is richer, Milton is more sonorous,
Hopkins more sensuous ... but Blake has no need of
qualifying epithets; he is simply poetic in imagination
and in expression."

739. Reid, Anthony. "Ralph Chubb, the Unknown: Part I: His
Life 1892-1960." *Private Library*, III (1970), 141-156.

Chubb was a painter-poet who led a very Blakean
existence. *The Child of Dawn* and *Flames of Sunrise* are
"masterpieces."

740. Reis, R.H. "George MacDonald: Founder of the Feast."
Tolkien Journal, II (1966), 3-5.

MacDonald's *Phantasies* and *Lilith* were the first in a
continuous tradition of mythopoeic fiction. Blake is
in this tradition, as are C.S. Lewis's Narnia books,
Charles Williams's works and Tolkien's.

741. Riede, David G. "Swinburne: A Study in Romantic Myth-
      making." *DAI*, XXXVII (1976), 2204A (University of
      Virginia).

      Chapter Two explores Swinburne's critical essay on
      Blake, pointing out Swinburne's misreadings of Blake
      "with regard to their implications to his own poetry."

742. See item 743.

743. Roszak, Theodore. *Where the Wasteland Ends*. Garden
      City, N.Y.: Doubleday, 1972.

      Blake, Wordsworth and Goethe--our Virgilian guides
      out of the contemporary wasteland. Important chapters
      on Blake. Roszak in *The Making of a Counterculture* had
      pointed to a regeneration of the imagination, of the
      unconscious, of energy and vision rather than the re-
      straining powers of rationality. Along with N.O. Brown,
      Roszak had defined the "hippie" Blake that Blake
      scholars tried not to notice.

744. Sandler, Eileen B. "William Blake: Poet of the City
      in the Industrial Age." *DAI*, XXXIII (1972), 764A
      (New York University).

      Blake protested "against the degradation of man in
      the industrialized city and ... was convinced that the
      city could be transformed, with human effort, into a
      utopian community of man--Jerusalem."

745. Sandler, Eileen B. "William Blake and the Technological
      Age." *Thought*, XLVI (1971), 577-591.

      Blake fused the human and religious with the new
      technology. A very anomalous view perhaps stemming from
      the author's belief that the renovation of place was
      very important to Blake.

746. Shain, Ronald. "A Sociological Study of the Romantic
      Imagination: Blake's Mythic Conception of Man's Fall
      into Outer Selfhood." *DAI*, XXXIX (1979), 6783A
      (University of California, Santa Barbara).

Argues that a study of Blake's work may provide
sociology with a speculative model regarding extreme
feelings of self-estrangement in the England of the
nineteenth century.

747. Sharrock, Roger. "Godwin on Milton's Satan." *Notes &
      Queries*, N.S. LX (1962), 463-465.

Godwin and Blake held the same view of Milton's
Satan and were both willing to point to the theological
implications of Satan-as-hero. Blake presented his
version in the *Marriage*, printed as early as 1790, and
may have been a source for Godwin's version of Satan
in *Political Justice*, 1793.

748. Spinks, C. William. "Blake's Spectre." *Studies in
      Relevance: Romantic and Victorian Writers in 1972*.
      Edited by Thomas Harwell. Salzburg: Institut für
      Englische Sprache und Literatur, 1973.

Blake's anticipation of Jung makes Blake more meaningful to Spinks.

749. Stevenson, Stanley W. "The Myth and the Mind: Towards
      a Theory of Creativity." *Personalist*, XLVI (1965),
      299-319.

Creativity leads to freedom in both Existentialism
and the Romantic theory of the imagination. Berdyaev's
relation of creativity and freedom parallels Blake's.

750. Sutherland, John. "William Blake and Non-violence."
      Nation, XXVIII (1969), 542-544.

Blake's turn from Orc the fiery prophet to love,
forgiveness and self-annihilation--Nonviolence.

751. Suvin, D. "The Shift to Anticipation: Radical Rhapsody
      and Romantic Recoil." *Metamorphoses of Science Fic-
      tion*. New Haven: Yale University Press, 1979, 115-
      144.

Argues that since science fiction is part of repressed subcultures and shines forth in periods of
convulsion, Blake among others displays in his work
a disposition to science fiction.

752. Thompson, E.P. *The Making of the English Working Class*.
      London: Victor Gollancz, 1964.

Fifteen references to Blake are made in the course of this class study.

753.   Thorslev, Peter L., Jr. "Some Dangers of Dialectic Thinking with Illustrations from Blake and His Critics." *Romantic and Victorian: Studies in Memory of William H. Marshall*. Edited by Paul W. Elledge. Rutherford, N.J.: Fairleigh Dickinson University Press, 1971, 43-74.

An important essay which attacks the growing criticism that refers to a dialectic based on Blake.

754.   Tolley, Michael J. "John Todhunter: A Forgotten Debt to Blake." *Blake Newsletter*, VIII (1974), 15-16.

Sample of Todhunter's very Blakean poetry.

755.   Walling, William. "The Death of God: William Blake's Version." *Dalhousie Review*, XLVIII (1968), 237-250.

Fine essay, which concludes that Blake anticipated Nietzsche, Sartre and Buber in regard to human reintegration.

756.   Weaver, Jack. "AE's Use of Blake in 'The Irish Homestead.'" *Journal of Irish Literature*, V (1976), 144-147.

George Russell quoted Blake often in his farm journal, the *Irish Homestead*.

757.   Whitla, William. "Sources for Browning in Byron, Blake and Poe." *Studies in Browning and His Circle*, II (1974), 7-16.

Plate 10 of Blake's *The Gates of Paradise* shows a drowning man, a possible influence on Browning's "Amphibian."

758.   Williams, Harry. "Dylan Thomas' Poetry of Redemption: Its Blakean Beginnings." *Bucknell Review*, XX (1972), 107-120.

Blake's idea of redemption through annihilation, "that is, the process in which the prophetic, wrath-like forces of imagination act against the abstracting forces of the reasoning negation in order to redeem the vulnerable forces of pity" is evident in Thomas's *Notebooks*.

759. Williams, Raymond. "Prelude to Alienation." *Stand*, VIII (1965), 36-44.

   Industrialization and urbanization create alienation, which leads to "the practice of individual preservation, within a grievous general condition, or to the practice of revolution, which would seek to end the condition. Blake and Wordsworth, this early, point the different ways."

760. Wilson, Colin. *Ritual in the Dark*. London: Victor Gollancz, 1960.

   The protagonist of this novel reads Blake, ponders Blake's proverb, "Sooner murder an Infant...." Wilson concludes that the murderer is mad, someone who has nursed unrealized desires, and therefore not a real follower of Blake's proverb.

761. Wilson, Colin. *Religion and the Rebel*. Boston: Houghton Mifflin, 1957.

   "... Blake's emphasis on pain is not sadism, but an Outsider's attempt to underline the concept of hell. He is simply striving for an intensification of consciousness...." Wilson tends to see Blake's vision as an escape from ennui--Blake is an outsider, and willing to do anything to create for himself a stimulating intensity.

762. Wittreich, Joseph A. "Dylan Thomas' Conception of Poetry: A Debt to Blake." *ELN*, VI (1969), 197-200.

   Thomas upheld the doctrines of contraries, of the spontaneity of art, of the artist as revolutionary--all in the Blakean style.

763. Woodman, Ross G. "James Reany." *Canadian Writers*, XII (1970), 1-64.

   Reany has adhered to the Romantic tradition and Freud's and Jung's views of the unconscious. Blake epitomizes both directions.

CHAPTER EIGHT

ENGRAVINGS, PAINTINGS AND DRAWINGS

This chapter includes items which are primarily about Blake's pictorial works and about the nature of Blake's composite art. Erdman's *Illuminated Blake* (item 41), Bindman's *Complete Graphic Works of William Blake* (item 19), and Easson and Essick's *William Blake: Book Illustrator* (Vol. I, 1972; Vol. II, 1979; item 32) are good sources of the pictorial art.

Erdman includes only Blake's illuminated work while Bindman includes everything Erdman includes plus all Blake's designs. Easson and Essick do not limit themselves to what Blake designed but also include work he engraved but did not design. They do not include Blake's illuminated books. *Blake Books* (item 5) lists Blake Trust and American Blake Foundation facsimiles, and the *Blake Newsletter* (now *Blake: An Illustrated Quarterly*) has published Essick's finding lists of Blake reproductions in about two hundred books and journals (items 809, 810).

The best single study of Blake's composite art is Mitchell's (item 215). He finds that Blake is not, as Hagstrum has argued (item 845), totally within or defined by the tradition of *ut pictura poesis* ("as a painting, so also a poem"). This tradition holds a notion of "complementarity," "the idea that the coupling of the two arts would provide a fuller imitation of the total reality" (Mitchell, 17). Mitchell summarizes Blake's use of composite art as opposed to the emblematists, who were in the tradition of *ut pictura poesis*:

> For the emblematists, painting was to be *added to* poetry, in order to imitate the larger sum of spatial and temporal reality; for Blake, poetry and painting were to be *multiplied* by one another to give a product larger than the sum of the parts, a reality which might include, but not be limited by, the world of space and time. (31)

A good number of critics are seeking some degree of traditional iconography in Blake's art (Wardle, items 568, 569; C. Taylor, item 920). Wardle cites George Richardson's *Iconology* as a source for Blake's iconography, in which Blake modified traditional images. The search for a recognizable, consistent iconography in Blake is based on an allegorical view of his art. Blake is partially within an esoteric tradition in which the sublime is best expressed through an allegorical image. This is all part of the tradition of ut pictura poesis, the sister arts tradition, a tradition Mitchell sees as not directly applicable to Blake's art.

In Mitchell's view, the poetry and the pictorial art are unified in the "goal of affirming the centrality of the human form ... in the structure of reality" (38). Although they must achieve that goal by each performing a distinct task,

> .... his poetry affirms the power of the human imagination to create and organize time in its own image, and his painting affirms the centrality of the human body as the structural principle of space. (34)

Mitchell also points out that one problem in explicating Blake's composite art is that art historians aren't familiar with Blake's system and literary people focus on text-related imagery in the designs and not on formal qualities. Adams, in a review in *Blake Newsletter* (item 119), cites the same problem and points out that if one imposes a *literary* reading on the designs, nothing is gained in understanding the text. He concludes that it "must be the formal relations of poetry and design which, beyond the *literary* symbolism, produce a single artistic whole or impression or effect."

An interesting article on this problem of interpretation is Grant's "You Can't Write About Blake's Pictures Like That" (item 835). In Grant's view every "adequate account of what Blake is about must be derived from as full an awareness of what Blake shows as of what he says" (194).

On the technical side, Morris Eaves's "Teaching Blake's Relief Etching" (item 803) outlines an interesting project to give students some sense of the techniques of illuminated printing. Todd's "The Techniques of Blake's Illuminated Printing" (item 926), Carr's "William Blake's Print-Making Process in *Jerusalem*" (item 795), and Kay Easson's "Blake and the Art of the Book" (item 800) provide interesting accounts of Blake's techniques. Lister's *Infernal Methods* (item 881) is for those who wish a fuller account of technical matters. As one would expect, however, alternative views of Blake's artistic techniques are available. Robert Essick's *William Blake Printmaker* (item 1671) is a lengthy study of Blake's graphic endeavors: "his [Blake's] commercial copy prints, his original line engravings, his special methods of color printing, and his invention of relief processes for publishing pictures and words from the same plate" (xxi).

Todd's chronological account of Blake the working artist is a helpful combination of biography and technical matters (item 923). A more readable combination of the two is Bindman's *Blake as an Artist* (item 96). Kay Easson's essay (item 800) is original in its treatment of the art of the book as a "separable artistic matter which is to the degree that Blake altered practices of his own day, revealing."

The Visionary Hand (item 144) and *Blake in His Time* (item 149) are useful, convenient collections of essays on Blake's composite art. The latter was the result of a "Blake in the Art of His Time" conference at Santa Barbara, California, March 1976. The fine book-length catalogue of that exhibit-conference, *William Blake in the Art of His Time* (item 933), is more useful than the essay collections in giving one a sense of Blake's debt to his contemporaries. Paley's *William Blake* (item 226) is a large-format introduction to Blake as both poet and artist. It contains a good sampling of Blake's art, and the commentary is balanced. Raine's *William Blake* (item 249) in the Praeger series is as richly illustrated, bound and printed a book as her two-volume *Blake and Tradition* (item 1096). Unfortunately, in a work which we assume will focus on the art she succeeds only in talking around the art, never encountering it in the fashion described by Mitchell or as fully as Bindman.

Specialized studies of individual works include Irene Tayler's *Blake's Illustrations to the Poems of Gray* (item 912), Bo Lindberg's *William Blake's Illustrations to the Book of Job* (item 878), the Erdman-Grant-Rose-Tolley edition of *William Blake's Designs for Edward Young's Night Thoughts* and Pamela Dunbar's *William Blake's Illustrations to the Poetry of Milton* (for these last two, see the Preface, above).

The popular Tate Gallery exhibit of 1978 was a highpoint in the recognition of Blake's art. Blake's work is selling for high prices in the marketplace (see items 802, 816), a circumstance more than partially generated by both the critical fervor and the acclaim and exposure Blake received in the 1960's. But, ironically, the force of a once-expanding sub-culture has subsided and Blake is left solely for the academic and art markets. I think, moreover, the Tate exhibit may mark the real end of a time when Blake's poetry could be separated from his designs, printed on a page, read and interpreted. Only when students of Blake see his work, from the very first, as a composite art will commentary emerge which is in neither the litterateur's camp nor the art historian's but in Blake's.

764. Allentuck, Marcia. "Dorothy Richardson on William Blake
      and the Broadside: An Unrecorded Appraisal." *Blake
      Studies*, III (1971), 195-196.

      Richardson in *Adelphi* (III [1925], 54-57), "The Status
      of Illustrative Art," showed herself to be a perceptive
      critic, especially in her comments on Blake.

765. Baine, Rodney M., and Mary R. Baine. "Blake's Sketch
      for *Hamlet*." *Blake Newsletter*, IX (1976), 117-119.

      In this sketch Blake equalled the intensity of Fuseli.

766. Behrendt, Stephen C. "Bright Pilgrimage: William Blake's
      Designs for *L'Allegro* and *Il Penseroso*." *Milton Studies*,
      VIII (1975), 123-147.

      The Milton of *L'Allegro* is associated with the material
      world and with conventional versifying, whereas the
      Milton of *Il Penseroso* is associated with the world of
      imagination and poetic genius.

767. Behrendt, Stephen C. "Liberating the Awakener: William
      Blake's Illustrations to John Milton's Poetry." *DAI*,
      XXXV (1975), 4415A (University of Wisconsin, Madison).

      The annihilation of Selfhood is carried out visually
      in Blake's designs to Milton's poems.

768. Behrendt, Stephen C. "The Mental Contest: Blake's *Comus*
      Designs." *Blake Studies*, VIII (1978), 65-88.

      Argues that the relationship between the *Comus* designs
      and *Milton* is striking not because the two are similar
      (Irene Tayler's view) but because they are different.

769. Behrendt, Stephen C. "Blake's Illustrations to Milton's
      Nativity Ode." *Philological Quarterly*, LV (1976),
      65-95.

      "Blake's designs evaluate both the nature and the
      consequences of Milton's choice, defining the historical,
      ethical, and mythological implications of Milton's re-
      jection of the pagan tradition in favor of the Christian."

770. Behrendt, Stephen C. "The Polished Artifact: Some Ob-
      servations on Imitative Criticism." *Genre*, X (1977),
      47-62.

      Distinguishes the imitative critic from the plagiarist
      and the allusive artist and goes on to consider the whole

mode of imitative criticism, focusing on Blake's illustrations of *Comus*.

771. Bentley, G.E., Jr. "The Accuracy of the Blake Trust Gray Catalogue." *Blake Newsletter*, VI (1973), 95.

The Blake Trust, i.e., Trianon Press, has produced facsimiles which "are available and beautiful, but not perfect."

772. Bentley, G.E., Jr. "Blakewell." *Blake: An Illustrated Quarterly*, XIII (1979), 152-153.

A cow-scape attributed to Blake is probably not his.

773. Bentley, G.E. "Byron, Shelley, Wordsworth, Blake and *The Seaman's Recorder*." *Studies in Romanticism*, IX (1970), 21-36.

Account of sea disasters contains six previously unknown Blake engravings among other items of interest to Byron, Shelley, Wordsworth scholars. See item 313 for a correction of this source.

774. Bentley, G.E. "The Inscription on Blake's Designs to *Pilgrim's Progress*." *Blake Newsletter*, VI (1973), 68-70.

Lists the inscriptions and suggests that Frederick Tatham between the years 1828 and 1863 numbered and identified them.

775. Bentley, G.E. "Blake's *Job* Copperplates." *Library*, XXVI (1971), 234-241.

Abortive plan to make another full-size facsimile of Job?

776. Bentley, G.E. "A Unique Prospectus for Blake's *Grave* Designs." *Princeton University Chronicle*, XXXV (1974), 321-324.

This prospectus states that Blake was to engrave 15 of the *Grave* designs.

777. Bentley, G.E. "An Apocryphal Blake Engraving: *The Minor's Pocket Book* (1814)." *Blake Newsletter*, IV (1971), 107-108.

778. Bindman, David. "An Announcement." *Blake Newsletter*, X (1976), 70.

Compares the first and second impression of the *Laocoön*.

779.   Bindman, David. "An Unpublished Blake Pencil Drawing of the Lambeth Period." *Blake Newsletter*, IV (1970), 39-40.

A description of "The Dead Bad-Doers" including reproductions of the drawing.

780.   Bindman, David. "Blake's 'Gothicised Imagination' and the History of England." *William Blake: Essays in Honour of Sir Geoffrey Keynes* (item 240), 29-49.

Blake's early copy work at Westminster "gothicised" his imagination. "Blake deliberately flaunts the anecdotal and mythological side of history against regular and elaborate inquiry into every ancient record and proof...."

781.   Bland, David. *A History of Book Illustration*. London: Faber and Faber, 1958.

"It was well that Blake was born to show what could happen to the book in the hands of a genius. But he is right outside the mainstream of development and it is difficult to see how even he could have travelled farther along that road. It is significant that he had no followers in book illustration."

782.   Blunt, Anthony. *The Art of William Blake*. New York: Columbia University Press, 1959.

Traces Blake's mastery of technical methods that would enable him to best convey his vision.

783.   Boase, T.S.R. *English Art 1800-1870*. Oxford: Clarendon Press, 1959.

A brief sketch in the *Oxford History of English Art* series.

784.   Bowden, Betsy. "The Artistic and Interpretive Context of Blake's 'Canterbury Pilgrims.'" *Blake: An Illustrated Quarterly*, XIII (1980), 164-190.

Outside of symbolizing the Wife of Bath as Whore of Babylon and the Parson as the Good Old Man, Blake's symbols derive from Chaucer's poem itself. However, the author proceeds to examine "precisely how he [Blake]

has changed each pilgrim away from artistic tradition
and, in several cases, away from the details of Chaucer's
poem." The artistic tradition discussed includes Dryden,
Stothard, John Lydgate, Caxton's 1483 edition, J.H.
Mortimer, Urry's edition of Chaucer (1721) and the
Ellesmere Ms.

785. Butlin, Martin. "The Inscription on *Evening Amusement*."
     Blake Newsletter, VI (1972), 74.

     Wording of Blake's engraving *Evening Amusement* is
     slightly different from Keynes's rendering of it in
     Engravings of William Blake.

786. Butlin, Martin. "Thoughts on the 1978 Tate Gallery
     Exhibition." *Blake: An Illustrated Quarterly*, XIII
     (1979), 16-23.

     Various reviews of the exhibition "showed a new
     acceptance of Blake's qualities as an artist." Comments
     on Blake's heads and expressions, problems in dating
     Blake's works in the 1790's, the development of Blake's
     late style, iconography and "various minor unconnected
     observations."

787. Butlin, Martin. "A New Portrait of William Blake."
     Blake Studies, VII (1975), 101-103.

     Believes that this drawing represents a spiritual
     form of Blake.

788. Butlin, Martin J. "The Catalogue of Blake's Designs
     Completed and a Last Minute Inclusion." *Blake News-
     letter*, IX (1975), 48-49.

     2250 designs are catalogued, and unrecorded works
     continue to appear.

789. Butlin, Martin. "An Extra Illustration to *Pilgrim's
     Progress*." *Blake Newsletter*, V (1972), 213-214.

     "I am sure that the picture referred to as 'A Warrior
     with Angels' in Robert Essick's *Finding List* [item
     810a] was an extra water color from the series of il-
     lustrations to Bunyan in the Frick Museum."

790. Butlin, Martin. "The Evolution of Blake's Large Color
     Prints of 1795." *William Blake: Essays for S. Foster
     Damon* (item 256), 109-130.

"... the large color prints of 1795 mark the point
at which Blake's primary and most successful means of
expression ceased to be poetry and its illustration
and became purely visual."

791. Butlin, Martin. "Blake, Varley, and the Patent Graphic
      Telescope." *William Blake: Essays in Honour of Sir
      Geoffrey Keynes* (item 240), 294-304.

      Mechanical device, patent graphic telescope used by
      Varley and/or Linnell to make copies of Blake's *Visionary
      Heads*.

792. Butlin, Martin. "Blake's 'God Judging Adam' Rediscovered."
      Burlington Magazine, CVII (1965), 86-89.

      Conjectures regarding large color prints of 1795 and
      the existence of a unifying theme. Was there a thirteenth
      design to supplement the twelve extant?

793. Butlin, Martin. "Blake's *Vala*, or, *The Four Zoas* and
      a New Watercolor in the Tate Gallery." *Burlington
      Magazine*, CVI (1964), 381-382.

794. Carlson, Marvin A. "A Fresh Look at Hogarth's *Beggar's
      Opera*." *Educational Theatre Journal*, XXVII (1975),
      31-39.

      Hogarth's painting was satirical and it would have
      been dangerous for him to do an engraving of it that
      would be widely distributed. Blake did the engraving
      in 1790.

795. Carr, Stephen C. "William Blake's Print-Making Process
      in *Jerusalem*." *ELH*, XLVII (1980), 520-541.

      The printmaking process enacts what his verbal and
      visual art describe.

796. Chard, Leslie F. "Two 'New' Blake Engravings: Blake,
      James Earle and the Surgeon's Art." *Blake Studies*,
      VI (1976), 153-165.

      The two engravings appear in James Earle's *Practical
      Observations on the Operation for the Stone*, 1793.

797. Cross, Colin. "A Direct Line to Heaven." *Observer*,
      Nov. 21, 1971, 23, 25-26.

      Discussion of Blake's Gray designs, which are re-
      produced.

798. Davies, James M.Q. "Blake's Designs for *Paradise Lost*:
     A Critical Analysis." *DAI*, XXXIII (1973), 6866A
     (University of Iowa).

     Contrast with Wittreich, item 941.

799. Douglas, Dennis. "Blake and the Grotesque." *Balcony*,
     No. 6 (1967), 9-16.

     Last engravings of *The Gates of Paradise* are macabre
     mixture of secularity and death. Influenced by Michel-
     angelo, Raphael, Romano and/or Goltzius.

800. Easson, Kay P. "Blake and the Art of the Book." *Blake
     in His Time* (item 149), 35-52.

     Blake used some typical eighteenth-century techniques.
     He also advocated an integral book structure and sought
     to free the illustrated book from the mechanized book
     production of the day.

801. Easson, Roger. "Blake's Artistic Strategy." *DAI*,
     XXXIII (1972), 1165A (University of Tulsa).

     Blake believed he was the victim of the commercializa-
     tion of the creative process, a process which he traced
     back to Rubens, Correggio, Rembrandt and others.

802. Easson, Roger. "Blake and the Contemporary Art Market."
     Blake Newsletter, IV (1971), 137-139.

     Art firms have arbitrarily equated Blake pieces--"a
     Blake original is a Blake original is a Blake original."
     Blake watercolors are selling for $25,000.

803. Eaves, Morris. "Teaching Blake's Relief Etching."
     Blake: An Illustrated Quarterly, XIII (1979), 140-
     147.

     Eaves has designed a course on linoleum block-cutting
     which is designed to acquaint students of Blake with
     the techniques of illuminated printing.

804. Ehrestine, John W. "William Blake's *King Edward the
     Third*." *Research Studies*, XXXVI (1968), 151-162.

     Some foreshadowing here of Blake's later work,
     especially in regard to the use of symbols.

805. Erdman, David V. "The Dating of William Blake's Engrav-
     ings." *Philological Quarterly*, XXXI (1952), 337-343.

     Joseph of Arimathea, Glad Day, The Accusers.

806. Erdman, David V. "Leonora, Laodamia, and the Dead
      Ardours." *Blake: An Illustrated Quarterly*, XIV (1980),
      96-98.

      "Bad doers" in a design not used in Burger's *Leonora*
      is really "ardours."

807. Essick, Robert. "The Art of William Blake's Early
      Illuminated Books." *DAI*, XXX (1969), 2020A (University
      of California, San Diego).

      "A study of the iconography of the early illuminated
      books (c.1789-1793) and the *Tiriel* drawings provide a
      better understanding of his development as an artist-
      poet...."

808. Essick, Robert. "A Finding List of Reproductions of
      Blake's Art. Part III: Illustrations in Series to
      Others' Writings. Part IV: Paintings, Drawings and
      Engravings Not Part of Any Series, Supplement:
      Blakeana." *Blake Newsletter*, III (1970), 1-23.

809. Essick, Robert. "A Finding List of Reproductions of
      Blake's Art: Part I, Illuminated Books." *Blake News-
      letter*, III (1969), 24-41.

      An important list since Blake's designs appeared in
      many works by others.

810. Essick, Robert. "Supplement to Part I, and Part II,
      Illustrations to Blake's Non-Illuminated Writings."
      Blake Newsletter, III (1969), 64-70.

810a. Essick, Robert. "Finding List of Reproductions of
      Blake's Art." *Blake Newsletter*, V (1971), 1-160.

      A revised and expanded version of items 808-810.

811. Essick, Robert. "The Art of William Blake's Early
      Illuminated Books." *Blake Studies*, II (1969), 89-90.

812. Essick, Robert. "Blake and the Traditions of Reproduc-
      tive Engraving." *Blake Studies*, V (1973), 59-103.

      Blake rebelled against the limiting, net-work of lines
      style of engraving.

813. Essick, Robert. "Blake, Linnell, and James Upton: An
      Engraving Brought to Light." *Blake Newsletter*, VII
      (1974), 78-79.

Important as the first product of Blake's relationship with Linnell.

814. Essick, Robert N. *William Blake's Relief Inventions*. Los Angeles: Press of the Pegacycle Lady, 1978.

815. See item 144.

816. Essick, Robert N. "Blake in the Marketplace, 1974-1975." *Blake Newsletter*, X (1976), 53-59.

Lists of sales, including prices.

817. Essick, Robert N. "The Figure in the Carpet: Blake's Engravings in Salzmann's *Elements of Morality*." *Blake Newsletter*, XII (1978), 10-14.

Blake was both designer and engraver of Pl.28.

818. Essick, Robert N., and Morton D. Paley. "The Printings of Blake's Designs for Blair's *Grave*." *Book Collector*, XXIV (1975), 535-552.

Describes the several printings of the Schiavonetti plates and identifies the books in which they appear.

819. Essick, Robert. "Blake's Newton." *Blake Studies*, III (1971), 149-162.

Blake's drawing "Newton" compared with "The Ancient of Days."

820. Fawcus, Arnold. "Blake's Job." *Illustrated London News*, CCLXIV (December 1976), 63, 65-67.

Essentially another advertisement for the Trianon Press facsimiles--this time of *Job*. Some colored illustrations and brief descriptions of "Blake's concept of the relationship between God and Man."

821. Fletcher, Angus. *The Transcendental Masque: Essay on Milton's Comus*. Ithaca, N.Y.: Cornell University Press, 1971.

Blake is the best at following Milton's ideas and at adhering to the details of the text.

822. Foley, Matthew J. "English Printing and Book Illustration 1780-1820." *DAI*, XXXVIII (1978), 6368A (University of California, Santa Cruz).

John Nash and Blake discussed in terms of the relationship between books and architecture.

823. Franson, J. Karl. "Christ of the Pinnacle: Interpretive
      Illustrations of the Crisis in *Paradise Regained*."
      Milton Quarterly, X (1976), 48-53.

      Only Blake of all illustrators interprets this scene
      in close accord with the text of the entire poem.

824. Frye, Northrop. "Blake's Reading of the Book of Job."
      William Blake: Essays for S. Foster Damon (item 256),
      221-234.

      Blake recreated the Book of Job in his engravings and
      did not simply illustrate it. Frye believes that Blake's
      vision of the Book of Job involved the imagination but
      that it was his critical mind which analyzed the work.

825. Frye, Northrop. "Poetry and Design in William Blake."
      Discussions of William Blake (item 182), 44-49; re-
      printed in items 144, 155.

      "A good many foolish ideas about Blake have resulted
      from staring at the naked text."

826. Gabbett-Mulhallen, Karen A. "Blake's Illustrations to
      Edward Young's *Night Thoughts*: Context, Christology
      and Composite Works." *DAI*, XXXIX (1979), 4269A (Uni-
      versity of Toronto).

      Argues that Blake's illustrations here demonstrate
      "one stage of the metamorphosis of Blake's Christianity."

827. Gage, John. "Blake's *Newton*." *Journal of the Warburg
      and Courtauld Institute*, XXXIV (1971), 372-376.

      In creating an image of Newton plotting the arc of
      a rainbow in a prism, Blake "invented one of the richest
      images of materialism in his art."

828. Gibson, William A., and Thomas L. Minnick. "William
      Blake and Henry Emlyn's Proposition for a New Order
      in Architecture: A New Plate." *Blake Newsletter*, VI
      (1972), 13-17.

      Plate is interesting because it is "among Blake's
      earliest commercial jobs...." It is the only work as-
      sociated with architects and is one of Blake's largest
      engravings.

829. Gleckner, Robert F. "Blake's Illustration of the Third
     Temptation in *Paradise Regained*." *Blake: An Illustrated
     Quarterly*, XI (1977), 126-127.

     Points out the importance of "positional dynamics and
     spatial movements" in describing Blake's illustration
     as one which dramatizes Milton's conception of Christ's
     unique nature.

830. Goslee, Nancy M. "From Marble to Living Form: Sculpture
     as Art and Analogue from the Renaissance to Blake."
     Journal of English and Germanic Philology, LXXVII
     (1978), 188-211.

     Contends that for Blake sculpture is not "subordinated
     to pictorial and then verbal art, but made an image for
     Milton's self and for Blake's composite, often competing
     arts." Traces Blake's response to Reynolds's view of
     general nature, Winckelmann's sedate grandeur and Flax-
     man's ideal forms.

831. Grant, John E. "Blake's Illustrations of the Book of
     Job." *Times Literary Supplement*, Nov. 30, 1973, 1484.

     Cites watercolors which Fawcus subsequently investi-
     gates (item 820).

832. Grant, John E. "Envisioning the First *Night Thoughts*."
     Blake's Visionary Forms Dramatic (item 139), 304-335.

     "... some commentators [believe] that the *Night Thoughts*
     designs are simpler and more obvious in meaning than
     the designs for Job or Dante.... Other commentators
     have indicated that Blake merely used Young's text for
     jumping-off points for his own visions. Both schools
     can find supporting evidence, but neither provides an
     adequate theory for understanding the whole series."

833. Grant, John E. "The Arlington Court Picture, Part I."
     Blake Newsletter, III (1970), 96-105.

     This is a rather important painting since it sum-
     marizes pictorially Blake's vision. A very particularized
     account.

834. Grant, John E. "The Arlington Court Picture, Part II."
     Blake Newsletter, IV (1970), 12-25.

     Corrects Raine's (item 1096) and Beer's (item 76)
     views of this work.

835.   Grant, John E. "You Can't Write About Blake's Pictures
        Like That." *Blake Studies*, I (1969), 193-202.

        Grant here corrects Clyde Taylor's interpretation
        of various iconographical themes. Although "this is
        not the first time that Blake's paradigm of vision has
        been misunderstood by a would-be exegete, it is probab-
        ly the most muddled since the explanations of Aradobo."

836.   Grant, John E. "Addenda and Some Solutions to Tolley's
        Blake Puzzles." *Blake Studies*, III (1971), 129-135.

        Grant has discovered a comparison for Tolley's re-
        cently discovered Anubis drawing.

837.   Grant, John E. "Blake's Designs for *L'Allegro* and *Il
        Penseroso*: With Special Attention to *L'Allegro* I,
        'Mirth and Her Companions.'" *Blake Newsletter*, IV
        (1971), 117-134; reprinted in item 144.

        A summary of remarks made at an MLA seminar. See item
        840 for a continuation.

838.   Grant, John E. "Redemptive Action in Blake's 'Arling-
        ton Court Picture.'" *Studies in Romanticism*, X (1971),
        21-26.

        A correction of Simmons and Warner's view of this
        picture (item 908).

839.   Grant, John E. "The Visionary Perspective of Ezekiel."
        Blake Studies, IV (1972), 153-157.

        Grant takes the opportunity to set the record straight
        and correct four scholars who have "inaccurately de-
        scribed one of Blake's greatest paintings." The paint-
        ing is "The Whirlwind: Ezekiel's Vision of the Eyed
        Wheels."

840.   Grant, John E. "The Meaning of Mirth and Her Companions
        in Blake's Designs for *L'Allegro* and *Il Penseroso*,
        Part II. Of Some Remarks Made and Designs Discussed
        at the MLA Seminar 12, 'Illuminated Books by William
        Blake,' 29 December, 1970." *Blake Newsletter*, V
        (1972), 190-202.

        "How is it then, that there has been much erroneous
        or irrelevant criticism of Blake? Ignorance of the
        range of Blake's symbolism seems to be the root of
        most misinterpretations. Or, what comes to the same

thing, exegetes have not tried hard enough to ascertain Blake's own opinion." See item 837.

841. Grant, Phillip B. "A Possible Source for a Blake Sketch and Drawing." *Blake Newsletter*, X (1976), 85-87.

Blake's "Female Figure with Head of a Horse" and his "Anubis" may have a common source, plate XIII of Jacob Bryant's *A New System*, 1774-76.

842. Greenberg, Mark. "The Canterbury Pilgrims by Stothard and Blake: An Account with Reproductions in 'The Architect.'" *Notes & Queries*, N.S. XXIII (1976), 401-402.

Architect, Nov. 1878 issue. The account follows Gilchrist. Cromek's manipulation of Blake and Stothard is sketched.

843. Hagstrum, Jean H. "Blake and the Sister-Arts Tradition." *Blake's Visionary Forms Dramatic* (item 139), 82-91.

Opposes Erdman (item 1294) and Mitchell (items 215, 889), who maintain that Blake is outside the tradition of *ut pictura poesis*, and believes that Blake remained indebted to the pictorialist masters of his youth.

844. Hagstrum, Jean H. "Blake and British Art: The Gifts of Grace and Terror." *Images of Romanticism*. Edited by Karl Kroeber and William Walling. New Haven: Yale University Press, 1978, 61-80.

British artists did not have as great an influence on Blake as did Michelangelo, Dürer and others but British artists, such as Fuseli, Flaxman and Stothard, did affect him.

845. Hagstrum, Jean H. *William Blake, Poet and Painter: An Introduction to the Illuminated Verse*. Chicago: University of Chicago Press, 1964.

Argues that Blake stands squarely in the pictorialist tradition. Although this view has been contested by Mitchell (item 215), Hagstrum's desire to see Blake's poetry and designs as strategically interrelated has done much to generate our present view that one must be introduced to the composite art.

846. Altizer, Thomas J. (rev., *William Blake, Poet and Painter*). *Christian Scholar*, XLVIII (1965), 165-167.

"A veritable renaissance in Blake studies has taken place since the Second World War, and perhaps nowhere else in the world of American scholarship may one discover such rich fruits of a reborn religious understanding."

847. Carruth, Hayden. (rev., *William Blake, Poet and Painter*). *Poetry*, CVII (1965), 193-195.

This work is interesting but flawed in its conception of Blake's use of design.

848. Chayes, Irene H. (rev., *William Blake, Poet and Painter*). *Modern Language Journal*, XLIX (1965), 261-262.

Hagstrum should have evaluated Blake's graphic work in comparison with his poetry. Second, Hagstrum fits the poetry to the art, while the opposite approach is utilized by the majority of Blake critics.

849. Grant, John E. (rev., *William Blake, Poet and Painter*). *Journal of Aesthetics and Art Criticism*, XXIV (1965), 126-127.

Hagstrum's "systematic account of Blake's antecedents in Medieval illumination and Renaissance painting, engraving, and emblems constitutes a vivid summary of how Blake understood the history of the visual arts."

850. Nurmi, Martin K. (rev., *William Blake, Poet and Painter*). *Modern Philology*, LXIV (1966), 166-168.

"Now that the Trianon facsimiles published for the Blake Trust have made almost all the illuminated books available ... Hagstrum's modest but valuable introduction to Blake's composite art will be able to achieve its desired effect...."

851. See item 844.

852. Hardie, Martin. "William Blake and Henry Fuseli." *Water Color Painting in Britain*. Vol. I: *The Eighteenth Century*. Edited by Dudley Snelgrove, et al. New York: Barnes & Noble, 1966-68.

Surveys Blake's watercolor work.

853. Harvey, J.R. "Blake's Art." *Cambridge Quarterly*, VII
     (1977), 129-150.

     Declares this the Age of Blake. Blake has marvelous
     works, incomprehensible works and dreadful works.

854. Helmstadter, Thomas H. "Blake and Religion: Iconographical
     Themes in the *Night Thoughts*." *Studies in Romanticism*,
     X (1971), 199-212.

     Helmstadter stresses Blake's departure from Young's
     themes. He reworked Young to suit his own needs.

855. Helmstadter, Thomas H. "Blake's *Night Thoughts*: Inter-
     pretations of Edward Young." *Texas Studies in Litera-
     ture and Language*, XII (1970), 27-54.

     See items 826, 832, 1128.

856. Helmstadter, Thomas H. "Blake and the Age of Reason:
     Spectres in the *Night Thoughts*." *Blake Studies*, V
     (1972), 105-139.

     Blake's designs to Young's work express his disagree-
     ment with Young's Urizenic orientation.

857. Helmstadter, Thomas H. "Bright Visions of Eternity:
     Blake's Design for Blair's *Grave*." *Blake Studies*,
     VIII (1978), 37-64.

     "The originality of pictures enlarging upon Blair's
     meaning will be best recognized and appreciated when
     they are examined in close connection to the text
     suggesting them." However, Helmstadter also approaches
     these designs as presenting their text via Blake's own
     vision.

858. Hoover, Suzanne. "Pictures at the Exhibitions." *Blake
     Newsletter*, VI (1972), 6-12.

     A description of the Manchester Art Treasures Exhibi-
     tion of 1857 and the two Blake watercolors on display:
     "Oberon and Titania on a Lilly" and "Visions of Queen
     Catherine."

859. Hughes, G. Bernard. "Blake's Work for Wedgewood."
     Country Life, CXXVI (1959), 194-196.

     Discusses *Wedgewood's Catalogue of Earthenware and
     Porcelain*, for which Blake did 18 plates.

860.   James, G.I. "Blake's Woodcuts, Plain and Coloured."
        Times Literary Supplement, May 18, 1973, 564.

        Blake's illustrations to Ambrose Philips's "Imitation
        of Virgil's First Eclogue." Some of the most satisfying
        woodcuts ever produced, according to the author.

861.   James, G. Ingli. "Blake's Mixed Media: A Mixed Blessing."
        Essays and Studies. Edited by W. Moelwyn Merchant.
        London: John Murray, 1977.

        Blake's composite art has long been a heaven on earth
        for the wealthy bibliophile and the bibliographer. But
        critical pronouncements necessitate a comparison of a
        considerable number of copies of a Blake work. And just
        a few wealthy people have access to them.

862.   James, G.I. "Blake's Woodcuts Illuminated." *Apollo*,
        XCIX (1974), 194-195.

        Blake's Virgil prints reproduced in color.

863.   Jones, Ben. "Blake on Gray: Outlines of Recognition."
        Fearful Joy. Edited by James Downey and Ben Jones.
        Montreal and London: McGill-Queens University Press,
        1974.

        Survey of Blake's illustrations of Gray's poems.
        Illustrations indicate that Blake read Gray carefully
        and depicted the poems perceptively.

864.   Jones, Warren. "Blake's Large Color-Printed Drawings
        of 1795." *DAI*, XXXIII (1973), 6873A (Northwestern
        University).

        General description, textual and historical, of
        "Elohim Creating Adam," "Satan Exulting Over Eve,"
        "God Judging Adam," "The Good and Evil Angels," "Newton,"
        "Nebuchadnezzar," "The House of Death," "Hecati," "Pity,"
        "Lamech and His Two Wives," "Ruth" and "Christ Appear-
        ing."

865.   Keynes, Geoffrey. "Blake's Visionary Heads and the
        Ghost of a Flea." *Bulletin of the New York Public
        Library*, LXIV (1960), 567-572.

        Account of Blake's relationship with Varley plus
        the suggestion that Blake's flea may have been modeled
        on a flea engraved in Hooke's *Micrographia*.

866. Keynes, Geoffrey. "Blake's *Little Tom the Sailor*." *Book Collector*, XVII (1968), 421-427.

A descriptive bibliographic study of Blake's text-etching and illustrations of Hayley's broadside ballad "Little Tom the Sailor."

867. Keynes, Geoffrey. "The Blake Trust Gray Catalogue and the Blake Trust Facsimiles." *Blake Newsletter*, VII (1973), 64-65.

Keynes's response to Bentley's discovery of "some serious minor defects" in the catalog. See item 771. Bentley is out "to undermine still further the status of the Blake Trust facsimiles."

868. Keynes, Geoffrey L. "A Newly Discovered Painting by William Blake." *Country Life*, II (1949), 1427.

Refers to the Arlington Court picture.

869. Keynes, Geoffrey. "Blake's Engravings for Gay's *Fables*." *Book Collector*, XXI (1972), 59-64.

A discussion of the independent qualities of Blake's engravings for John Gay's *Fables*, 1793. Illustrations included.

870. Keynes, Geoffrey. "A Blake Engraving in Bonnycastle's *Mensuration*, 1782." *Book Collector*, XII (1963), 205-206.

Book in Keynes's possession; Blake engraving after Stothard's design.

871. Keynes, Geoffrey. "The William Blake Trust." *William Blake: Essays for S. Foster Damon* (item 256), 414-420.

A business report of the Trust: its projects, achievements, etc.

872. See item 607a.

873. Kup, Karl. "The Engraved Work of William Blake 1757-1827." *American Artist*, XI (1947), 25-29, 49.

A brief, general account of Blake's life and art.

874. LaBelle, Jenijoy. "Blake's Visions and Re-visions of Michelangelo." *Blake in His Time* (item 149), 13-22.

By tracing seven monochrome wash drawings after the engravings by Adam Ghisi, one can see the great influence Michelangelo had on Blake.

875. LaBelle, Jenijoy. "Michelangelo's Sistine Frescoes and Blake's 1795 Color-Printed Drawings: A Study in Structural Relationships." *Blake: An Illustrated Quarterly*, XIV (1980), 66-84.

Blake borrowed motifs and styles from Michelangelo as well as the organizational patterns of the Sistine ceiling.

876. Lange, Thomas V. "Blake in American Almanacs." *Blake: An Illustrated Quarterly*, XIV (1980), 94-96.

Two early American piratings of Blake plates.

877. Lange, Thomas V. "Blake's Engraving of Wollstonecraft After Opie." *Blake: An Illustrated Quarterly*, XIII (1979), 36-37.

The original copper plate is in the Department of Drawings and Prints of the Pierpont Morgan Library and is rectangular in shape, having been reworked from its original oval shape.

878. Lindberg, Bo. *William Blake's Illustrations to the Book of Job*. Dissertation, published in 1973 in the *Acta Academiae Aboensis*.

A catalogue raisonné of the *Job* designs which includes comprehensive discussions of each design. Highly praised work.

879. Grant, John E. (rev., *William Blake's Illustrations to the Book of Job*). *Philological Quarterly*, LIII (1974), 651.

"The frequent consideration of Blake's designs from the point of view of art history is particularly salutary."

880. Lipking, Lawrence. "Blake and the Book." *The Ordering of the Arts in Eighteenth Century England*. Princeton: Princeton University Press, 1970, 64-69.

Blake attacks Reynolds's *Discourses* in such a dynamic way as to make it his book.

881. Lister, Raymond. *Infernal Methods: A Study of William Blake's Art Techniques*. London: G. Bell & Sons, 1975.

Dwells on *how* rather than *why* Blake did what he did. Lister is primarily interested in Blake's "tremendous versatility as a practical workman...." Blake was as original in his artistic execution as he was in his conceptions. Very interesting on purely technical, artistic matters.

882. Harvey, J.R. "Blake's Art." (rev., *Infernal Methods*). *Cambridge Quarterly*, VII (1977), 129-150.

"... it so presses to the foreground of our sight the man working on paper, wood, and metal with ground pigments, wax, acid, glue, and so maintains the necessary relegation of poet, radical and visionary, that it gives, as few studies do, a clear picture of Blake the Artist, as distinct from the other Blakes."

883. McCord, James D. "William Blake's Experiments in Illuminated Printing: 1793-1795." *DAI*, XXXVIII (1978), 4142A (University of California, Santa Barbara).

A reading of the Lambeth Books which reveals that "variation and experimentation more than consistency or development characterize Blake's methods as composite artist."

884. Mangravite, Peppino G. "Dante Through Three Artists' Eyes." *Columbia Library Columns*, XV (1965), 17-27.

The artists are Botticelli, Blake and Rauschenberg. Blake's Dante engravings are considered.

885. Margoliouth, Herschel M. "William Blake: Historical Painter." *Studio*, CLIII (1957), 97-103.

Blake was an imaginative rather than an imitative portrait painter.

886. Merchant, W. Moelwyn. *Shakespeare and the Artist*. London: Oxford University Press, 1959.

Blake's Shakespeare illustrations "have a unique place in the history of Shakespeare illustration."

887. Merchant, W. Moelwyn. "Blake's Shakespeare." *Apollo*,
      LXXIX (1964), 318-325.

      Interesting reproduction of Blake's tempera on canvas,
      William Shakespeare, plus seven Shakespeare character
      heads. "... in addition to their highly personal comment
      on Shakespeare's thinking, they form a quite substantial
      comment on certain aspects of Blake's private mythology."

888. Miner, Paul. "The Apprentice of Great Queen Street."
      Bulletin of the New York Public Library, LXVII (1963),
      639-642.

      Some of Blake's apprentice engravings can be found in
      Richard Gough's *Sepulchral Monuments in Great Britain*
      (1786).

889. Mitchell, W.J.T. "Blake's Composite Art." *Blake's
      Visionary Forms Dramatic* (item 139), 57-81.

      "This essay claims that the illuminated poems con-
      stitute a composite art, a single, unified aesthetic
      phenomenon in which neither form dominates the other
      and yet in which each is incomplete without the other."

890. Mitchell, W.J.T. "Blake's Composite Art: The Relation-
      ship of Text and Illustration in the Illuminated Poetry
      of William Blake." *DAI*, XXIX (1968), 1874A (Johns
      Hopkins University).

      "... Blake's illuminated books constitute a 'composite
      art,' a unified aesthetic phenomenon in which each art-
      form fulfills the particular artistic demands of its
      own medium and yet in which each depends for its full
      appreciation on the other." Opposes Hagstrum's view
      (item 845).

891. Mitchell, W.J.T. "Style and Iconography in the Illustra-
      tion of Blake's *Milton*." *Blake Studies*, VI (1973),
      47-71.

      Mitchell's studies on the composite art are superb.
      This is no exception.

892. Mulhallen, Karen G. "For Friendship's Sake: Some Addi-
      tions to Blake's Sheet for 'Designs to a Series of
      Ballads' (1802)." *Studies in Bibliography*, XXIX (1976),
      331-341.

Identifies 11 more sheets of Blake's scratch paper,
paper which was originally proof sheets of *Designs to
a Series of Ballads*.

893. Mulhallen, Karen. "William Blake's Milton Portraiture
      and Eighteenth Century Milton Iconography." *Colby
      Library Quarterly*, XIV (1978), 7-21.

      Examines the Milton iconographic tradition as it is
      reflected in three portraits by Blake. Agrees with
      Wittreich (item 1286) that Blake's head of Milton is an
      amalgam of "motifs previously used." "My work ... seeks
      to extend Wittreich's by showing how Blake's altering
      of his sources illuminates his iconography."

894. Nelms, Ben F. "Text and Design in *Illustrations of the
      Book of Job*." *Blake's Visionary Forms Dramatic* (item
      139), 336-358.

      There is an interdependence of text and design which
      is mutually enriching.

895. Norvig, Gerda. "Images of Wonder, Images of Truth: Blake's
      Illustrations to *The Pilgrim's Progress*." *DAI*, XXXIX
      (1979), 7360A (Brandeis University).

      Blake's illustrations here define not only Bunyan's
      work but Blake's.

896. Paley, Morton D. "Blake's *Night Thoughts*: An Explora-
      tion of the Fallen World." *William Blake: Essays
      for S. Foster Damon* (item 256), 131-157.

      Close description of how Blake in his illustrations
      to *Night Thoughts* utilized Young's imagery to reveal
      a Blakean vision.

897. Paley, Morton D. "'Wonderful Originals'--Blake and
      Ancient Sculpture." *Blake in His Time* (item 149),
      170-197.

      Discusses Blake's theory and practice of art in the
      light of traditions about ancient sculpture and concludes
      that Blake's originality shines through.

898. Paley, Morton D. "John Camden Hotten, A.C. Swinburne,
      and the Blake Facsimiles of 1868." *Bulletin of the
      New York Public Library*, LXXIX (1976), 259-296.

A long survey of Hotten in an attempt to answer the question of why he forged Blake drawings at a time when original Blakes were inexpensive.

899.   Pevsner, Nikolaus. *The Englishness of English Art*. Harmondsworth, Middlesex: Penguin Books, 1956.

Chapter entitled "Blake and the Flaming Line."

900.   Read, Dennis M. "A New Blake Engraving: Gilchrist and the Cromek Connection." *Blake: An Illustrated Quarterly*, XIV (1980), 60-65.

Cromek destroyed Blake's frontispiece engraving to Malkin's *A Father's Memoirs of His Child* but kept Blake's proof, which was eventually given to the British Museum by Cromek's son.

901.   Read, Dennis M. "William Blake and the *Grave*." *DAI*, XXXVII (1977), 6478A (University of Wisconsin, Milwaukee).

Concludes that the *Grave* project "significantly advanced Blake's notions of an ultimate reconciliation of mankind through imaginative apocalypse."

902.   Reisner, M.E. "Effigies of Power: Pitt and Fox as Canterbury Pilgrims." *Eighteenth Century Studies*, XII (1979), 481-503.

Traces the descent, "on the basis of astonishing resemblance, of Blake's Pardoner and Summoner in Chaucer's *Canterbury Pilgrims* from satirical portraits of William Pitt the Younger and Charles James Fox, so common in contemporary political prints."

903.   Rhodes, Judith. "Blake's Designs for *L'Allegro* and *Il Penseroso*: Thematic Relationships in Diagram." *Blake Newsletter*, IV (1971), 135-136.

Constructs a diagram which supposedly relates thematic aspects with direction and level for interpretation of Blake's illustrations. Blake's designs or Rhodes's diagram?

904.   Rose, Edward J. "Blake's Illustrations for *Paradise Lost*, '*L'Allegro*,' and '*Il Penseroso*': A Thematic Reading." *Hartford Studies in Literature*, II (1970), 40-67.

These designs can be read thematically and reveal Blake's commentary on Milton.

905. Ryan, Robert M. "Poisonous Blue." *Blake Newsletter*, VII
      (1974), 87, 89.

      The blue Blake used was not woad but Prussian blue.

906. Ryskamp, Charles. "Blake's Drawing of Cowper's Monument."
      Princeton University Library Chronicle, XXIV (1962),
      32-35.

      William Blake did the sketch of the Cowper monument
      found opposite page 188 of volume four of Upcott's *Cowper's
      Works*.

907. Sewter, A.C. "William Blake and the Art of the Book."
      Manchester Review, VIII (1959), 360-373.

      A study of Blake's method of illustrating his own works.

908. Simmons, Robert E., and Janet Warner. "Blake's 'Arling-
      ton Court Picture': The Moment of Truth." *Studies in
      Romanticism*, X (1971), 3-20.

      A Blakean interpretation of the painting. See Grant's
      trysts with this painting, items 833, 834, 838.

909. Singer, Charles. "The First English Microscopist: Robert
      Hooke (1635-1703)." *Endeavor*, XIV (1955), 12-18.

      Blake's "Ghost of a Flea" drawing is like a drawing
      of a flea in Hooke's *Micrographia*, 1665.

910. Stevenson, Warren. "Interpreting Blake's Canterbury
      Pilgrims." *Colby Library Quarterly*, XIII (1977), 115-
      126.

      Describes each member of the party and relates their
      depiction to Blake's own vision while maintaining a
      reasonable fidelity to Chaucer's text.

911. Tannenbaum, Leslie. "Blake and the Iconography of Cain."
      Blake in His Time (item 149), 23-34.

      There is a commensurateness between Blake's depiction
      of Cain and Abel and his belief that in the fallen world
      man is doomed to be both murderer and victim.

912. Tayler, Irene. *Blake's Illustrations to the Poems of
      Gray*. Princeton: Princeton University Press, 1971.

      Monochrome reproduction plus thorough commentary.

913.   Helmstadter, Thomas H. (rev., *Blake's Illustrations
       to the Poems of Gray*). *Blake Newsletter*, IV (1971),
       140-142.

       "Tayler offers no rules for interpreting the
       illustrations and proffers no theories to which
       all the pictures must ascribe. Her careful ex-
       ploration of design and text and her persuasive
       allusions to Blake's work to support her findings
       make this a fine contribution...."

914.   Rieger, James. (rev., *Blake's Illustrations to the
       Poems of Gray*). *Philological Quarterly*, LI (1972),
       646-647.

       "Mrs. Tayler's study seems finally myopic in
       its denial of Blake's humor and multivalence--
       its unexamined, operative assumption that Blake
       spoke everywhere a narrowly parabolic language,
       and that the 'knowledgeable' have its key."

915.   Tayler, Irene. "Metamorphoses of a Favorite Cat." *Blake's
       Visionary Forms Dramatic* (item 139), 285-303.

       Blake's illustrations to Gray's *Ode on the Death of a
       Favorite Cat* are discussed in terms of "the shifting re-
       lationship between fable and moral...." A satiric view
       of the fallen world and a glance at eternity.

916.   Tayler, Irene. "Blake's *Comus* Designs." *Blake Studies*,
       IV (1972), 45-80.

       A study of the series of eight illustrations to *Comus*.
       They mark the beginning of Blake's attempt to illustrate
       interpretively almost all of Milton's English poetry.

917.   Tayler, Irene. "Visionary Forms Dramatic: William Blake's
       Illustrations to the Poetry of Thomas Gray." *DAI*,
       XXIX (1968), 881A (Stanford University).

       This dissertation is the first complete study of the
       116 Gray illustrations which were rediscovered recently.
       See item 912.

918.   Tayler, Irene. "Blake's Laocoon." *Blake Newsletter*, X
       (1976), 72-81.

       The Laocoön is a summary of Blake's later thought.

919. Tayler, Irene. "Two Eighteenth Century Illustrators of Gray." *Fearful Joy*. Edited by James Downey and Ben Jones. Montreal: McGill-Queens University Press, 1974, 119-126.

Discusses the differences between Richard Bentley's illustrations to Gray and Blake's.

920. Taylor, Clyde R. "Iconographical Themes in William Blake." *Blake Studies*, I (1968), 39-85.

"... if we approach Blake's art as he conceived it, we would proceed on the realization that seeing Blake *whole* means 'reading' every one of his pictures in relation to every passage of his prose and poetry."

921. Taylor, Peter A. "Blake's Text for the *Enoch* Drawings." *Blake Newsletter*, VII (1974), 82-86.

Attempts to demonstrate that Allan R. Brown's reading of the *Enoch* drawings rests on a text Blake couldn't have seen. Brown's essay appeared in the *Burlington Magazine*, LXXVII, 1940.

922. Thompson, Raymond E. "The 'Double' of the Double Portrait of Blake: A Description of Tatham's Replica Portrait." *Blake: An Illustrated Quarterly*, XIII (1979), 29-32.

The replica portrait was made for the Butts family and is on public display in the Denver Art Museum.

923. Todd, Ruthven. *William Blake, the Artist*. New York: E.P. Dutton; London: Studio Vista, 1971. 158pp.

A chronological handbook of Blake's daily artistic activities, enhanced because Todd has experimented with Blake's techniques and speaks knowledgeably about them. Also serves as a fine biographical sketch of Blake's life. Numerous illustrations in black and white.

924. Anon. (rev., *William Blake, the Artist*). *Philological Quarterly*, LI (1972), 648.

"... by all odds the most satisfactory survey of Blake's art ever designed for the general public."

925. Wackrill, H.R. (rev., *William Blake, the Artist*). *Blake Studies*, IV (1972), 168-169.

"On the subject of the Color Printed Drawings,
Mr. Todd writes less fully ... than he does on
relief etching, tempera technique and engraving."

926. Todd, Ruthven. "The Techniques of William Blake's Illumi-
      nated Printing." *The Visionary Hand* (item 144), 19-44.

      Notes on technique provided by the author with the
      assistance of William Hayter and Joan Miro.

927. Todd, Ruthven. "'Poisonous Blues' and Other Pigments."
      Blake: An Illustrated Quarterly, XIV (1980), 31-35.

      Suggests that nitric acid is the poisonous blue.

928. Todd, Ruthven. "Two Blake Prints and Two Fuseli Drawings
      with Some Possibly Pertinent Speculations." *Blake News-
      letter*, V (1972), 173-181.

      Todd found Fuseli's original drawings for the plates
      engraved by Blake as the frontispiece for Lavatar's
      Aphorisms and as the last page of Fuseli's *Lectures on
      Painting*.

929. Todd, Ruthven. "A Tentative Note on the Economics of the
      Canterbury Pilgrims." *Blake: An Illustrated Quarterly*,
      XI (1977), 30-31.

      The painting was cheap to produce but the art is great.

930. Todd, Ruthven. "The Identity of 'Hereford' in *Jerusalem*:
      With Observations on Welsh Matters." *Blake Studies*,
      VI (1976), 139-147.

      Contends that Thomas Johnes of Hafod is "the only
      plausible candidate for Hereford."

931. Tolley, Michael J. "Some Blake Puzzles--Old and New."
      Blake Studies, III (1971), 107-128.

      Hidden sketches revealed beneath the mounted Blake
      sketches in the British Museum Department of Prints and
      Drawings. Illustrations reproduced and commentary pre-
      sented.

932. Tomory, Peter. "A Blake Sketch for Hayley's Ballad 'The
      Lion' and a Connection with Fuseli." *Burlington Maga-
      zine*, CXVII (1975), 376-378.

      Compares Blake's drawing with the engravings. Fuseli's
      Odysseus Killing the Suitors has the same compositional
      arrangement as "The Lion."

933. University of California, Santa Barbara. Faculty-Graduate Student Project. *William Blake in the Art of His Time.* Santa Barbara: University of California, 1976.

   Ostensibly a catalogue of an exhibit which focuses on Blake and his contemporaries. "There is no doubt that they share many characteristics with William Blake in both style and content." Therefore, a catalogue with an important thesis regarding Blake's art.

934. Warner, Janet A. "Blake's Figures of Despair: Man in His Spectre's Power." *William Blake: Essays in Honour of Sir Geoffrey Keynes* (item 240), 208-224.

   Blake portrays despair in various pictorial ways.

935. Warner, Janet. "Blake and the Language of Art: From Copy to Vision." *Colby Library Quarterly,* XIII (1977), 99-114.

   Blake knew the general iconographic tradition and felt certain that his visual symbols would be recognized by his public.

936. Watson, Alan M. "William Blake's Illustrated Writings: The Early Period." *DAI,* XXX (1969), 1538A (University of New Mexico).

   Attempts to answer questions regarding the what, how, when and why of Blake's illustrations.

937. Wills, James T. "An Additional Drawing for Blake's Bunyan Series." *Blake Newsletter,* VI (1972-73), 63-67.

   Proposes that there are 29 genuine designs in the *Pilgrim's Progress* series.

938. Wills, James T. "William Blake's Designs for Bunyan's *Pilgrim's Progress.*" *DAI,* XXXVIII (1977), 3525A (University of Toronto).

   Attempts to establish a continuity between the Blake of the Prophetic Books and the Blake of the 1820's "who devoted the majority of his time to the illustration of the works of others."

939. Wills, James T. "'For I Discern Thee Other Than Thou Seem'st': An Extra Illustration for Blake's *Paradise Regained* Series." *Blake Studies,* VIII (1979), 109-119.

Suggests that this drawing in the Frick is a pivot for a sequence including "The First Temptation" and "A Prophet in the Wilderness."

940.   Wilton, Andrew. "A Fan Design by Blake." *Blake Newsletter*, VII (1973), 61-63.

Rare for Blake because it is decorative and frivolous.

941.   Wittreich, Joseph A. "William Blake: Illustrator-Interpreter of *Paradise Regained*." *Calm of Mind*. Cleveland: Press of Case Western Reserve, 1971, 93-132.

Blake was a perceptive critic whose illustrations of others' work, in this instance Milton's, gives evidence of that fact.

942.   Wright, Andrew. *Blake's Job: A Commentary*. Oxford: Clarendon Press, 1972.

"This study discriminates between Blake's effort in the late prophetic books to project his vision into a personal myth and, after a recognition of relative failure, the attempt in his ultimate illustrations to insinuate that same meaning into the works of Dante and Job."

943.   Wright, John W. "Blake's Relief Etching Method." *Blake Newsletter*, IX (1976), 94-114.

Discusses Blake's relief-etched plates and distinguishes the electrotypes from the *America* fragment, the only surviving Blake plate.

944.   Wright, John. "Toward Recovering Blake's Relief-Etching Process." *Blake Newsletter*, VII (1973), 32-39.

Techniques used by Blake for copies and original relief-etched designs.

CHAPTER NINE

SOURCES AND ANALOGUES

In his historical approach to Blake, Erdman (item 129)
attempts to locate Blake within his own time. To what extent,
he asks, is Blake's work comprehensible in terms of the political and social events of his day? He reconstructs that milieu
so clearly that the reader can affix the importance of any
event or person upon Blake, while at the same time apprehending
the unique course of Blake's own development. In *Natural
Supernaturalism*, Abrams (item 945) describes the ways in which
the Romantics, including Blake, secularized both traditional
and esoteric religious thought. His description of the Hebrew
Cabbala and Hermetic lore, both originating in the Bible,
Neoplatonism, Gnosticism and pagan mythology, is presented in
a way which illuminates Blake, although he, like Erdman, is
not source-hunting:

> The concurrence in topics and design among these very
> diverse writers was less the result of mutual influence
> than it was of a common experience in the social, in-
> tellectual, and emotional climate of the post-Revolu-
> tionary age, and of a grounding in a common body of
> materials--above all in the Bible, especially as expounded
> by radical Protestant visionaries, many of whom had
> assimilated a modicum of Neoplatonic lore. (256)

Both Erdman and Abrams attempt to describe the milieu from
which Blake emerged--Erdman the political-social, Abrams the
intellectual. Abrams's work serves to make us aware of views
analogous to Blake's own. Both Erdman and Abrams succeed in
locating Blake for us, but they do so without reducing Blake
to the level of instrument of either esoteric or traditional
thought, or the circumstances of his day. Blake's work is always, we are led to believe, something different from the
factors that may or may not have influenced it.
    In truth, finding a source for some part or all of Blake's
work implies that the source can be substituted for his work.

This is ridiculous, especially when one is speaking of an artist-poet-prophet such as Blake. If the source and Blake's work are not equatable then we are faced with the problem of ascertaining to what degree Blake made use of that source. We must study Blake's work in terms of the suggested source. The suggested source becomes an analogous work. Whatever illumination we derive from such a comparison derives from the fact that we have treated the suggested source not as a source but as an analogue.

We do not handle analogues as we do suggested sources--with great trepidation. The autonomy, the originality of Blake's work is not at stake. What we desire to do is to see Blake's work as fully as possible within its historical and intellectual setting, to perceive concurrent modes of thought and expression and to finally perceive the uniqueness of Blake's own work. While rich descriptions of various analogues cause us to come to Blake with reawakened senses, pronouncements based on the establishment of supposedly unarguable sources cause us to wonder why Blake more than any other author is looked upon as needing buttressing by this or that tradition or individual. Such an impulse to reinforce Blake is probably caused by an unfortunate doubt about the ability of Blake's work to stand alone. If a much-needed grand critical assessment of all of Blake takes place in the future, the fact that Blake was a spokesman for this or that tradition will not affect that assessment in the slightest.

On the side of source-hunting, we find in a preeminent position Raine's *Blake and Tradition* (item 1096). Raine believes that Blake would have been mute without the Perennial Philosophy. Cruttwell (item 982), in a rejoinder, wonders what is left of Blake's work if one decides the perennial philosophy is "an ill-digested corpus of elaborate nonsense"? The unfortunate aspect of Raine's work is that Blake is made to fit into the perennial philosophy whether or not a good part of him is left sticking out. Harper's *The Neoplatonism of William Blake* (item 1025) holds Neoplatonism away from Blake for a while, giving us the sense that here indeed is a useful analogue, before forcing Blake into it. J.G. Davies (item 988) can persistently see an orthodox Blake in spite of much evidence to the contrary.

In actuality, source-hunters are not dangerous. Whether or not they deem their suggested sources as essential to understanding Blake, students are advised to treat the sources as analogues and to distinguish attempts at applying the analogue to Blake unimaginatively from illuminating descriptions of the analogue. There are, however, a number of commentators who do write both imaginatively and perceptively regarding analogues, thus establishing immediately a bond of trust and mutual endeavor with the reader.

Hagstrum (item 1020) defines Blake's notion of the spiritual body as something quite different from Neoplatonic or mystical views. Paley (item 1079) is very interesting regarding the Millenarians, Brothers and Southcott. Fisher (item 1004) discusses Blake's treatment of Druidism. Morton (item 1072) and Lindsay (item 204) point out many interesting parallels between Blake and the Antinomian tradition of the seventeenth century, but both enlist Blake under that banner without hesitation. Wagenknecht (item 1137) enlists Blake under the banner of Pastoralism without hesitation. Wittreich (item 1156) feels that the Spenser-Milton epic tradition is the best guide to understanding Blake. Bloom (item 101) dismisses every tradition but that of the Bible and Milton. Brogan (item 976) places Blake firmly within the occult tradition and Trawick (item 1130) places him firmly outside it. Paley (item 1082) traces Blake's attitude toward Swedenborgianism. John Beer (item 962) cavalierly surveys the field as if nothing had ever been written. Thus one can see that in a selected listing that attempts to focus on reliable presentation of sources, there persists a tendency to equate Blake with the suggested source. The analogue disguise vanishes and the key to all Blake's myth appears--alas.

To summarize, the works which prove most rewarding are not those which go to great and unnatural lengths to accommodate the source to Blake or vice-versa, but those which present analogues in so compelling a fashion that we re-see Blake's work, in both its uniqueness and its indebtedness.

945. Abrams, Meyer H. *Natural Supernaturalism*. New York: W.W. Norton, 1971.

Though Abrams uses Wordsworth rather than Blake as a constant paradigm, one can perceive connections with Blake on almost every page. Most interesting is his account of the Romantic notion of the circular or spiral quest: "the journey is a spiritual way through evil and suffering which is justified as a necessary means to the achievement of a greater good.... This process is conceived as a fall from unity into division and into a conflict of contraries which in turn compel the movement back toward a higher integration." In general, a study of the Romantics' use of esoteric tradition.

946. Adlard, John. "The Annandale Druids: A Blake Crux." *Notes & Queries*, N.S. XIV (1967), 19-20.

Did Blake confuse Annandale with Nithsdale? Adlard's research seems to point to that.

947. Adlard, John. "Mr. Blake's Fairies." *Neuphilologische Mitteilungen*, LXV (1964), 144-160.

Traces Blake's use of fairies without advancing any particular hypothesis.

948. Adlard, John. "Blake and Thomas Taylor." *English Studies*, XLIV (1963), 353-354.

Blake perhaps saw a sentence referring to a clod of earth in T. Taylor's *A Vindication of the Rights of Brutes*.

949. Adlard, John. "Blake and *Rasselas*." *Archiv für das Studium der Neueren Sprachen und Literaturen*, CCI (1964), 47.

If Blake had read *Rasselas*, Imlac's views of the poet would have upset him.

950. Adlard, John. *The Sports of Cruelty*. London: Cecil and Amelia Woolf, 1972.

"Fairies, Folksongs, Charms and Other Country Matters in the Work of William Blake." Something of a survey of eighteenth-century folklore. Adlard maintains that "though the English fairies are conspicuous through twenty years of his [Blake's] creative work, the folklore sources have been largely neglected."

951. Adlard, John. "Triumphing Joyfulness: Blake, Boehme and the Tradition." *Blake Studies*, I (1969), 109-122.

Esoteric sources for Blake's symbolism in Milton. "Once and for all, we must establish whether Blake's philosophy is, as Eliot thought, 'ingenious' but 'home-made,' or whether it belongs to the theosophical tradition. More important, will a study of this tradition make Blake easier to understand?"

952. Ansari, Asloob A. "Blake and the Kabbalah." *William Blake: Essays for S. Foster Damon* (item 256), 199-220.

"Blake's genius is radically Christian rather than Jewish in inspiration. Blake, like Milton, did owe something to the Hebraic sources."

953. Ansari, Asloob. *Arrows of Intellect: A Study of William Blake's Gospel of the Imagination*. Aligarh: Naya Kitabghar, 1965; Folcroft, Pa.: Folcroft, 1970.

Interesting for its comparison of Blake and Sir Mohammed Iqbal's *The Reconstruction of Religious Thought in Islam*. Both Blake and Iqbal present views which oppose Buddhist doctrine.

954. Ault, Donald D. "Visionary Physics: Blake's Response to Newton." Dissertation, University of Chicago, 1969.

955. Ault, Donald D. *Visionary Physics: Blake's Response to Newton*. Chicago: University of Chicago Press, 1974.

Ault claims "that Blake's epic prophecies constitute a *Principia* which subsumes and reverses Newton's." This is a book that could have been written by Bacon, Newton or Locke and annotated by Blake.

956. Chayes, Irene. (rev., *Visionary Physics*). *ELN*, XIII (1975), 28-29.

"... in matters of practical criticism it tends to be too rigidly systematic in its own right, a creation of Urizen rather than Los."

957. Faulkner, Dewey. (rev., *Visionary Physics*). *Yale Review*, LXIV (1974), 271-274.

"On the negative side, however, his ideas-- and prose--often grow so dense as to make those Blakean passages upon which he periodically alights appear havens of light and air...."

958. Skelton, Susan. (rev., *Visionary Physics*). *Southern Humanities Review*, XII (1978), 389-390.

"According to Ault, Blake is fundamentally concerned with what he considers as the Satanic usurpation of universality, activity, and vision through their assimilation to a system which effectively consolidates the error of earlier systems while at the same time providing a dangerously seductive appeal to the imagination."

959. Welch, Dennis M. (rev., *Visionary Physics*). *Philological Quarterly*, LIV (1975), 901-902.

"While at times fascinating, Ault's study is extremely complex."

960. Baine, Rodney M., and Mary R. Baine. "Then Mars wast our center." *ELN*, XIII (1975), 14-18.

Lines refer to the symbolic cosmology of Swedenborg.

961. Beer, John. "Blake's 'Donald the Hammerer.'" *Blake Newsletter*, V (1972), 165-167.

Tracing a source, Scott's *The Abbot*.

962. Beer, John. "Influence and Independence in Blake." *Interpreting Blake* (item 245), 196-261.

Presents at length possible sources for certain particulars in both Blake's designs and poetry. Considers Whichcote's *Aphorisms* (1703) to have "generated various echoes on Blake over a long period of time." Also considers Pope's "Eloisa to Abelard" and John Ogilvie's *The Theology of Plato*. Briefly surveys alchemy's effect on Blake's thought.

963. Bentley, G.E., Jr. "Blake and Percy's Reliques." *Notes & Queries*, CCI (1956), 352-353.

Argues that Blake was familiar with the third volume of *Reliques of Ancient English Poetry*, 1765, and that it is safe to source-hunt in all three volumes.

964. Bentley, G.E., Jr. "Blake and Swedenborg." *Notes & Queries*, CXCIX (1954), 264-265.

Blake adhered to Swedenborg's view of which books in the Bible had the internal sense.

965. Bentley, G.E., Jr. "A Jewel in an Ethiop's Ear." *Blake in His Time* (item 149), 213-240.

Blake found confirmation of his own visions in the apocryphal Book of Enoch.

966. Bentley, G.E., Jr. "Blake's Annotations to Swedenborg's *Heaven and Hell*." *University of Toronto Quarterly*, XXXIV (1965), 290-293.

Adds further to the connection between Swedenborg and Blake.

967. Bentley, Gerald E., Jr. "William Blake and the Alchemical Philosophers." B.Litt. Thesis, Oxford University, 1954.

968. Bindman, David. "Blake's Theory and Practice of Imitation." *Blake in His Time* (item 149), 91–98.

   Argues that "Blake's attitudes toward art are in a profound sense eighteenth century in spirit, and are predominantly determined even to the end of his career by classical idealism."

969. Bishop, Morchard. "Blake and Buckingham." *Times Literary Supplement*, April 2, 1964, 277.

   Blake quoted lines from the Duke of Buckingham's play *The Rehearsal*.

970. Bogan, James. "Vampire Bats and Blake's Spectre." *Blake Newsletter*, X (1976), 32–33.

   In 1792, Blake engraved John Stedman's *Narrative of a Five Year's Expedition Against the Revolted Negroes of Surinam*. It contains an account of a vampire bat or spectre.

971. Bogen, Nancy. "Blake's Debt to Gillray." *American Notes and Queries*, VI (1967), 35–38.

   In his depiction of Burke in *Europe*, Blake was making a direct rejoinder to the political cartoonist Gillray.

972. Bogen, Nancy. "Blake and the Ohio." *Notes & Queries*, N.S. XV (1968), 19–20.

   Blake's allusion to the Ohio in an untitled poem in the Rossetti Notebook may have come from Gilbert Imlay's *A Topographical Description of the Western Territory of North America*.

973. Bogen, Nancy. "The Problem of William Blake's Early Religion." *Personalist*, XLIX (1968), 509–522.

   Blake's early Anglicanism merits study.

974. Borck, Jim S. "William Blake: A Prophetic Tradition." *DAI*, XXXI (1970), 1750A (University of California, Riverside).

   Milton and *Jerusalem* are prophecies; and that form is placed in historical context: eighteenth-century chiliasts' rhetorical devices, Brothers and Southcott, Robert Lowth and Newton.

975. Brinkley, Robert A. "Romanticism and the Desire Called
      Milton." *DAI*, XL (1980), 4603A (University of Massa-
      chusetts).

      "The thesis locates the dilemma of dialectic in
      Wordsworth, charts its critique in Bloom, seeks its
      origin in Milton, and discovers its annihilation in
      Blake."

976. Brogan, Howard O. "Blake and the Occult: 'The Real Man
      the Imagination Which Liveth Forever.'" *Wordsworth
      Circle*, VIII (1977), 147-160.

      Sees Blake as being firmly within the occult tradi-
      tion—Neoplatonism, Gnosticism, Manichaeism, etc.

977. Brown, John E. "Neo-Platonism in the Poetry of William
      Blake." *Journal of Aesthetics and Art Criticism*, X
      (1951), 43-52.

      Blake operated fully within the Neoplatonic tradition.

978. Carothers, Yvonne M. "Romantic Enthusiasm: Blake,
      Coleridge and Shelley." *DAI*, XXXVIII (1978), 5492A
      (University of California, Irvine).

      Blake countered rationalism with enthusiasm and
      aligned himself with biblical prophets such as Isaiah
      and Ezekiel. *Jerusalem* outlines the means by which
      rationalism may be elevated to a perception of the
      infinite.

979. Chayes, Irene H. "Plato's *Statesman* Myth in Shelley
      and Blake." *Comparative Literature*, XIII (1961),
      358-369.

      "... within the framework of generally similar con-
      ceptions of the nature of man and the universe and a
      common relationship to Plato's *Statesman*, Shelley and
      Blake make use of the common pattern."

980. Chayes, Irene H. "The Presence of Cupid and Psyche."
      Blake's Visionary Forms Dramatic (item 139), 214-243.

      "... in spite of his strictures on 'the classics'
      his work itself shows that Blake was sufficiently a
      product of his age to draw on the traditional Greek
      and Roman myths as well as on more esoteric material
      for the complex purposes of his two parallel arts."

981. Cohen, Sandy. "Is William Blake's Concept of Marriage Kabbalistic?" *Notes & Queries*, N.S. XX (1973), 100-101.

Maybe yes, maybe no.

982. Cruttwell, Patrick. "Blake, Tradition and Miss Raine." *Hudson Review*, XXIII (1970), 133-142.

"... what if one has to answer with the conclusion that the 'perennial philosophy' is an ill-digested corpus of elaborate nonsense? What is then left of the prophetic books?" See item 1096.

983. Curran, Stuart. "Blake and the Gnostic Hyle: A Double Negative." *Blake Studies*, IV (1972), 117-133.

Hyle is Greek for matter, and all matter can be "humanized--spiritualized--when we see through, not with the eye." "I would like to enumerate what appear to me the three major fallacies that beset our view of Blake's relationship with tradition, then proceed to take a limited--and somewhat esoteric--tradition of Christian theology and illustrate to what use, or abuse, Blake put it."

984. Curtis, F.B. "Blake and the 'Moment of Time': An Eighteenth Century Controversy in Mathematics." *Philological Quarterly*, LI (1972), 460-470.

Blake was aware of math articles published in 1800 in the *Monthly Review*. Blake reinterprets the math term to gain ontological status.

985. Curtis, F.B. "William Blake and Eighteenth Century Medicine." *Blake Studies*, VIII (1979), 187-199.

Presents eighteenth-century medical writing as an analogue to certain passages in the Lambeth books; contends that Blake knew anatomy and critically evaluates "the function of this anatomical imagery in Blake's verse."

986. Daly, Michael J. "The Marriage Metaphor and the Romantic Prophecy: A Study of the Uses of the Epithalamium in the Poetry of Blake, Wordsworth, and Coleridge." *DAI*, XXIX (1969), 2254A (University of Southern California).

Each poet struck upon the marriage metaphor to juxta-
pose Romantic unity with mechanistic division.

987.   Davenport, A. "Blake's Minute Particulars." *Notes &
       Queries*, CXCIII (1948), 7.

       Related to Boswell's introduction to the *Life*.

988.   Davies, J.G. *The Theology of William Blake*. Oxford:
       Clarendon Press, 1948.

       According to Davies, Blake is an orthodox Christian.
       The student simply has to plug Blake into Christianity
       and all questions will be answered.

989.   Davis, Patricia. "William Blake's New Typology and the
       Revaluation of Prophecy in the Eighteenth Century."
       DAI, XL (1980), 6288A.

       Argues that Blake's view of prophecy "evolved as he
       matured in his response to prevailing forms of biblical
       exegesis in the 18th century."

990.   Deck, Raymond. "Blake and Swedenborg." *DAI*, XXXIX
       (1978), 3594A (Brandeis University).

       A thorough examination of the relationship, tracing
       all its changes.

991.   Dillon, Ralph G. "Source for Blake's 'The Sick Rose'?"
       American Notes and Queries, XII (1974), 157-158.

       The source is Jeremiah iv:30: "And when thou art
       spoiled, what wilt thou do?"

992.   Dillworth, Thomas R. "Blake's Babe in the Woods."
       Blake: An Illustrated Quarterly, XI (1977), 35-37.

       "The Little Girl Lost" and "The Little Girl Found"
       may have been influenced by the English sixteenth-
       century ballad "Babe in the Wood."

993.   DiSalvo, Jacqueline A. "War of Titans: Blake's Con-
       frontation with Milton; *The Four Zoas* as Political
       Critique of *Paradise Lost* and the Genesis Tradition."
       DAI, XXXVIII (1977), 3456A (University of Wisconsin,
       Madison).

       Argues that Blake transformed the tradition of radical
       prophecy into an "historical materialist one." This
       latter involves a "decline from tribal communism through

a series of stratified societies, from ancient slavery to modern industrialism."

994. Doxey, William S. "William Blake, James Basire, and the *Philosophical Transactions*: An Unexplored Source of Blake's Scientific Thought?" *Bulletin of the New York Public Library*, LXXII (1968), 252-260.

Blake may have worked on engravings for the Royal Society of London's *Philosophical Transactions*. Includes an appendix with plates autographed by Basire.

995. Doxey, William S. "William Blake and the Lunar Society." *Notes & Queries*, N.S. XVIII (1971), 343.

The Lunar Society held meetings in Soho, where Blake lived in 1778. Did Blake attend? Was he influenced?

996. Easson, Roger R. "Blake and the Gothic." *Blake in His Time* (item 149), 145-154.

"The Gothic revival is a crucial element in the creation of Blake's poetic and pictorial aesthetic."

997. Erdman, David V. "Blake's Early Swedenborgianism: A Twentieth Century Legend." *Comparative Literature*, V (1953), 247-257.

Pierre Berger and Edwin Ellis initiated the myth that young Blake was taught Swedenborgianism at home by James Blake, Jr.

998. Erdman, David V. "William Blake's Debt to Joel Barlow." *American Literature*, XXVI (1954), 94-98.

Discusses the relationship between Blake's *America* and Book V of *The Vision of Columbus*, Barlow's portrayal of the American Revolution. Many scenes of Barlow are echoed in Blake.

999. Evanoff, Alexander. "The Visions of William Blake." *Antigonish Review*, II (1971), 11-18.

The author believes that Blake was a medium in the hands of occult forces. He concludes: "Blake's critics must break away from the tyranny of reason if they are to treat his world with the appropriate balance."

1000. Evans, James C. "Blake, Locke and the Concept of 'Generation.'" *Blake Newsletter*, IX (1975), 47-48.

"Locke's definition of generation both epitomizes ...
a narrow, physical, totally rational concept of man and
perfectly describes the mental state of those who dwell
in so circumscribed a world."

1001.   Fisch, Harold. *Jerusalem and Albion: The Hebraic Factor
        in Seventeenth Century Literature*. New York: Schocken
        Books, 1964.

        Focuses on "the spiritual and intellectual conflicts
        of the seventeenth century, which Blake did something
        to illuminate, since his chief dramatis personae were
        Milton, Bacon, Locke and Newton." The author concludes
        that Blake was certainly influenced by Hebrew poetry
        and its free system of versification.

1002.   Fisch, Harold. "Blake's Miltonic Moment." *William
        Blake: Essays for S. Foster Damon* (item 256), 36-56.

        Argues that Blake's poetry belongs in the last anal-
        ysis to a tradition essentially different from Milton's.

1003.   Fisher, Peter F. "The Doctrine of William Blake in the
        Background of the Eighteenth Century. Part I: The
        Doctrine in Its Larger Historical Setting." Disserta-
        tion, University of Toronto, 1949.

1004.   Fisher, Peter F. "Blake and the Druids." *Journal of
        English and Germanic Philology*, LVIII (1959), 589-
        612.

        Blake relied on Bryant, Davies, Williams. Considers
        Blake "a professed Christian" who saw in Druidism a
        progenitor of contemporary Deism.

1005.   Fisher, Peter F. *The Valley of Vision*. Toronto: Uni-
        versity of Toronto Press, 1961. 261pp.

        Places Blake within the Enlightenment and sees him
        as attempting to present a point of view not exclusively
        his own. It is the imagination which forms the basis
        of Blake's attack on both "rationalistic naturalism
        and dogmatic theism."

        1006.   Adkinson, R.V. (rev., *The Valley of Vision*).
                Revue des Langues Vivantes, XXI (1966), 431.

                "There is much that is useful and erudite
                in this study, but one leaves the book with
                a distinct impression that the baby has been

thrown out with the bath-water; that in placing
Blake in a fuller philosophical context, Fisher
has condemned him to the sort of abstraction
he so abhorred."

1007. Erdman, D.V. (rev., *The Valley of Vision*).
Philological Quarterly, XLI (1962), 658.

"The great value of the book is its philosophical clarity, brought to bear on the elucidation
of Blake's thinking in its widest context."

1008. Franz, Rolaine M. "All the Ship's Company: A Wesleyan
Paradigm for the Poetry of Christopher Smart, William
Cowper, and William Blake." *DAI*, XXXIX (1979), 5523A
(Brown University).

A study of the relationship between the folk theology
of the Wesleys and the religious lyrics of Smart, Cowper
and Blake.

1009. Frye, Northrop. "Blake's Case Against Locke." *English
Literature and British Philosophy: A Collection of
Essays*. Edited by S.P. Rosenbaum. Chicago and London:
University of Chicago Press, 1971, 119-135.

This is a reprint of Chapter One of *Fearful Symmetry*.
A fine discussion of the philosophical milieu from which
Blake emerged and departed.

1010. Frye, Northrop. "Blake's Reading of the Book of Job."
Spiritus Mundi. Bloomington: Indiana University Press,
1976, 228-244.

"... perfect unity is potential in the poem itself,
and is really achieved by the reader. The sense of
unity that one feels about the Job engravings considered
as a series, indicates that Blake extracted a correspond-
ing unity out of his text."

1011. Fussell, Paul, Jr. "Writing as Imitation: Observation
on the Literary Process." *The Rarer Action: Essays
in Honor of Francis Fergusson*. Edited by A. Cheuse and
R. Koffler. New Brunswick, N.J.: Rutgers University
Press, 1970, 218-239.

Mostly on Johnson, although the author suggests that
Blake was involved in "the compositional process of
imitation" and cites Chatterton's *Bristowe Tragedie*
and Matthew Prior's "A True Maid."

1012.   Gallant, Christine. *Blake and the Assimilation of Chaos*.
        Princeton: Princeton University Press, 1978.

        Strives for a Jungian interpretation of Blake which
        respects aesthetic autonomy. The book is not altogether
        readable because of its extended explication approach,
        going from one Blake work to another and bringing in
        the Jung analogy in segments.

        1013.   Tannenbaum, Leslie. (rev., *Blake and the Assimila-
                tion of Chaos*). *Blake: An Illustrated Quarterly*,
                XIII (1980), 200-202.

                Gallant pursues identification of Blake and
                Jung and does not use Jung simply as an analogy,
                as a co-worker emerging from the same Romantic
                tradition. Notes that Gallant affirms that
                "only through ... the Jungian archetypes" can
                we understand changes in *The Four Zoas*.

        1014.   Wilkie, Brian. (rev., *Blake and the Assimilation
                of Chaos*). *Wordsworth Circle*, XI (1980), 158-
                159.

                "The word is not 'assimilate' but 'reject.'"

1015.   Gallant, Christine. "Regeneration Through Archetype:
        William Blake's Changing Myth in *The Four Zoas*." *DAI*,
        XXXVIII (1977), 3480A (University of Minnesota).

        Basis of her book *Blake and the Assimilation of Chaos*
        (item 1012). Blake's regeneration is very much like
        Jung's individuation.

1016.   Gershgoren, Sid C. "Millenarian and Apocalyptic Litera-
        ture from Thomas Burnet to William Blake." *DAI*, XXXI
        (1969), 2385A (University of California, Davis).

        A theme presented also by Paley and Lindsay, most
        notably. See items 1079 and 204.

1017.   Gleckner, Robert F. "Blake and the Four Daughters of God."
        ELN, XV (1977), 110-115.

        Suggests that Blake may have had some knowledge of the
        Four Daughters tradition.

1018.   Gleckner, Robert F. "Blake, Gray and the Illustrations."
        Criticism, XIX (1977), 118-140.

Gray's Ode I: "On the Spring" is the source of Blake's "The Fly."

1019. Gleckner, Robert F. "Blake's Miltonizing of Chatterton." *Blake: An Illustrated Quarterly*, XI (1977), 27-29.

Chatterton's lines in *Bristowe Tragedie* are "the vehicle for Blake's manipulation of Milton to his own, and ultimately, to Milton's benefit."

1020. Hagstrum, Jean H. "Christ's Body." *William Blake: Essays in Honour of Sir Geoffrey Keynes* (item 240), 129-156.

The Neoplatonic and traditional mystical views in regard to Blake's notion of the body, a Spiritual Body, are refuted here. Not Milton but Michelangelo anticipated fully the extremely physical Christ of Blake's vision.

1021. Hagstrum, Jean H. "William Blake Rejects the Enlightenment." *Blake: A Collection of Critical Essays* (item 155), 142-155.

A fine background essay, quite like Frye's "The Case Against Locke," a chapter in item 157.

1022. Hagstrum, Jean H. "Romney and Blake: Gifts of Grace and Terror." *Blake in His Time* (item 149), 201-212.

Romney's "terrible sublime" art prefigures Blake's visual landscape and psychological iconography.

1023. Hall, Mary S. "Materialism and the Myths of Blake." *DAI*, XXIX (1968), 1208A (Princeton University).

Blake's myth is a reaction to the materialist philosophers James Watt, Joseph Priestley, Richard Price, Erasmus Darwin, William Hamilton, Richard Payne Knight and D'Hancarville.

1024. Harding, Eugene J. "Jacob Boehme and Blake's *The Book of Urizen*." *Unisa English Studies*, VIII (1970), 3-11.

Traces many of the Boehme-like ideas in Blake's "Genesis."

1025. Harper, George M. *The Neoplatonism of William Blake*. Chapel Hill: University of North Carolina Press, 1961.

Explores in depth the Neoplatonic influence, via
Thomas Taylor, on Blake.

1026.   Bentley, G.E., Jr. (rev., *The Neoplatonism of
        William Blake*). *Modern Philology*, LXII (1964),
        169-172.

        The facts: no connection between Taylor and
        Blake exists; Blake never refers to Taylor;
        Taylor never refers to Blake; all Blake refer-
        ences to Plato are hostile ones. Conclusion:
        Harper attempts to prove that Blake's writings
        were from 1788 on crucially influenced by
        Taylor's Neoplatonism.

1027.   Dowden, Wilfrid S. "Blake's Neoplatonism" (rev.,
        The Neoplatonism of William Blake). *Sewanee
        Review*, LXXII (1964), 139-141.

        "... he has certainly proved that Neoplatonism--
        from whatever source--is inherent in Blake's
        work...."

1028.   Erdman, D.V. (rev., *The Neoplatonism of William
        Blake*). *Philological Quarterly*, XLI (1962),
        659.

        The author is tempted to push for a direct
        relationship between Taylor and Blake.

1029.   Rostvig, Maren-Sofie. (rev., *The Neoplatonism
        of William Blake*). *English Studies*, XLVIII
        (1967), 81-82.

        No real criticism of Harper's Neoplatonic
        Blake, but raised eyebrows at Harper's disre-
        spect for Renaissance Neoplatonists. Advises
        students to read Hirst also.

1030.   Harper, George M. "Thomas Taylor and Blake's Drama
        of Persephone." *Philological Quarterly*, XXXIV (1955),
        378-394.

        Argues that *Thel* and *Visions* are based on the Perse-
        phone myth and that both poems are similar to Taylor's
        Mysteries.

1031.   Harper, George M. "Blake's Neo-Platonic Interpretation
        of Plato's Atlantis Myth." *Journal of English and
        Germanic Philology*, LIV (1955), 72-79.

Argues that in "his intimate acquaintanceship with the Atlantis myth and the theory of the earth which the Neo-Platonists associated with it ... as well as in his symbolic use of the myth's main outlines, Blake reveals that the source of his knowledge is Thomas Taylor."

1032. Helms, Randel. "Why Ezekiel Ate Dung." *ELN*, XV (1978), 279-281.

The voice of prophetic inspiration residing within man and not without can break the Mosaic law.

1033. Helms, Randel. "Artful Thunder: A Literary Study of Prophecy." *DAI*, XXIX (1969), 3612A (University of Washington).

Blake's link with the genre of prophecy. Provides a study of *The Code of Handsome Lake*, its form and its conception of prophet.

1034. Herzing, Thomas W. "Ceaseless Mental Fight: William Blake and Eighteenth Century Thought." *DAI*, XXXIII (1973), 4345A (University of Wisconsin, Madison).

"Blake was forced to adopt both the premises and the processes of rational dispute in his poetic attempts to undercut the hegemony of rationalism."

1035. Hirst, Desiree. "On the Aesthetics of Prophetic Art." *British Journal of Aesthetics*, IV (1964), 248-252.

"A more recent example of this type of artist [prophetic-sacred] is the poet and painter William Blake. The sculptor Eric Gill could be quoted as a later example and the Welsh artist and poet, David Jones as a living exemplar."

1036. Hirst, Desiree. *Hidden Riches: Traditional Symbolism from the Renaissance to Blake*. New York: Barnes and Noble, 1964.

Blake is not the only writer considered, as in Raine's study (item 1096) of esoteric traditions. Harper (item 1025), Raine and Hirst describe such traditions but not to such good effect as Abrams in *Natural Supernaturalism* (item 945).

1037. Anon. "What Did Blake Read?" (rev., *Hidden Riches*). *Times Literary Supplement*, April 9, 1964, 282.

Hirst's criticism is not in the dominant
positivist tradition. She is aware of the
"perennial philosophy," the esoteric traditions, of which most critics are oblivious.

1038.   Bloom, Harold. (rev., *Hidden Riches*). *Yale Review*,
        LIV (1964), 143-149.

"With Desiree Hirst's *Hidden Riches* we momen-
tarily forsake responsible scholarship, and
plunge into the bathos of the British or occult
school of myth criticism."

1039.   Malekin, P. (rev., *Hidden Riches*). *Review of
        English Studies*, XVI (1965), 436-437.

"*Hidden Riches* is great in range and partially
valuable in content, but it is marred by its
lack of scholarly objectivity, its confusion of
judgment with fact, and the unreliability of
some of its supposedly factual accounts."

1040.   Nolde, Sr. M. Simon. (rev., *Hidden Riches*).
        Manuscripta, IX (1965), 58-59.

Blake is really considered only in the first
and last chapters and what is in between doesn't
always relate.

1041.   Horn, William. "Blake's Gnosticism: The Material World
        as Allegor.." *DAI*, XXXIX (1979), 5527A (UCLA).

Fully explores the relationship in the hope that "an
understanding of Blake's Gnosticism helps us appreciate
not only Blake's art, but also Romanticism's reinterpretation of Christian themes."

1042.   Howard, John. "The Child-Hero in the Poetry of Blake,
        Shelley, Byron, Coleridge, and Wordsworth." *DAI*,
        XXVIII (1968), 2647A (University of Maryland).

The strangely powerful child who is isolated in nature
and endangered by worldliness, by experience.

1043.   Howard, John. "Swedenborg's *Heaven and Hell* and Blake's
        Songs of Innocence." *Papers on Language and Literature*,
        IV (1968), 390-399.

Swedenborg's work provided the moral framework for
the *Songs of Innocence*.

1044. Hughes, Daniel. "Blake and Shelley: Beyond the Uroboros."
      William Blake: Essays for S. Foster Damon (item 256),
      59-83.

      The snake with its tail in its mouth is traced in
      Blake and Shelley.

1045. Jackson, Mary V. "A Study of the Use of Poetic Myth in
      the Work of William Blake from 1783 to 1794." *DAI*,
      XXX (1970), 5410A (Washington University).

      Blake's use of "mythic elements as a poetic device
      to give visible and comprehensible form to complex and
      elusive insights."

1046. Jackson, Mary. "Blake and Zoroastrianism." *Blake News-
      letter*, XI (1977), 72-85.

      External evidence includes: section in *A Descriptive
      Catalogue* of 1809, Blake illuminations which parallel
      illustrations in Thomas Hyde's *Historica Per Sacrum*.

1047. See item 483.

1048. Jones, Myrddin. "Blake's 'To Spring': A Formative
      Source?" *Notes & Queries*, N.S. XVII (1970), 314-315.

      Psalm 19 as a probable source of angel-sun image.

1049. Keith, William J. "The Complexities of Blake's 'Sun-
      flower': An Archetypal Speculation." *Blake: A Collec-
      tion of Critical Essays* (item 155), 56-64.

      Sources of Blake's myth inhere in Ovid and Shakespeare.

1050. Kellogg, Seth. "Tragic Generation: A Commentary on Some
      Works of William Blake and on the Book of Genesis."
      DAI, XXXIV (1973), 3346A (University of Massachusetts).

      The idea is to show that Blake recreated the cos-
      mogony and theogony of the Bible's Genesis.

1051. Keynes, Geoffrey. "Blake and Wesley." *Notes & Queries*,
      CCII (1957), 181.

      Keynes cites a Blake signature on a collection of
      Wesley hymns, proving Blake knew these hymns.

1052. King, James. "The Meredith Family, Thomas Taylor and
      William Blake." *Studies in Romanticism*, II (1972),
      153-157.

      Thomas Taylor gave Blake geometry lessons.

1053.   King, James. "A New Piece of Tayloriana." *Blake News-
           letter*, VI (1972), 72.

           Ms. notebook at McMaster University entitled "The
           Only Fragments Which Remain of the Writings of the
           Philosopher Celsus" may have been the working notes
           for Thomas Taylor's 1830 *Arguments of Celsus ... Against
           the Christians*.

1054.   Kolker, Robert P. "The Altering Eye: William Blake's
           Use of Eighteenth-Century Poetics." *DAI*, XXX (1969),
           1987A (Columbia University).

           "The fact is that Blake does not stand so much at
           the beginning of a new poetic movement as he stands at
           the end of a line of poetic development."

1055.   Kremen, Kathryn R. "The Imagination of the Resurrection:
           The Poetic Continuity and Conversion of the Religious
           Motif in Donne, Blake and Yeats." *DAI*, XXXI (1971),
           5366A (Brandeis University).

1056.   Kremen, Kathryn R. *The Imagination of Resurrection:
           The Poetic Continuity of a Religious Motif in Donne,
           Blake, and Yeats*. Lewisburg, Pa.: Bucknell University
           Press, 1972.

     1057.   Anon. (rev., *The Imagination of the Resurrection*).
               Choice, X (1973), 440.

                   Kremen's conclusion--"that transcendent
                   unity, artistic, and human, is dependent upon
                   divine reality"--is not convincing.

     1058.   Chapin, Chester. (rev., *The Imagination of the
               Resurrection*). *Philological Quarterly*, LIII
               (1974), 649-651.

                   "... I am left with the suspicion that Blake's
                   eschatological beliefs fail to save his version
                   of Christianity, generous and humane as it
                   certainly is, from that subjectivity and con-
                   sequent loss of power which occurs ... when
                   theological beliefs lose their shared charac-
                   ter insofar as they cease to belong to a
                   definable ecclesiastical community."

     1059.   Wittreich, Joseph A. (rev., *The Imagination of
               the Resurrection*). *Blake Newsletter*, VI (1973),
               97-99.

"... fascinating in conception, flawed in
execution, and careless in documentation. One
would like to believe that a scholar who invokes
names knows them, but Kremen provides little
nourishment for such faith."

1060. Kuhn, Albert J. "Blake on the Nature and Origins of
Pagan Gods and Myths." *Modern Language Notes*, LXXII
(1957), 563-572.

Blake did not criticize the imaginative myth makers
but the corruptors and allegorizers of them. For beneath
pagan myth and art was original inspiration derived
from emblems in the Scriptures.

1061. Lefcowitz, Barbara. "Blake and the Natural World."
PMLA, LXXXIX (1974), 121-131.

Asserts that Blake didn't have the same regard for
nature as did traditional mystics.

1062. Lento, Thomas V. "The Epic Consciousness in Four Romantic and Modern Epics by Blake, Byron, Eliot and Hart
Crane." *DAI*, XXXV (1975), 7911A (University of Iowa).

Blake altered the epic tradition in regard to his
choice of a hero and in his affirmation of unifying
creativity over "divisive destructiveness as a cultural
ideal."

1063. Lovell, Ernest J., Jr. "The Heretic in the Sacred Wood;
or, the Naked Man, the Tired Man, and the Romantic
Aristocrat: William Blake, T.S. Eliot, and George
Wyndham." *Romantic and Victorian*. Edited by Paul
Elledge and Richard Hoffman. Rutherford, N.J.: Fair-
leigh Dickinson University Press, 1969.

1064. McClellan, Jane, and George Mills Harper. "Blake's
Demonic Triad." *Wordsworth Circle*, VIII (1977), 172-
182.

Argues that Blake's rejection of triplicity is based
on Boehme and Thomas Taylor, who held that four is the
first effable deity.

1065. McClellan, Jane M. "William Blake's Concept of Man in
The Four Zoas, Milton and *Jerusalem*." *DAI*, XXXVII
(1977), 4371A (Florida State University).

Argues for a Neoplatonic cosmogony and theogony in Blake.

1066.   Margoliouth, Herschel M. "Notes on Blake." *Review of English Studies*, XXIV (1948), 303-316.

A compilation of biblical references found in Blake.

1067.   Mellor, Anne K. "Physiognomy, Phrenology, and Blake's Visionary Heads." *Blake in His Time* (item 149), 53-74.

Argues that the Visionary Heads reveal Blake's close adherence to Spurgheim's physiognomical charts.

1068.   Middleman, Louis I. "'Bring out number, weight & measure in a year of dearth.'" *Blake Newsletter*, IV (1971), 147.

This Proverb of Hell is rather like "mene, mene, tekel, upharsin" (Daniel V:25-28): "numbered, numbered, weighed, divided."

1069.   Miner, Paul. "William Blake: Two Notes on Sources. 1. Blake's Use of Gray's Fatal Sisters. 2. A Source for Blake's Enion?" *Bulletin of the New York Public Library*, LXII (1958), 203-207.

"Fatal Sisters" and Night VII of *Four Zoas*, *Milton* and *Jerusalem*. Enion and the sixth song of Michael Drayton's *Poly-Olbion*.

1070.   Miner, Paul. "William Blake's 'Divine Analogy.'" *Criticism*, III (1961), 46-61.

Argues for the influence the Pentateuch had upon Blake's imagery.

1071.   Minnick, Thomas L. "On Blake and Milton: An Essay in Literary Relationship." *DAI*, XXXIV (1973), 2641A (Ohio State University).

"The influence of Milton on Blake--the profoundest example of literary relationship which the English language affords--is a case study in the varieties of literary relationship."

1072.   Morton, Arthur L. *The Everlasting Gospel: A Study in the Sources of William Blake*. London: Lawrence & Wishart, 1958.

Blake's place in the Antinomian tradition of the
seventeenth century: the greatest English Antinomian
and the last. Antinomians held the following beliefs:
(1) God existed in man—most held that he existed in
all created things, and many held that he had no other
existence; (2) there was no moral or ceremonial law;
(3) there was an Everlasting Gospel; (4) they employed
symbolism to represent the destruction of Babylon and
the building of Jerusalem. Chapter on "Blake and the
Ranters."

1073.   Muir, Kenneth. "William Blake and the Eighteenth Cen-
        tury." *Literary Half-Yearly*, XII (1971), 87-97.

        Frye's and Hagstrum's essays on Blake and the eigh-
        teenth century supplement this essay.

1074.   Nanavutty, Piloo. "Blake and Emblem Literature." *Jour-
        nal of the Warburg and Courtauld Institute*, XV (1952),
        258-261.

        Alciati's emblem of Icarus falling sideways and the
        birth of Orc in the *First Book of Urizen*. Mentions
        Claude Paradin's *Devises Heroiques* (1557), and cites
        others briefly.

1075.   Natoli, Joseph P. "A Study of Blake's Contraries with
        Reference to Jung's Theory of Individuation." *DAI*,
        XXXIV (1973), 3351A (SUNY, Albany).

        Jung's theory of self-development, of the creation
        of a dialectic between conscious and unconscious ener-
        gies through the imagination's capacity to form symbols,
        is presented as an illuminating analogy to Blake's own
        vision of reintegration.

1076.   Newsome, David. *Two Classes of Men: Platonism and
        English Romantic Thought*. New York: St. Martin's
        Press, 1975.

        Blake is classed on the side of the Platonic tradi-
        tion in opposition to eighteenth-century empiricism
        in the tradition of Aristotle and Locke.

1077.   Nurmi, Martin K. "Negative Sources in Blake." *William
        Blake: Essays for S. Foster Damon* (item 256), 303-
        318.

        "... hazardous to accept prior analogues to his ideas
        as sources, especially on the basis of mere conceptual

analogy, and even more hazardous to practice the kind
of algebraic substitution in which Blake is made to
mean what a supposed source meant."

1078.   O'Higgins, Elizabeth. "The Fairy in the Streaked Tulip
        of Suibhne Geilt, Cennfaeladh O Neill and William
        Blake." *Dublin Magazine*, XXVII (July-Sept. 1952),
        17-29; XXVII (Oct.-Dec. 1952), 7-19.

        Based on the belief that Blake was Irish.

1079.   Paley, Morton D. "William Blake, the Prince of the
        Hebrews, and the Woman Clothed with the Sun." *William
        Blake: Essays in Honour of Sir Geoffrey Keynes* (item
        240), 260-293.

        "It is interesting to compare Blake's treatment of
        the millennial theme with those of Joachim, the Free
        Spirit, and the Ranters; but it is at least as interest-
        ing to compare Blake to the millenarian movements of
        his own time, the chief of these being those of Richard
        Brothers and Joanna Southcott."

1080.   Paley, Morton D. "The Truchsessian Gallery Revisited."
        Studies in Romanticism, XVI (1977), 1965-1977.

        Contends that Blake's visit to the Truchsessian
        Gallery caused Blake to reaffirm his dedication to
        Michelangelo and condemn Rubens, Rembrandt, Titian
        and Correggio. "... Blake had an eclectic middle period
        in which he was willing to absorb lessons in colorism
        and chiaroscuro from sources which he later rejected
        as inimical to true art."

1081.   Paley, Morton, and Deirdre Toomey. "Two Pictorial
        Sources for *Jerusalem 25*." *Blake Newsletter*, V (1972),
        185-190.

        Nicolas Poussin's *The Martyrdom of St. Erasmus* and
        The Giant Polypheme.

1082.   Paley, Morton D. "A New Heaven Is Begun: William
        Blake and Swedenborgianism." *Blake: An Illustrated
        Quarterly*, XIII (1979), 64-90.

        Traces Blake's attitude toward Swedenborgianism.

1083.   Peckham, Morse. "Blake, Milton and Edward Burney."
        Princeton University Library Chronicle, XI (1950),
        107-126.

Burney influenced the illustrations to *Paradise Lost*.

1084. Peterfreund, Stuart S. "A Program Toward Prophecy: Eighteenth Century Influences on the Poetry of William Blake." *DAI*, XXXVI (1975), 3700A (University of Washington).

Blake "corrected" those authors whom he found to be in error.

1085. Pointon, Marcia R. *Milton and English Art*. Manchester: Manchester University Press, 1970.

Blake was ambivalent about Milton, admiring Lucifer and the description of Adam and Eve in the garden but disliking Milton's puritanical bent.

1086. Preston, Kerrison. "A Note on Blake's Sources." *Apollo*, LXXX (1965), 133.

Blake's engravings compared with those of Rembrandt, Dürer, Bonasone and Bronzino.

1087. Raine, Kathleen. *From Blake to A Vision*. Dublin: Dolmen Press, 1979.

Blake and Yeats and the Perennial Philosophy.

1088. Raine, Kathleen. "Blake's Christ-Consciousness." *Studies in Comparative Religion*, X (1976), 213-218.

Surveys Blake's opposition to deistic-humanistic views and states that we find in Swedenborg's teachings the ground of Blake's system.

1089. Raine, Kathleen. "The Use of the Beautiful." *Southern Review* (Adelaide), II (1966), 245-263.

Blake among others sought and created in lyrical form the ideal of the Beautiful.

1090. Raine, Kathleen. "Blake and Tradition." *Times Literary Supplement*, Jan. 8, 1970, 34.

Raine refers to a *TLS* reviewer's charge (*TLS*, Dec. 25, 1969, p. 146) that she pigeonholed Blake as a Neoplatonist. Her defense.

1091.   Raine, Kathleen. "Blake's Debt to Antiquity." *Sewanee Review*, LXXI (1963), 352-450.

See comment on *Blake and Tradition* (item 1096).

1092.   Raine, Kathleen. "On the Mythological." *CEA Chap Book*, Supplement to *The CEA Critic*, XXXII (1969), 1-14.

Blake mentioned throughout in this general survey essay.

1093.   Raine, Kathleen. "Berkeley, Blake, and the New Age." *Thought*, LI (1976), 356-377.

"Blake was not an original thinker...." He owes a debt in the *Marriage* to Swedenborg and Berkeley.

1094.   Raine, Kathleen. "Thomas Taylor, Plato, and the English Romantic Movement." *Sewanee Review*, LXXVI (1968), 230-257.

Blake was dependent upon Taylor's philosophic objections to Bacon and Locke. Blake's aphorisms were an "impassioned summary of Taylor's work."

1095.   Raine, Kathleen. "Blake and Tradition." *Encounter*, VII (1956), 51-54.

Criticizes Eliot's view of Blake and argues for Blake's place in the "perennial philosophy of absolute spiritual knowledge and its unchanging symbols."

1096.   Raine, Kathleen. *Blake and Tradition*. 2 vols. Princeton: Princeton University Press, 1968.

Neoplatonism as defined by Thomas Taylor is seen as the "tradition" which affected Blake. Unfortunately, Blake is tailored whenever necessary to fit the requirements of this tradition. The Blake work most distorted is the *Marriage* and it's interesting to note that that work, which in itself would refute many of Raine's notions, is never really directly discussed. This work was sponsored and published for the Bollingen Foundation, copyright held by the Trustees of the National Gallery of Art. It is the 11th volume of the A.W. Mellon Lectures in the Fine Arts. It is nevertheless very wrongheaded in its approach to Blake.

1097.   Bronowski, Jacob. (rev., *Blake and Tradition*). *Nation*, Dec. 22, 1969, 700-701.

"She [Raine] implies that Neo-platonism is the only tenable form of this philosophy; and she strains to make it the crucial and over-riding content first of Blake's thought and then of his poems. Both are endeavors which seem to me ill-judged; they are extravagant and in the end damaging."

1098. Gleckner, Robert F. (rev., *Blake and Tradition*). *Virginia Quarterly Review*, XLV (1969), 540-544.

"*Blake and Tradition* ... completed in 1958, submitted in 1969 to the Bollingen Foundation with some 'additions and amendments,' parts of it given as the Mellon lectures in 1962, and appearing early in 1969 virtually unchanged, I find a monumental disappointment."

1099. Hagstrum, Jean H. "Kathleen Raine's Blake" (rev., *Blake and Tradition*). *Modern Philology*, LXVIII (1970), 76-82.

In actuality, this review serves as a complete refutation of Raine's belief that Blake lies completely within the Neoplatonic tradition.

1100. Hirst, Desiree. "With a Poet's Discernment" (rev., *Blake and Tradition*). *Kenyon Review*, XXXI (1969), 684-694.

"... they [Raine and Harper] have raised the central issues in Blake studies and re-affirmed, once more, the importance of the vigorous and influential line of idealist thought that has come down to us in the West."

1101. Hirst, Desiree. (rev., *Blake and Tradition*). *Journal of English and Germanic Philology*, LXVIII (1969), 708-714.

"*Blake and Tradition* will remain then, as a classic study in the mythological system of a great Western genius. More than that, it is a work which draws attention ... to the Platonic" tradition.

1102. McGann, Jerome. "Blake and a Tradition" (rev., *Blake and Tradition*). *Poetry*, CXVII (1970), 45-49.

"Of course the times are degenerate, yet,
in God's eyes, is the loss of the perennial
philosophy really so catastrophic a matter?"

1103.   Paley, Morton. (rev., *Blake and Tradition*). *ELN*,
        VII (1970), 304-310.

        Another tactful though censorious review of
        Raine's work and her theme that Blake was a
        Neoplatonist via Thomas Taylor.

1104.   Rose, Edward J. (rev., *Blake and Tradition*).
        Dalhousie Review, L (1970), 269-271.

        "... like most source studies, *Blake and
        Tradition* is often on shaky ground, since to
        assert an influence and to prove it are two
        very different things. While it is unfortunate
        that Miss Raine is often single-minded and at
        crucial points surprisingly uncertain, it is
        more unfortunate that she goes on at such
        great length."

1105.   Russell, Peter. "Jerusalem's Blake" (rev., *Blake
        and Tradition*). *Southern Review*, VII (1971),
        1145-1156.

        "... I do not hesitate to call Kathleen
        Raine's the crowning achievement of Blake
        criticism."

1106.   Weeks, Donald. (rev., *Blake and Tradition*).
        Journal of Aesthetics and Art Criticism,
        XXIX (1971), 424-425.

        Doesn't particularly like Raine's insensi-
        tivity revealed in various comments, such as
        Jews having a natural racial bent toward
        commerce.

1107.   Reisner, Thomas A. "Blake's 'To Tirzah.'" *Explicator*,
        XXXIII (1974), Item 3.

        "The transliterated, romanized version of the mosaic
        commandment prohibiting murder in the Hebrew text of
        Exodus is Lo tirzah...."

1108.   Schlieper, Reinhold. "William Blake, Philosopher: An
        Analysis of the Metaphysical System Underlying his
        Poetry." *DAI*, XXXV (1975), 6158A (Ball State Univer-
        sity).

Argues that Blake is a subjective idealist, like Berkeley, who chose poetic language, as did Nietzsche.

1109.   Schuchard, Marsha K. "Freemasonry, Secret Societies and the Continuity of the Occult Traditions in English Literature." *DAI*, XXXVI (1975), 2792A (University of Texas, Austin).

Believes Blake's involvement with the Swedenborg Society also involved him in European Masonry.

1110.   Shook, Margaret L. "Visionary Form: Blake's Prophetic Art and the Pictorial Tradition." *DAI*, XXVII (1967), 4265A (University of California, Berkeley).

Blake's doctrine of art. Blake had a "profound commitment to the Neo-classical tradition of ut pictura poesis...." His intemperate attack on Reynolds, frequently considered to be the manifesto of the nascent romantic, in fact shows Blake defending the past, and resisting innovations."

1111.   Singer, June K. *The Unholy Bible: A Psychological Interpretation of William Blake*. New York: Putnam, 1970.

Mostly concerned with a Jungian interpretation of the *Marriage*, although Blake the man is too frequently analyzed.

  1112.   Corey, Robert L. (rev., *The Unholy Bible*). *Blake Studies*, V (1972), 167–168.

    "*The Unholy Bible* is a book written around the questionable thesis that William Blake explains Jung." Actually, Singer proceeds on Jung's own clue that Blake's work represents the visionary mode; she thus discusses Blake in Jungian terms.

  1113.   Erdman, David. (rev., *The Unholy Bible*). *ELN*, IX (1971), 33.

    "Not recommended reading, since Blake and his work are seldom in focus...."

  1114.   Grimes, Ronald L. (rev., *The Unholy Bible*). *Journal of the American Academy of Religion*, XLI (1973), 460.

Believes Singer's view is interesting and
different.

1115.   Shaefer, Margret. (rev., *The Unholy Bible*).
        Blake Newsletter, VI (1973), 100-104.

Singer translates one myth into another--
Blake into Jung. "Unfortunately, this process
neither explains nor clarifies, but merely
obfuscates Blake's thought."

1116.   Spaulding, James C. "Sermons Before Parliament (1640-
        1649) as a Public Puritan Diary." *Church History*,
        XXXVI (1967), 24-35.

Preachers during the Long Parliament preceded Blake
in their concern for making England "this our Jerusalem
a paradise in the midst of the earth."

1117.   Spicer, Harold O. "The Chariot of Fire: A Study of
        William Blake's Use of Biblical Typology in the Minor
        Prophecies." *DA*, XXIII (1962), 2141 (Indiana Uni-
        versity).

Traces certain thematic symbols and myths from the
Bible in the minor prophecies.

1118.   Stanculescu, Liana P. "William Blake and the English
        Renaissance." *DAI*, XXXVII (1976), 2902A (University
        of Miami).

Argues that Blake's strongest affinities are with
the hermetical seventeenth century. Christian Neoplatonic world outlook.

1119.   Stein, Kenneth. "Blake's Apocalyptic Poetry: A Study
        of the Genre of Blake's Prophetic Books." *DAI*, XXX
        (1969), 2500A (Brandeis University).

"... indebtedness to the apocalyptic books of the
Bible and the intertestamental era.... Blake employed
the genre, however, to suit his own artistic perspective."

1120.   Stempel, Daniel. "Blake's Monadology: The Universe
        of Perspectives." *Mosaic*, VIII (1975), 77-98.

Argues that Blake knew and used Leibnizian doctrines.
"What links Blake and Leibniz in their parallel quest
for total order is their acceptance of the primacy of

cognition.... Like Leibniz, Blake spurns the Cartesian
res cogitans ... for the ens cognoscens...."

1121. Stevenson, W.H. "'Death's Door.'" *Blake Newsletter*,
IV (1970),

An old mine entrance in Coverdale?

1122. Stevenson, Warren. *Divine Analogy: A Study of the
Creation Motif in Blake and Coleridge*. Salzburg:
Institut für Englische Sprache und Literatur, 1972.

A study of major myths before Blake. Then Blake's
myth is traced through his works. "The Tyger" and
"Kubla Khan" are contrasted.

1123. Curran, Stuart. (rev., *Divine Analogy*). *Blake
Studies*, VII (1975), 180-182.

This comparison serves as a negative example
since Stevenson tries to clothe Blake and
Coleridge in the same garments.

1124. Strickland, Edward. "John Dennis and Blake's Guinea
Sun." *Blake: An Illustrated Quarterly*, XIV (1980),
36.

Blake echoes Dennis's contrast between Vulgar Passion
and Enthusiastick Passion in the conclusion to "A
Vision of the Last Judgment."

1125. Tayler, Edward W., and Everett C. Frost. "The Source
of 'Bring out number, weight, & measure in a year
of dearth.'" *Blake Newsletter*, V (1972), 213.

Marvell's lines found in Blake's edition of John
Milton are really the source of this Proverb of Hell.

1126. Tolley, Michael J. "William Blake's Use of the Bible
in a Section of 'The Everlasting Gospel.'" *Notes &
Queries*, N.S. IX (1962), 171-176.

Shows how important a knowledge of biblical references can help the reader, although not the whole way.
See item 643.

1127. Tolley, Michael, and Michael Ferber. "Thel's Motto:
Likely and Unlikely Sources." *Blake Newsletter*, X
(1976), 35-38.

A lesson in source study.

1128. Tolley, Michael J. "*The Book of Thel* and *Night Thoughts*."
       Bulletin of the New York Public Library, LXIX (1965),
       375-385.

       Thel most likely derives from Young's work.

1129. Trawick, Leonard M. "William Blake's German Connection."
       Colby Library Quarterly, XIII (1977), 229-245.

       Fuseli and Lavater, familiar with German thought of
       the period, were apparently confirming influences on
       Blake.

1130. Trawick, Leonard. "Blake's Empirical Occult." *Words-
       worth Circle*, VIII (1977), 161-171.

       Argues that Blake's ideas are incompatible with
       occult traditions. There is some similarity between
       Blake's visions and what Underhill calls the "unitive
       life."

1131. Vogler, Thomas A. *Preludes to Vision: The Epic Venture
       in Blake, Wordsworth, Keats, and Hart Crane*. Berkeley:
       University of California Press, 1971.

       Vogler's thesis is that certain writers had to first
       vindicate the human imagination as a source of knowl-
       edge before they could begin their epic as Dante and
       Virgil and Milton had begun theirs. Thus, Blake's
       Milton is essentially a prelude to vision--to *Jerusalem*.
       It is the testing ground, purely on the psychological
       level, of the poet's ability to create visionary mean-
       ing out of a fallen world.

       1132. Antippas, Andy P. (rev., *Preludes to Vision*).
              Blake Newsletter, VI (1972), 34-36.

              "... Vogler comes to Blake, Wordsworth and
              Keats with certain critical predispositions
              gathered over the years from his work on
              Crane's *Bridge*. Whether these criteria illumi-
              nate the *Four Zoas* and *Milton* and contribute
              something new to our understanding of Blake
              is questionable."

       1133. Grant, Patrick. (rev., *Preludes to Vision*).
              Malahat Review, XX (1971), 128-129.

              "... Vogler's stage is cluttered, and his
              lighting diffuse ... too many issues coincide
              with too broad a scope."

1134. LaBelle, Jenijoy. (rev., *Preludes to Vision*).
      Blake Studies, IV (1972), 163-164.

> "... one should not look to Vogler for a
> full exploration of the ways Blake made speci-
> fic borrowings from and revisions of Milton's
> verse."

1135. McFarland, Thomas. (rev., *Preludes to Vision*).
      Yale Review, LXI (1972), 294-295.

> "On balance, I found this a subtle book,
> and an original one."

1136. Wilkie, Brian. (rev., *Preludes to Vision*).
      Journal of English and Germanic Philology,
      LXXI (1972), 255-260.

> "Vogler agrees with those literary historians
> who believe that the traditional epic, as
> formally defined, had died by the middle of
> the eighteenth century. But the epic impulse,
> the desire by individual poets to create
> epics, has survived in full vitality, Vogler
> argues, and has certainly not been absorbed
> into the novel...."

1137. Wagenknecht, David. *Blake's Night: William Blake and
      the Idea of Pastoral*. Cambridge, Mass.: Belknap
      Press of Harvard University Press, 1973.

> "... it interprets the whole of Blake's poetical
> career in terms of a single, unifying thematic concern
> or idea; the idea of pastoral ... the largest histori-
> cal implication of the present study is ... that
> pastoralism is the great unexplored link between
> Romantic and Renaissance ideas.... Blake's Night,
> equally filled with eroticism and with death, is the
> ultimate *locus* of the idea of pastoral."

1138. Anon. (rev., *Blake's Night*). *Choice*, X (1974),
      1723.

> Wagenknecht's thesis, that Blake wrote in
> a Christianized Pastoral Tradition, is con-
> sidered an important addition to Blake
> scholarship.

1139. Anon. (rev., *Blake's Night*). *Library Journal*,
      XCVIII (1973), 3005.

Wagenknecht's "background material, discussion of Blake's illustrations, and commentary
on individual poems will be helpful to critics,
whether or not they accept his emphasis on
pastoralism."

1140.   Faulkner, Dewey. (rev., *Blake's Night*). *Yale
        Review*, LXIII (1974), 590-599.

"The author assumes, I think falsely, that
all of Blake is contained in any part of Blake
and that complicated ideas from later poetry
can be read wholesale into simpler early
poems...."

1141.   Torchiana, Donald T. (rev., *Blake's Night*).
        Philological Quarterly, LIII (1974), 655-656.

"To bring a few of his statements ... into
the open air may then be merely to point to
the impossibility of forcing a single system
or mode on Blake and to hold up the extremes
of distortion awaiting those who try."

1142.   Wardle, Judith. "Blake's Leutha." *ELN*, V (1967), 105-
        106.

Could derive from the Greek goddess Leucothea, the
goddess of dawn who appears in *Paradise Lost*, Book XI.

1143.   Wardle, Judith. "The Influence of Wyne's *Emblems* on
        Blake." *Blake Newsletter*, IX (1975), 46-47.

1144.   Warner, Janet A. "Blake and English Printed Textiles."
        Blake Newsletter, VI (1973), 85-92.

"... it seems possible that Blake's inspiration for
his floral designs was found in eighteenth century
embroidery patterns and textile designs."

1144a. Webber, Joan. "Milton's God." *ELN*, LX (1973), 514-531.

Blake had an accurate understanding of Milton's
ideas.

1145.   Welch, Dennis M. "William Blake's Apocalypse: A Theo-
        Psychological Interpretation." *DAI*, XXXIII (1972),
        732A (University of Southern California).

"The intention of this work ... is to show how
Blake sought to permanently escape history.... Blake's

view of history is essentially linear ... while his
critics' understanding of his view ... is cyclic."
And further, "the linear view of history is Christian
and transcendent, while the cyclic view is Platonic
and immanent."

1146. Welch, Dennis M. "*America* and *Atlantis*: Blake's Ambivalent Millennialism." *Blake Newsletter*, VI (1972),
50.

"The poet's doubts are subtly reflected in Orc's
questionable heritage and in the imagery and allusions
of the poem's millennial passage."

1147. See item 1144a.

1148. White, Harry. "Blake and the Mills of Induction."
Blake Newsletter, X (1977), 109.

"Blake's larger purpose in attacking the logic of
experimentalism was ... to re-affirm the idea of scientific progress in light of explanation which implied
that science could succeed only within an essentially
fixed and stable world order."

1149. Wimsatt, W.K. "Imitation as Freedom--1717-1798."
New Literary History, I (1970), 215-236.

Survey of English poets in the years 1717-1798 who
imitated other English poets as well as the classics.
Blake's *Poetical Sketches* is very imitative.

1150. Witke, Joanne. "Blake's Tree of Knowledge Grows Out
of the Enlightenment." *Enlightenment Essays*, III
(1972), 71-84.

Berkeley and Hume and not Plato.

1151. Wittreich, Joseph A. "Blake and Tradition: A Prefatory
Note." *Blake Studies*, V (1972), 7-11.

"Blake invokes tradition only to subject it to
radical transformation. Without tradition Blake would
have been speechless."

1152. Wittreich, Joseph A. "Blake's Philosophy of Contraries:
A New Source." *ELN*, IV (1966), 105-110.

Milton's *Reason of Church Government* is a likely
source for the doctrine of contraries and Blake's
view of the poet as prophetic legislator.

1153. Wittreich, Joseph A. "Blake's Milton: 'To Immortals ...
       a Mighty Angel.'" *Milton Studies*, XI (1978), 51-82.

       Contends that without Milton "Blake's own epic vision
       would have had no vehicle."

1154. Wittreich, Joseph A. "Domes of Mental Pleasure: Blake's
       Epics and Hayley's Epic Theory." *Studies in Philology*,
       LXIX (1972), 101-129.

       Blake owes a debt to Hayley's *An Essay on Epic
       Poetry*, although in general he adheres to Milton's
       sense of epic.

1155. Wittreich, Joseph A. "Opening the Seals: Blake's Epics
       and the Milton Tradition." *Blake's Sublime Allegory*
       (item 118), 23-58.

       "Blake's deepest roots are planted in the epic tra-
       dition that by Spenser and Milton was tied to the
       tradition of prophecy. These are the traditions, un-
       explored by Raine but continually invoked by Blake,
       that stand behind this poetry from *Poetical Sketches*
       to *Jerusalem* and that provide the best guide to under-
       standing it."

1156. Wittreich, Joseph A. "'Sublime Allegory': Blake's
       Epic Manifesto and the Milton Tradition." *Blake
       Studies*, IV (1972), 15-44.

       Blake's "Sublime Allegory" is in the Spenser-Milton
       epic tradition, yet it moves toward myth, poet as God,
       and thus engages the reader in finding his own deity.

1157. Woodman, Ross G. "Milton's Urania and Her Romantic
       Descendants." *University of Toronto Quarterly*,
       XLVIII (1979), 189-208.

       Blake demoted Milton's Urania, made her a pagan-
       like Daughter of Beulah.

1158. Woodman, R.G. "Satan in the 'Vale of Soulmaking':
       A Survey from Blake to Ginsberg." *Humanities Associa-
       tion Review*, XXV (1974), 108-121.

       "Romanticism in our time submits to 'le Neant' rather
       than overcome it by the projection of a human image."
       Blake possessed radical religious genius.

1159. Worrall, David. "Blake's Derbyshire: A Visionary Locale in Jerusalem." *Blake: An Illustrated Quarterly*, XI (1977), 34-35.

Reference in *Jerusalem* 23 is probably to the Devil's Arse caverns in Derbyshire.

1160. Worrall, David. "William Blake and Erasmus Darwin's Botanic Garden." *Bulletin of the New York Public Library*, LXXVIII (1975), 397-417.

"Darwin's real worth to Blake lay in the riches of *The Botanic Garden* as a repository of contemporary, even prophetic, scientific knowledge."

CHAPTER TEN

CRITICAL COMPARISONS

This chapter lists items that are more concerned with
mutual illumination of the authors involved than with assert-
ing Blake's influence or influences upon Blake. I find the
following particularly noteworthy: Frye's essay on Albion
and Finnegan (item 1196), de Sola Pinto's essay on Lawrence
and Blake (item 1256), Adams's essay on Blake and Gulley
Jimson (item 1163), Scrimbeour's essay on Kierkegaard's sick
man and Blake's spectre of Urthona (item 1268); Peschel's
essays on Blake and Rimbaud (items 1253, 1254); Helms's on
Orc in Tolkien and Blake (item 1210); Green's on Dante and
Blake (item 1205); DiSalvo's on Blake and Milton in terms
of bourgeois individualism and sexism (item 1186); Bloom's
on first and last romantics (item 1174); Beer's on political
parallels in Blake, Coleridge and Wordsworth (item 1172);
Rose's on Blake and Dürer (item 1265); Stevenson's on Blake
and Berdyaev (item 749).

Adams's book on Blake and Yeats (item 1164) is the best
on that important relationship. Irving Fiske on Blake and
Shaw stresses Shaw (item 1192). Some interesting comparisons
exist only as dissertations: Bandy's on Shelley and Blake
(item 1171); Abel's on Blake and Baudelaire (item 1161).

1161. Abel, Elizabeth. "The Married Arts: Poetry and Paint-
       ing in Blake and Baudelaire." *DAI*, XXXVII (1976),
       290A (Princeton University).

       Uses a structuralist approach to find a relationship
       between Blake and Baudelaire in regard to a view of
       painting and poetry that holds them to be analogous
       yet different enough to necessitate a synthesis which
       defines the complete art form.

1162. Adams, Hazard. "The Structure of Myth in the Poetry
       of William Blake and W.B. Yeats." *DA*, XIV (1954),
       105-106 (University of Washington).

       Concludes that both men kept alive a tradition of
       mythic ideation.

1163. Adams, Hazard. "Blake and Gulley Jimson: English
       Symbolists." *Critique*, III (1959), 3-14.

       The best of several articles paralleling Gulley and
       the Blakean vision.

1164. Adams, Hazard. *Blake and Yeats: The Contrary Vision*.
       New York: Russell and Russell, 1955, 1968.

       The best available work on Yeats and Blake.

       1165. Erdman, D.V. (rev., *Blake and Yeats*). *Philolog-
              ical Quarterly*, XXXV (1956), 107.

              "... there is a certain plangency at Yeats's
              failure to measure up to Blake...."

1166. Adlard, John. "Blake and the 'Geeta.'" *English Studies*,
       XLV (1964), 460-462.

       Passages in *The Marriage of Heaven and Hell* remind
       one of the "Geeta."

1167. Allen, Orphia J. "Blake's Archetypal Criticism: The
       Canterbury Pilgrims." *Genre*, XI (1978), 173-189.

       Argues that on the deeper level Blake's sense of
       irony of human existence was similar to Chaucer's.

1168. Allentuck, Marcia. "Fuseli's Translations of Winc-
       kelmann: A Phase in the Rise of British Hellenism
       with an Aside on William Blake." *Studies in the
       Eighteenth Century*. Edited by R.F. Brissenden.
       Toronto: University of Toronto Press, 1973.

       "... both Blake and Fuseli, as artists and critics,
       invested ideas with senses, instead of submerging
       senses in schemata, and elevated the emblems of clas-
       sical allegory to the symbols of unique vision."

1169. Bacon, M.E. "Blake and Gray: A Case of Literary Sym-
       biosis." *Culture*, XXIX (1968), 42-50.

Blake intended that his poem "To Mrs. Ann Flaxman" be read with Gray's "Elegy."

1170. Baird, Julian. "Swinburne, Sade and Blake: The Pleasure-Pain Paradox." *Victorian Poetry*, IX (1971), 49-75.

Swinburne's poems contain a purpose, and point to the kind of development Blake declared.

1171. Bandy, Melanie F. "The Idea of Evil in the Poetry of Blake and Shelley: A Comparative Study." *DAI*, XXXII (1971), 5218A (University of New Mexico).

Blake held a relative view of evil; Shelley, an absolute one in some cases. They have similar views regarding the evils of marriage, lust and prostitution as distinct from passion. Shelley holds women equal while Blake defines them in terms of men.

1172. Beer, John. "Blake, Coleridge, and Wordsworth: Some Cross-Currents and Parallels, 1789-1805." *William Blake: Essays in Honour of Sir Geoffrey Keynes* (item 240), 231-259.

Discusses certain parallel themes and preoccupations in all three in regard to political ferment.

1173. Bloom, Harold. "Yeats and the Romantics." *Modern Poetry*. Edited by John Hollander. Oxford: Oxford University Press, 1968, 501-520.

Excellent summary of Yeats's relationship to the Romantics, including Blake.

1174. Bloom, Harold. "First and Last Romantics." *Studies in Romanticism*, IX (1970), 225-232.

Distinction between Romantics (including Blake) who adhere to the "Romantic invention" of the English Renaissance and those (Yeats, Lawrence, Graves) who lose themselves in obscure sources.

1175. Bowering, George. "The Solitary Everything." *Walt Whitman Review*, XV (1969), 13-26.

Connection made between Blake, Hegel, Emerson and Whitman.

1176. Brereton, Geoffrey. "Imagination Enthroned: Blake and Romanticism." *Principles of Tragedy*. Coral Gables, Fla.: University of Miami Press, 1969.

Blake interestingly contrasted with Pascal in regard
to imagination, the heart, nature and God. Blake's
supposed Platonism attacked. "His [Blake's] claims
to be a lawgiver, a prophet, a spiritual guide and
even leader, were not unjustified in the absence of
rival claims. Not only bourgeois materialism, but
science itself, hit back at him through Positivism...."

1177.   Bromberg, Pamela. "Blake and the Spectre of Milton."
        DAI, XXXIV (1973), 2548A (Yale University).

        Blake's "poetic relationship" with Milton--why,
        how manifested and its effects.

1178.   Chaffee, Alan J. "The Rendezvous of Mind." *Wordsworth
        Circle*, III (1972), 196-203.

        Distinguishes Blake's view of imagination from
        Wordsworth's. Blake is myth and symbol oriented; Words-
        worth, nature and metaphor oriented.

1179.   See item 1180.

1180.   Clarke, John. "Joyce and the Blakean Vision." *Criti-
        cism*, V (1963), 173-180.

        Argues that Blake and Joyce are operating in mutually
        exclusive spheres--Blake is "cosmic, eternal, uni-
        versal and absolute" and Joyce is "social, temporal,
        typical and relative." You cannot read *Ulysses* pro-
        phetically.

1181.   Cleaver, James. "William Blake and Thomas Bewick."
        A History of Graphic Art. London: Owen, 1963, 95-
        107.

        A brief account of both which indicates they are
        very unlike indeed.

1182.   Clifford, Mallory Y. "The Storyteller's Apology: A
        Study of Truth and Storytelling in the *Odyssey*,
        Genesis, Spenser, Milton, and Blake." *DAI*, XL
        (1980), 5041A (SUNY, Buffalo).

        Truth for Blake is revealed through art and there-
        fore Blake is not suspicious of storytelling.

1183.   Crook, J. Mordaunt. "A Neo-Classical Visionary: The
        Architecture of Thomas Harrison--III." *Country Life*,
        May 6, 1971, 1089.

Harrison is briefly compared with Blake—both are Neo-Classical visionaries (?).

1184. Davie, D. "Dissent and the Wesleyans, 1740-1800." *A Gathered Church*. Oxford: Oxford University Press, 1978, 37-54.

The Wesley-Blake relationship. Sharp differences.

1185. Deboo, Kitayun E. "The Principle of the Cycle in James Joyce's *Ulysses* and William Blake's *The Mental Traveller*." *DA*, XXVIII (1967), 623A (SUNY, Buffalo).

The cycle in both works is an ironic rather than epic device.

1186. DiSalvo, Jackie. "Blake Encountering Milton: Politics and the Family in *Paradise Lost* and *The Four Zoas*." *Milton and the Line of Vision*. Edited by Joseph Wittreich. Madison: University of Wisconsin Press, 1975, 143-184.

"When, in *Milton*, Blake challenges the Puritan bard to criticism and self-criticism, he has him reject two errors of his Spectre or false selfhood (bourgeois individualism) and his sexism (his domination of women)."

1187. Downing, Richard. "Blake and Augustine." *Times Literary Supplement*, June 18, 1970, 662.

Letter suggesting that there are certain similarities between Blake and the *Confessions*.

1188. Druian, Michael G. "Visual Imagination in Blake's *Jerusalem* and Goethe's *Faust* II." *DAI*, XXXIV (1973), 1238A (University of Oregon).

An attempt to prove the breadth of Romanticism, manifested through a character who stands for "imaginative activity."

1189. Duerksen, Roland A. "Plinlimmon in Blake's 'Jerusalem' and Melville's 'Pierre.'" *Journal of Popular Culture*, III (1969), 348-351.

Plinlimmon is a Blakean prophet with a Blakean message.

1190.   England, Martha W. "Blake and the Hymns of Charles Wes-
         ley." *Bulletin of the New York Public Library*, LXX
         (1966), 7–26.

         Blake's songs are like Wesley's poems in many ways--
         except conceptually.

1191.   Engsberg, Richard C. "Two by Two: Analogues of Form
         in Poetry and Music." *DAI*, XXX (1969), 278A (New York
         University).

         Comparison of structure in music and poetry: the
         period, the double-period, the phrase groups, the
         binary song-form and the ternary song-form.

1192.   Fiske, Irving. "Bernard Shaw and William Blake." *G.B.
         Shaw*. Edited by R.F. Kaufmann. Englewood Cliffs,
         N.J.: Prentice-Hall, 1965.

         Shaw and Blake shared common opinions of art, science,
         literature, religion and "virtually every question of
         human nature and human destiny."

1193.   Fite, Monte D. "Yeats as an Editor of Blake." *DAI*,
         XXXI (1970), 355A (University of North Carolina,
         Chapel Hill).

         "The purpose of this study is to relate Yeats's edi-
         torial emendations to his critical and interpretive
         commentary, and to conclude how he held Blake's subject
         matter, symbology, and poetics."

1194.   Flynn, James. "The Everlasting Gospel: Blake in Retro-
         spect." *Paunch*, No. 27 (1966), 58–67.

         A reading.

1195.   Frye, Northrop. "Yeats and the Language of Symbolism."
         University of Toronto Quarterly, XVII (1947), 1–17.

         A contrast between Yeats's symbolism and Blake's.

1196.   Frye, Northrop. "Quest and Cycle in *Finnegans Wake*."
         James Joyce Review, I (1957), 39–47.

         Blake's vision of Albion parallels Joyce's vision
         of Finnegan.

1197.   Gandolfo, Anita. "Whose Blake Did Joyce Know and What
         Difference Does It Make?" *James Joyce Quarterly*, XV
         (1978), 215–221.

         Yeats-Ellis edition.

1198. Gleckner, Robert. "Joyce and Blake: Notes Toward Defining a Literary Relationship." *A James Joyce Miscellany*,
3rd Series. Edited by M. Magalaner. Carbondale:
Southern Illinois University Press, 1962, 188-225.

Joyce borrowed from Blake but remolded what he borrowed
to suit his own vision.

1199. Gleckner, Robert F. "Blake and Wesley." *Notes & Queries*,
CCI (1956), 522-524.

The irony in Blake's "Holy Thursday" of *Songs of
Innocence* is heightened when one contrasts the poem
to several Wesley hymns for charity children.

1200. Gleckner, Robert F. "Blake and Yeats." *Notes & Queries*,
CC (1955), 38.

Refers to Blake's "Public Address" regarding an "Em-
broider'd Coat" as an inspiration for Yeats's poem "A
Coat" and as a turning point in his career.

1201. Goldstein, Laurence A. "The Mercy of Eternity: Aspects
of Regeneration in *The Prelude* and *Milton*." *DAI*,
XXXI (1971), 6548A (Brown University).

Study of accounts of the theme of degeneration previous to Blake's *Milton* and Wordsworth's *The Prelude*.
Spiritual regeneration is their theme.

1202. Goslee, Nancy M. "Mutual Amity: *Paradise Lost* and the
Romantic Epic." *DAI*, XXX (1969), 723A (Yale University).

"Through their independent fiction they [Blake,
Shelley, Keats] argue that the vast energies shown
by Milton's Satan or the search for god-like knowledge
he prompts in Eve shape the divine image in man far
more than the earlier poet would admit or praise."

1203. Gould, Thomas. "Four Levels of Reality in Plato,
Spinoza, and Blake." *Arion*, VIII (1969), 20-50.

Compares Blake's fourfold vision with Plato's levels
of reality in *Republic* VI. Blake's espousal of Boehme's
"way" is discussed.

1204. Grant, John E. "The Female Awakening at the End of
Blake's Milton." *Milton Reconsidered: Essays in
Honour of Arthur E. Barker*. Edited by J.K. Franson.
Salzburg, Austria: Institut für Englische Sprache
und Literatur, 1976.

A reading of *Milton* plates 42, 48, 49 and 50.

1205.   Green, Richard G. "Blake and Dante on Paradise." *Comparative Literature*, XXVI (1974), 51–61.

         Comparison of the conceptions of Eternity and Paradise in the visions of Blake and Dante. Both ascribed to a theme of restored spiritual beatitude. Does eventually point out that "Dante's God is ontological, circumscribing humanity in both space and time ... while for Blake all deities reside in the human breast."

1206.   Haight, Richard R. "Pope's *Dunciad* and Blake's *Jerusalem*: An Epic Eighteenth Century Dialogue." *DAI*, XXXII (1971), 6375A (Ohio State University).

         Pope is satiric, Blake prophetic. Satire employs the shame in the hope of asserting rationality. Prophecy seeks to abolish shame and generate a reintegration of self.

1207.   Hanke, Amala. "Spatio-Temporal Consciousness in English and German Romanticism: A Comparative Study of Novalis, Blake, Wordsworth and Eichendorff." *DAI*, XXXIX (1979), 4226A (UCLA).

         Attempts to show that Romantics seek a union of the temporal world, the eternal world and the unity of self in time and space. Blake is a transcendental idealist who believes the physical world is a manifestation of the spiritual world.

1208.   Harrold, William. "Blake's *Tyger* and Vaughan's *Cockcrowing*." *Notes & Queries*, N.S. XIV (1967), 20–21.

         Blake's *Tyger* imitates Vaughan's *Cockcrowing*.

1209.   Helms, Randel. *Tolkien's World*. Boston: Houghton Mifflin, 1974.

         Blake's Orc and Tolkien's Orcs are "symbols or representatives of a disruptive power inimical to established order." In Blake, status quo is sterile, in Tolkien it is desirable.

1210.   Helms, Randel. "Orc: The Id in Blake and Tolkien." *Literature and Psychology*, XX (1970), 31–35.

         Orc appears in Blake and in Tolkien, although in the former he is opposed to order and in the latter he is repressed and represents sterile conformity to order.

1211. See item 1581.

1212. Hoagwood, Terence A. "Prophecy and the Philosophy of
Mind in the Poetry of Blake and Shelley." *DAI*, XL
(1979), 2696A (University of Maryland).

Discovers political purposes, technical philosophy,
literary traditions and biblical aesthetics in the
poetry of both poets.

1213. Hoagwood, Terence A. "Holbach and Blake's Philosophical
Statement in 'The Voice of the Devil.'" *ELN*, XV
(1978), 181-186.

Holbach's *System of Nature* and Blake's *Marriage* share
common ideas, including contraries and their view of
body and soul.

1214. Hoeveler, Diane L. "The Erotic Apocalypse: The An-
drogynous Ideal in Blake and Shelley." *DAI*, XXXVII
(1977), 6498A (University of Illinois, Urbana-Champaign).

Argues that for Blake and Shelley the androgyne is
a symbol which permits them to "transcend the limitations implicit in the single-sexed mind."

1215. Holmberg, Carol E. "A Study of William Blake's Fourfold Perceptive Process as Interpreted by William
Butler Yeats." *DAI*, XXXII (1971), 2666A (University
of Minnesota).

Glosses Blake's theory of perception with Yeats's
"The Necessity of Symbolism."

1216. Hopkins, Robert H. "Postscript: Blake and Lamb."
Bulletin of the New York Public Library, LXVIII
(1964), 257-258.

More a comment on Lamb's "The Praise of Chimney-
Sweepers" than on Blake.

1217. Ingamells, John. "An Image Shared by Blake and Henri
Rousseau." *British Journal of Aesthetics*, III (1963),
346-352.

Lion watching over a sleeping girl.

1218. Kay, Wallace G. "Blake, Baudelaire, Beckett: The Romantics of Nihilism." *Southern Quarterly*, IX (1971),
253-259.

Blake is seen as one who denies the existence of
values and whose apocalyptic vision is a contradiction
to his nihilism.

1219.   Keane, Christopher. "Blake and O'Neill: A Prophecy."
        Blake Studies, II (1970), 23-24.

        Hairy Ape finalizes the end of humanity prophesied
        by "The Tyger."

1220.   King, Anne R. "Hopkins's 'Windhover' and Blake."
        English Studies, XXXVII (1956), 245-252.

        Hopkins might have seen Blake's second painting for
        L'Allegro, "Night Startled by the Lark."

1221.   Kiralis, Karl. "William Blake as an Intellectual and
        Spiritual Guide to Chaucer's Canterbury Pilgrims."
        Blake Studies, I (1969), 139-190.

        Blake was an impressionistic critic judging by his
        painting of the *Canterbury Tales*.

1222.   Kiralis, Karl. "Joyce and Blake: A Basic Source for
        Finnegans Wake." *Modern Fiction Studies*, IV (1958-
        59), 329-334.

        Blake was one of Joyce's favorite poets; thematically
        and structurally *Jerusalem* and *Finnegans Wake* are quite
        similar. Both deviated from Vico in several ways.
        Characters are parallel. They deal with space and time
        in the same way.

1223.   Kiralis, Karl. "Blake's Criticism of Milton's *L'Allegro*
        and *Il Penseroso* and of Its Author." *Milton Recon-
        sidered*. Edited by J.K. Franson. Salzburg: University
        of Salzburg, 1976, 46-77.

        Contends that Blake didn't think these companion
        poems pointed to a poet-prophet role for Milton, who
        was, according to Blake, sexually repressed, overly
        rationalistic and deceived by the Female Will.

1224.   Koper, Peter T. "Authentic Speech: An Essay with In-
        vestigations of the Rhetoric of Samuel Johnson,
        Edmund Burke, and William Blake." *DAI*, XXXIV (1974),
        6594A (Texas Christian University).

        "The *Ramblers*, the *Reflections* and the *Marriage* all
        have the structure of a montage. This characteristic
        accounts for the sense of breadth and of openness

which is the common denominator of their rhetorical effect."

1225. Kramer, Jane. "Paterfamilias--I." *New Yorker*, XLIV (1968), 32-73.

An undocumented connection between Blake and Ginsberg.

1226. LaBelle, Jenijoy. "William Blake, Theodore Roethke, and Mother Goose: The Unholy Trinity." *Blake Studies*, IX (1980), 74-86.

The Songs and Roethke's Nonsense Poems.

1227. LaBelle, Jenijoy. "Archetypes of Tradition." *The Echoing Wood of Theodore Roethke*. Princeton: Princeton University Press, 1976, 84-103.

Blake and Roethke both focus on innocence and experience and the child's encounter with the other.

1228. LaValley, Albert J. *Carlyle and the Idea of the Modern: Studies in Carlyle's Prophetic Literature and Its Relation to Blake, Nietzsche, Marx and Others*. New Haven, Conn.: Yale University Press, 1968.

Discusses four central themes: a concern with the unconscious, an exploration of alienation in self and society, the awareness of multiplicity, and the urge to verify these concerns through mythmaking activity.

1229. Lefcowitz, Barbara. "The Shaping Flame: Self, Nature and Madness in the Poetry of Christopher Smart and William Blake." *DAI*, XXXI (1971), 4125A (University of Maryland).

Physiognomy of objects reveals mental aberration. Aberration is defined as existing when subjectivism impedes communication.

1230. Lefcowitz, Barbara. "Omnipotence of Thought and the Poetic Imagination: Blake, Coleridge, and Rilke." *Psychoanalytic Review*, LIX (1972), 417-432.

In our own century, these men would be considered megalomaniacs because of the importance they placed on the imagination.

1231. Levitt, Annette E.S. "The Poetry and Thought of William Blake in Joyce Cary's *The Horse's Mouth*." *DAI*, XXX (1970), 4778A (Pennsylvania State University).

"... there is, in *The Horse's Mouth*, a meaningful progression through Blake's poetry and thought which parallels the development of Gulley Jimson's paintings and which coincides with the movements in his life and ideas."

1232.   Levitt, Annette S. "The Miltonic Progression of Gulley Jimson." *Mosaic*, XI (1977), 77-91.

The artist manqué of *Milton* is a paradigm for the life and work of Gulley Jimson.

1233.   Lister, Raymond. "Beulah to Byzantium: A Study of Parallels in the Works of W.B. Yeats, William Blake, Samuel Palmer and Edward Calvert." *The Dolmen Press Yeats Centenary Papers*, 1965, 29-68.

Palmer and Calvert became less strongly influenced by Blake as they grew older; Yeats's connection has baffled scholars.

1234.   Lodge, David. "'Crow' and the Cartoons." *Critical Quarterly*, XIII (1971), 37-42.

Hughes's crow and Blake's tyger symbolize energy beyond the confines of tradition and convention.

1235.   Lowenstein, Amy. "Annals of the Poor: Social Fact and Artistic Response in Gray, Goldsmith, Cowper, Crabbe, Blake, Burns." *DA*, XXIX (1969), 4009A (New York University).

Blake transforms the poor via metaphor into an image of all society's victims.

1236.   McGhee, Richard D. "Thalassius: Swinburne's Poetic Myth." *Victorian Poetry*, V (1967), 127-136.

Points out essentially minor similarities between Blake and Swinburne, failing to note the more important differences.

1237.   Massey, Irving. "An End to Innocence." *Queen's Quarterly*, LXXII (1965), 178-194.

This theme is found in Blake, Lawrence, Kafka and Nietzsche among others.

1238.   Melchiori, Giorgio. "Cups of Gold for the Sacred Fount: Aspects of James's Symbolism." *Critical Quarterly*, VII (1965), 301-316.

The theme of *Roderick Hudson* is similar to the theme of the *Songs* and "Mental Traveller."

1239. Messenger, Ann P. "A Painter's Prose: Similes in Joyce Cary's *The Horse's Mouth*." *RE: Arts and Letters*, XIII (1970), 16-27.

Gulley Jimson attempts to embody Blake's beliefs.

1240. Miller, Hugh. "Blake and Gulley Jimson in Joyce Cary's *The Horse's Mouth*." *Antigonish Review*, XXXIII (1978), 79-81.

Gulley moves through the same cycle as Blake's cyclic myth as defined by Frye in *Fearful Symmetry*.

1241. Miller, James E., Jr. "The Mysticism of Whitman: Suggestions for a Seminar Discussion." *Emerson Society Quarterly*, No. 22 (1961), 15-18.

Whitman's "Crossing Brooklyn Ferry," "When Lilacs Last in the Dooryard Bloom'd," "Out of the Cradle," and "Passage to India" indicate that Whitman held a kind of "mysticism" similar to Blake's.

1242. Minnick, Thomas L. "Blake and Cowper's Tame Hares." *Blake Newsletter*, IV (1970), 11-12.

1243. Mitchell, Jeffrey. "Blake's Milton as a Problem of Conscience." *DAI*, XXXV (1974), 1113A (Columbia University).

St. Thomas Aquinas, Erik Erikson and John Barth are considered. "This dissertation 'studies' Blake; it also records, though it does not resolve, the problem of conscience Blake has become for its author."

1244. Morkan, Joel. "Milton's *Eikonoklastes* and Blake's Mythic Geography: A Parallel." *Blake Newsletter*, VII (1974), 87-89.

Comparison between a passage in *Eikonoklastes* and Blake's conflation of Biblical and English geography.

1245. Moss, John G. "William Blake and Wilson Harris: The Objective Vision." *Journal of Commonwealth Literature*, IX (1975), 29-40.

"Harris's novels, like Blake's poetry, embody not so much a dimension or dimensions, of reality as an implicitly defined perception of it."

1246.   Nemerov, Howard. "Two Ways of the Imagination." *Re-
        flexions on Poetry and Poetics*. New Brunswick, N.J.:
        Rutgers University Press, 1972.

        Both Blake and Wordsworth focused on the poet's task
        and the role of the imagination. Blake now seems more
        pertinent than Wordsworth in regard to theories of
        imagination and nature and in regard to symbolic presen-
        tation.

1247.   O'Malley, Frank. "The Wasteland of William Blake."
        Review of Politics, IX (1947), 183-204.

        Scholarship is not at all equal (in 1947) to handling
        the richness of Blake. Blake compared with Berdyaev,
        Bernanos and Kafka.

1248.   Pache, Walter, and Ursula Salacki. "Blake and Ovid."
        Blake Studies, IV (1971), 89-92.

        Contrasts Ovid's *Fasti*, II, 711-712, with Blake's
        "I Saw a Chapel All of Gold."

1249.   Paley, Morton D. "Blake in Nighttown." *James Joyce
        Miscellany: Third Series*. Carbondale: Southern Illinois
        University Press, 1962, 175-187.

        Blake and Joyce and common experiences.

1250.   Paniker, K. Afyappa. "Myth and Machine in Hart Crane."
        Literary Criterion, IX (1971), 27-41.

        Crane and Blake.

1251.   Pearcy, R.J. "Blake's Tyger and Richard Crashaw's
        Paraphrase of Thomas of Celane's *Dies Irae*." *Blake
        Newsletter*, VII (1974), 80-81.

        Crashaw's translation has the same distinctive sub-
        limity of expression as does Blake's "Tyger." And their
        themes are supposedly similar.

1252.   Pederson, Glenn M. "Blake's Urizen as Hawthorne's
        Ethan Brand." *Nineteenth Century Fiction*, XII (1958),
        304-314.

        Significant similarity between the two artists'
        concepts of the psychology of living.

1253.   Peschel, Enid R. "Themes of Rebellion in William Blake
        and Arthur Rimbaud." *French Review*, XLVI (1973),
        750-761.

Rebellion for Blake and Rimbaud is a positive force, one which was inspired in them by similar repressive institutions in society.

1254. Peschel, Enid R. "Violence and Vision: A Study of William Blake and Arthur Rimbaud." *Revue de Littérature Comparée*, XLVI (1972), 376-395.

Both poets held that violence is a prerequisite for vision and regeneration. Violence is not defined in the essay.

1255. Pfefferkorn, Eli. "The Question of the Leviathan and the Tyger." *Blake Studies*, III (1970), 53-60.

The tyger and Moby Dick. Different philosophical content but each uses sublime rhetorical questions.

1256. Pinto, Vivian de Sola. "William Blake and D.H. Lawrence." *William Blake: Essays for S. Foster Damon* (item 256), 84-106.

Lawrence's polarities, his reliance on energy, vision based on the body, are some of the important themes.

1257. Pittman, Philip. "Blake, Rossetti, and Reynolds: A Detail." *Notes & Queries*, N.S. XXI (1974), 215-216.

A detail in their paintings.

1258. Prickett, Stephen. *Romanticism and Religion: The Tradition of Coleridge and Wordsworth in the Victorian Church*. Cambridge: Cambridge University Press, 1976.

In comparing Wordsworth and Blake, considers Blake first a Christian and then a Platonist.

1259. Privateer, Paul. "The Romantic *Cogito*: Poetic Identity in Blake and Wordsworth." *DAI*, XXXIX (1979), 7361A.

Argues for an alternative, non-historical understanding of the poetic identities of both poets.

1260. Raine, Kathleen. "A Traditional Language of Symbols." *Listener*, LX (1958), 559-560.

Blake in his "The Mental Traveller" and Yeats in "Resurrection" share a mutual symbolic tradition and gloss each other.

1261.   Reeves, William J. "Blake and Dickens: The Similar
        Vision." *American Notes & Queries*, XVII (1978), 37-
        40.

        On similarities: *Oliver Twist* and the *Songs*, in which
        there is a comparable vision of the world of city life,
        exploitation of children and the harlot's cry.

1262.   Roberts, Neil. "The Spirit of *Crow*." *Delta*, No. 50
        (1972), 3-15.

        The spirit of Hughes's *Crow* is Blake's spirit.

1263.   Rogers, Neville. "The Poetic Process: Notes on Some
        Observations by Keats, Rilke and Others." *Keats-
        Shelley Memorial Bulletin* (Rome), XVIII (1967), 26-
        35.

        Blake was wrapped in the struggle to acquire negative
        capability. Blake's tyger is like Rilke's panther.

1264.   Rose, Edward J. "The 'Gothicized Imagination' of
        'Michelangelo Blake.'" *Blake in His Time* (item 149),
        155-169.

        Both Michelangelo and Blake can be seen as end results
        of all Gothic thought.

1265.   Rose, Edward J. "Blake and Dürer." *Colby Library Quar-
        terly*, XVI (1980), 166-176.

        Affinity of creative minds, not influence, is in-
        volved here. There are theoretical and doctrinal simi-
        larities: Michelangelesque judgments and Gothicized
        imaginations.

1266.   Rudd, Margaret. *Divided Image: A Study of William Blake
        and W.B. Yeats*. London: Routledge & Kegan Paul, 1953.

        Looks to Blake's vision to gloss Yeats's.

1267.   Scholz, Joachim J. "Blake and Novalis: A Comparison
        of Romanticism's High Arguments." *DAI*, XXXVIII (1978),
        4808A (University of Chicago).

        Argues that the work of these two poets is comparable
        in regard to the effectiveness of poetry in life. They
        ultimately synthesize infinite desire and infinite
        fulfillment, imagination and reality, aesthetics and
        ethics.

1268. Scrimbeour, J.R. "Great Example of Horror and Agony:
A Comparison of Soren Kierkegaard's Demoniacally
Despairing Individual with William Blake's Spectre
of Urthona." *Scandinavian Studies*, XLVII (1975),
36-41.

The similarity in the visions of these two point out
the valid psychological insights in Blake's view of
the human condition. Both figures (Kierkegaard's despairing individual and the spectre of Urthona) portray
distraught human consciousness in a fragmented, ab-
surdist world.

1269. Senior, John. "Hermetic Vessels: Blake and Hugo." *The
Way Down and Out*. Ithaca, N.Y.: Cornell University
Press, 1959.

Argues that Blake's world view is occult in a tradition which says the poet's function is to communicate
vision.

1270. Sharrock, Roger. "Godwin on Milton's Satan." *Notes &
Queries*, N.S. IX (1962), 463-465.

Godwin's Satan and Blake's "have in common splendid
energy, virtuous in its self-aggrandisement."

1271. Singleton, Marvin K. "Deuced Knowledge as Shandean NUB:
Paracelsian Hermetic as Metaphoric Bridge in *Tristram
Shandy*." *Zeitschrift für Anglistik und Amerikanistik*,
XVI (1968), 274-284.

Tristram Shandy presents a Blakean view of evil and
the Devil and not a Judaic-Christian one.

1272. Skelton, Susan. "Blake, Novalis, and Nerval: The Poetics
of the Apocalypse." *DAI*, XXXIV (1974), 7247A (University of Southern California).

Common ideas on primordial unity, fall, restoration
and the role of the poet.

1273. Stavrou, Constantine M. "William Blake and D.H. Lawrence." *University of Kansas City Review*, XXII (1956),
235-240.

Obvious points of similarity mentioned: polarities,
body-soul, energy.

1274. Stavrou, Constantine M. "William Blake and D.H. Lawrence: A Comparative Study in the Similarity of

Their Thought." *DA*, XII (1952), 430-431 (SUNY at Buffalo).

Considers their anti-rationalism and their overall similarity in thought.

1275. Tannenbaum, Leslie. "Lord Byron in the Wilderness: Biblical Tradition in Byron's *Cain* and Blake's *The Ghost of Abel*." *Modern Philology*, LXXII (1975), 350-364.

The Ghost of Abel uses biblical tradition to comment lucidly and profoundly on Byron's *Cain*. Byron, like Elijah, has done the negative work of slaying false prophets and now Blake will lead him to a positive vision.

1276. Tarr, Rodger L. "'The Eagle' Versus 'The Mole': The Wisdom of Virginity in *Comus* and *The Book of Thel*." *Blake Studies*, III (1971), 187-194.

Blake challenges Milton's doctrine. *The Book of Thel* is a refutation of *Comus*'s championship of chastity.

1277. Tidwell, Paul, and Norman Morgan. "A Blake-Joyce Note." *A Wake Newslitter*, XIII (1976), 112-114.

History is cyclic to both and imagination occurs individually, in moments.

1278. Tzougros, Penelope. "Hopkins and Blake: A New Heaven and a New Earth." *DAI*, XXXIX (1979), 4290A (University of Toronto).

Argues that the two worked with the same mythological framework and used terms which are metaphors of perception.

1279. Uphaus, Robert. "Thomas Traherne: Perception as Process." *University of Windsor Review*, III (1968), 19-27.

Traherne's idea of perception is compared and contrasted with Blake's.

1280. Valdes, Mario J. "Archetype and Recreation: A Comparative Study of William Blake and Miguel de Unamuno." *University of Toronto Quarterly*, XL (1971), 58-72.

1281. Vickery, John B. "William Blake and Eudora Welty's *Death of a Traveling Salesman*." *Modern Language Notes*, LXXVI (1961), 625-632.

Blake and Welty have the same view of Beulah--"a
middle ground between spiritual and temporal forms of
existence."

1282. Wagner, Brian J. "Affinities of Imaginative Conception
and Expressive Form Between Primitive Initiation
Rituals and Major Works of William Blake and D.H.
Lawrence." *DAI*, XL (1979), 3326A (Kansas State University).

Argues that Blake and Lawrence try to produce "an
existential change in the reader by altering his perception" and that this desire is similar to many puberty
initiation rituals.

1283. Waters, Gregory. "Blake and Rossetti." *English Record*,
XXIX (1978), 23-27.

Blake anticipated problems which overwhelmed Rossetti.
He also achieved a visionary form of art which is far
superior to Rossetti's, who unfortunately seemed to
learn so little from the man he "discovered."

1284. Whittaker, Edward K. "Sorrow and the Flea." *Tri-Quar-
terly*, No. 19 (1970), 35-55.

This article reviews Edward Dahlberg, *The Fleas of
Sodom* and *The Sorrows of Priapus*. Blake and Dahlberg
had similar views of the body-soul amalgam.

1285. Wilson, William. "Process and Imagination: The Romantic
Absolute in William Blake and D.H. Lawrence." *DAI*,
XXXVIII (1977), 1421A (Emory University).

Argues that both Blake and Lawrence sought dialectical
wholeness through embracing significant human experience within a religious vision.

1286. Wittreich, Joseph A. *Angel of Apocalypse: Blake's Idea
of Milton*. Madison: University of Wisconsin Press,
1975.

Argues that Blake viewed Milton as a revolutionary,
apocalyptic visionary.

1287. Chayes, Irene. (rev., *Angel of Apocalypse*).
ELN, XIV (1976), 32.

"The 'idea' of Milton advanced here--in-
volving betrayed political radicalism, the

errors of orthodoxy, late repentance and the
use of tradition for the corrective subversion
of tradition--may seem to some readers to be-
long as much to the politico-cultural ambience
of the late 1960's as to Blake."

1288.   Dargan, Tom. "Blake and Hayley in Wittreich's
         Angel of Apocalypse" (rev., *Angel of Apocalypse*).
         Blake Newsletter, X (1977), 130-135.

         "A close reading of *Angel of Apocalypse* re-
         veals double disaster: the evidence is not evi-
         dence, and the arguments won't stand to a posi-
         tion."

1289.   Davies, J.M.Q. (rev., *Angel of Apocalypse*).
         Modern Language Review, LXXIII (1978), 886-887.

         "Systematically though the argument is
         presented, it reflects an uncertain grasp of
         the systematic element in both Milton and Blake."

CHAPTER ELEVEN

INDIVIDUAL WORKS

Articles and books which focus on one particular Blake work are included in this chapter. Titles of Blake works are arranged in accordance with the alphabetical order of *Blake Books*, Part I (item 5). Items on the *Songs of Innocence and of Experience* are listed in one alphabetical sequence under that title whether or not one or more songs are discussed.

America

1290.   Bentley, G.E., Jr. "The Printing of Blake's *America*." *Studies in Romanticism*, VI (1966), 46-57.

Tries to establish the printing order of copies of *America*.

1291.   Dorfman, Deborah. "'King of Beauty' and 'Golden World' in Blake's *America*: The Reader and the Archetype." *ELH*, XLVI (1979), 122-135.

Reading of Plate 10 in *America*. Argues that the Ariston passage is part of the story, illuminates character and supports the "dialectical consciousness of the poem."

1292.   Doskow, Minna. "William Blake's *America*: The Story of a Revolution Betrayed." *Blake Studies*, VIII (1979), 167-186.

There is a recognition of the flaws and ultimate betrayal of the American Revolution in Blake's *America*. America did not spread its revolution as Trotsky advocated.

1293. Erdman, David V. "*America*, Everyone?" *Blake Newsletter*,
       IX (1975), 123-126.

       Discusses the American Blake Foundation's *America*
       and the *Blake Newsletter*'s *America*.

1294. Erdman, David V. "*America*: New Expanses." *Blake's
       Visionary Forms Dramatic* (item 139), 92-114.

       Argues that the poetry and the designs work indepen-
       dently of each other and neither is a simple gloss for
       the other.

1295. James, David E. "Angels Out of the Sun: Art, Religion
       and Politics in Blake's *America*." *Studies in Roman-
       ticism*, XVIII (1979), 235-252.

       The coincidence of material and spiritual realities
       envisioned in *America* already existed in Blake's amal-
       gamation of painter's and poet's skills, intellectual
       and manual activity.

1296. Spicer, Harold O. "Biblical Sources of William Blake's
       America." *Ball State University Forum*, VIII (1967),
       23-29.

       Argues that there are in *America* more spiritual con-
       cerns than political-social concerns.

1297. Tebbetts, Terrell. "A Critical Study of Blake's *America*."
       DAI, XXXII (1971), 987A (University of Arkansas).

       America is discussed in terms of insight and predic-
       tion.

                        The Book of Ahania

1298. Paley, Morton. "Method and Meaning in Blake's *Book of
       Ahania*." *Bulletin of the New York Public Library*,
       LXX (1966), 27-33.

       Fuzon, energy, achieves only a temporary victory
       over repressive law.

The Book of Thel

1299.   Adlard, John. "Blake, Thel and *The Wisdom of Angels*."
        Studia Neophilologica, XLVI (1974), 172-174.

        Blake circled a passage from Swedenborg's *Wisdom*
        which he may have had in mind when working on *The Book
        of Thel*.

1300.   Baine, Rodney. "Thel's Northern Gate." *Philological
        Quarterly*, LI (1972), 957-961.

        Not Taylor's but Pope's translation of *The Odyssey*
        may have been Blake's source.

1301.   Bogen, Nancy. "A Critical Edition of William Blake's
        'Book of Thel,' with a New Interpretation." *DAI*,
        XXXII (1971), 908A (Columbia University).

        Became a facsimile edition published by Brown Uni-
        versity Press, 1971.

1302.   Duerksen, Roland A. "The Life-in-Death Theme in *The
        Book of Thel*." *Blake Studies*, II (1970), 15-22.

        The Book of Thel presents a fourfold vision.

1303.   Ferber, Michael. "Blake's *Thel* and the Bride of Christ."
        Blake Studies, IX (1980), 45-56.

        "I propose to dwell on the Biblical imagery surround-
        ing the creatures, draw out its implications, and con-
        nect it with the rest of the poem."

1304.   Ferber, Michael. "A Possible Source for 'Thel's Motto.'"
        Blake Newsletter, IX (1975), 43-44.

        Hebrews 9.3-4.

1305.   Ferber, Michael. "Thel's Motto: Likely and Unlikely
        Sources." *Blake Newsletter*, X (1976), 36-38.

        Hebrews 9.3-4 is "a frame of reference for symbolic
        meanings, and certainly an analogue of greater impor-
        tance and helpfulness to the reader than Ecclesiastes
        12.6."

1306.   Gleckner, Robert. "Blake's *Thel* and the Bible." *Bulletin
        of the New York Public Library*, LXIV (1960), 573-
        580.

To present his view that Thel was incorrect in turning her back on experience and trying to prolong innocence, Blake alluded to the Book of Job, the prophets Isaiah, Jeremiah and Ezekiel, and to various isolated passages in the Bible.

1307.   Heppner, Christopher. "'A Desire of Being': Identity and *The Book of Thel.*" *Colby Library Quarterly*, XIII (1977), 79-98.

Argues that Swedenborg is an important influence in this poem and that Thel explores "modes of being in the world" and finally decides to give up the search.

1308.   Johnson, Mary Lynn. "Beulah, Seraphim, and Blake's *Thel.*" *Journal of English and Germanic Philology*, LXIX (1970), 258-277.

Thel is simply an isolated creature in our own world who must rely on her own instincts. A kind of existential freedom is open to her.

1309.   Levinson, Marjorie. "'The Book of Thel' by William Blake: A Critical Reading." *ELH*, XLVII (1980), 287-303.

Argues that the fact of speech, the act of speech, is the hero of this poem. The story exists for the sake of the dialogue, which is dialectic.

1310.   Levitt, Annette S. "Comus, Cloud and Thel's Unacted Desires." *Colby Library Quarterly*, XIV (1978), 72-83.

Clarifies the role of the Cloud and Thel's response to it by referring to Milton's *Comus.*

1311.   Mellor, Anne Kostelanetz. "Blake's Designs for *The Book of Thel*: An Affirmation of Innocence." *Philological Quarterly*, L (1971), 193-207.

Argues that Thel is in Innocence and that her refusal to enter experience is wise. Thel eventually finds fulfillment in the Vales of Har. A very anomalous view.

1312.   Pearce, Donald R. "Natural Religion and the Plight of Thel." *Blake Studies*, VIII (1978), 23-35.

Argues that Thel's flight is not due to weakness of character but occurs because she has been victimized by false religious instruction.

The Book of Urizen

1313. Anderson, William D. "'Awake Ye Dead': A Study of
Blake's *The Book of Urizen*, *The Four Zoas*, and
Jerusalem." *DA*, XXVIII (1967), 1386A (University of
Texas, Austin).

A context of motifs reveals meaning at any point in
these works.

1314. Curtis, F.B. "The Geddes Bible and the Tent of the
Eternals in the *Book of Urizen*." *Blake Newsletter*,
VI (1973), 93-94.

A description in Geddes is perhaps the source of a
passage in *The Book of Urizen*.

1315. Doggett, John R. "A Reading of William Blake's 'The
Book of Urizen.'" *DAI*, XXXV (1974), 2936A (University
of Texas, Austin).

A reading of *Urizen* that ignores external sources
and other Blake works.

1316. Eaves, Morris. "The Title-Page of *The Book of Urizen*."
*William Blake: Essays in Honour of Sir Geoffrey
Keynes* (item 240), 1-28.

The title page of *The Book of Urizen* is "Blake's
report on the state of the arts--which is the state of
the nation--in 1794.... The principal object of satire
is Law."

1317. Elliott, Patricia D. "A Critical Variorum Edition of
William Blake's *The Book of Urizen*." *DAI*, XXXVIII
(1977), 2804A (University of Arkansas).

Believes that the characters in *The Book of Urizen*
have been presented previously in the *Marriage* and the
Songs. Second part is a variorum *Urizen*.

1318. Kittel, Harald A. "*The Book of Urizen* and *An Essay
Concerning Human Understanding*." *Interpreting Blake*
(item 245), 111-144.

Tries to connect "significant symbolic correlatives"
in *Urizen* with aspects of Locke's theory of knowledge,
thus demonstrating that Blake's satire against Locke's
theory of knowledge is contained in *Urizen*. Blake's
own vision is implicit in that satire.

1319. Kroeber, Karl. "Graphic-Poetic Structuring in Blake's
      Book of Urizen." *Blake Studies*, III (1970), 7-18.

      "What follows is not an interpretation of William
      Blake's *Book of Urizen*. It is a definition of formal
      principles of interaction between verse and pictures
      by which Blake realizes his prophetic vision."

1320. Marks, Mollyanne. "Structure and Irony in Blake's
      'The Book of Urizen.'" *Studies in English Literature*,
      XV (1975), 579-590.

      Argues that the poem's structure is an attempt to
      transcend the ordinary limits of plot and language.
      The structure attempts to reenact the Fall it describes.

1321. Rosenberg, Marc. "Style and Meaning in *The Book of
      Urizen.*" *Style*, IV (1970), 197-212.

      Argues that "Blake's style corresponds in a signifi-
      cant manner with his explicitly stated ideas."

1322. Simmons, Robert E. "*Urizen*: The Symmetry of Fear."
      Blake's Visionary Forms Dramatic (item 139), 146-173.

      Symmetry to Blake is equated with finiteness and
      fixity whereas the eternal world is in a state of ener-
      getic flux, housing all forms.

1323. See item 1326.

1324. Tannenbaum, Leslie W. "Blake's Art of Crypsis: *The Book
      of Urizen* and Genesis." *Blake Studies*, V (1972), 141-
      164.

      Blake's special treatment of Genesis in his *Book of
      Urizen*.

1325. Tannenbaum, Leslie W. "Dark Visions of Torment: Symbol
      and Structure in William Blake's *The Book of Urizen*."
      DAI, XXXIII (1973), 6328A (University of Wisconsin,
      Madison).

      Discerns a symbolic unity in the *Book of Urizen*
      which creates a coherent structural framework.

1326. Tannenbaum, Leslie W. "Transformations of Michelangelo
      in William Blake's *The Book of Urizen*." *Colby Library
      Quarterly*, XVI (1980), 19-50.

"As a prophetic call to fallen man, *The Book of Urizen*
employs images from Michelangelo both to articulate
man's fall and to point the way back to wholeness."
Blake reinvested Michelangelo's forms with his own
prophetic fury.

Europe

1327. Bogen, Nancy. "Blake's Debt to Gillray." *American Notes
and Queries*, VI (1967), 35-38.

In his depiction of Burke in *Europe*, Blake was making
a direct rejoinder to the political cartoonist Gillray.

1328. Douglas, Dennis. "Blake's *Europe*: A Note on the Preludium." *Aulla*, No. 23 (1965), 111-116.

Parallels between images and concepts in "Preludium"
and the same in the work of Taylor, Robert Fludd,
Richard Clarke and Cornelius Agrippa.

1329. Erdman, David V. "William Blake's Debt to James Gillray." *Art Quarterly*, XII (1949), 165-170.

Believes Blake's *Europe* illuminations were influenced
by Gillray's political cartoons.

1330. Kowle, Carol P. "Plate III and the Meaning of *Europe*."
Blake Studies, VIII (1978), 89-99.

This plate, composed at the same time as the others,
was originally suppressed by Blake. It is in Kowle's
view an "important guide to the meaning of the entire
prophecy." It was probably suppressed because Blake
felt it was too obvious.

1331. Lincoln, A.W.J. "Blake's *Europe*: An Early Version?"
Notes & Queries, N.S. XXV (1978), 213.

Argues that *Europe*, 1794, is a composite work.

1332. Pierce, Hazel M.B. "A Critical Study of William Blake's
Europe." *DAI*, XXXI (1970), 5372A (University of
Nebraska, Lincoln).

Europe was a testing ground in regard to form,
metrics, imagery and mythic framework.

1333.   Tolley, Michael J. *"Europe:* 'to those ychain'd in
        sleep.'" *Blake's Visionary Forms Dramatic* (item 139),
        115-145.

        Everyone in *Europe* is ignorant of the future, chained
        to the past and blind to the present.

1334.   Wardle, Judith. *"Europe* and *America." Notes & Queries,*
        N.S. XV (1968), 20-21.

        An interpretation of designs on Plates 8 and 10 of
        America which parallels the acknowledged theme of the
        work.

                              The Four Zoas

1335.   Bentley, Gerald E., Jr. "The Failure of Blake's *Four
        Zoas." Texas Studies in English,* XXXVII (1958), 102-
        115.

        Two failures: failure of critics expounding and
        scholars editing and failure as a poem. The "real
        trouble with *The Four Zoas* is that it was revised far
        too frequently and from too many divergent points of
        view."

1336.   Benzel, Michael A. "Vision and Revision in *The Four
        Zoas:* The Evidence of the Manuscript." *DAI,* XXXVII
        (1977), 6492A (University of Toledo).

        Argues that Blake abandoned *Four Zoas* because of
        "a deepening Christian vision during the years he
        worked on it (c.1795-1810)."

1337.   Bidney, Martin. "Urizen and the Comedy of Automatism
        in Blake's *The Four Zoas." Philological Quarterly,*
        LVI (1977), 204-220.

        Applies Bergson's principle of comic automatism to
        The Four Zoas: "The rigid, the ready-made ... in con-
        trast with the supple ... the living...."

1338.   Bloom, Harold. "States of Being: *The Four Zoas." Blake:
        A Collection of Critical Essays* (item 155), 104-118.

        Essentially a fine paraphrase of the major movements
        of this work. A good introductory essay. A chapter
        of *Blake's Apocalypse* (item 101).

1339. Erdman, David V. "Night the Seventh: The Editorial
       Problem." *Blake Newsletter*, XII (1978), 135-139.

       Reviews the work of Kilgore and Lincoln on "Night
       the Seventh's" two versions.

1340. Erdman, David V. "*The Four Zoas*: New Text for Pages
       5, 6, & 7, Night the First." *Blake: An Illustrated
       Quarterly*, XII (1978), 96-99.

       Changes in the Doubleday and Longman texts based on
       Andrew Lincoln's demonstration that *Four Zoas* 143 is
       not necessarily later than *Four Zoas* 7. See items 1351-
       1352.

1341. Evans, James C. "The Apocalypse as Contrary Vision:
       Prolegomena to an Analogical Reading of *The Four
       Zoas*." *Texas Studies in Literature and Language*,
       XIV (1972), 13-28.

       Argues that the structure of the poem "reflects the
       poem's thematic statement that 'salvation' is achieved
       through proper perception of the environment as an
       organic whole."

1342. Grant, John E. "Visions in Vala: A Consideration of
       Some Pictures in the Manuscript." *Blake's Sublime
       Allegory* (item 118), 141-202.

       An exhaustive consideration of the drawings. For
       example: "His sketchily indicated left hand extends
       beneath her left armpit and a crab advances toward
       her crotch. This scene may be regarded as a version
       of the cuckolding of Hephaestus by Aphrodite and Ares."

1343. Harper, George H. "Apocalyptic Vision and Pastoral
       Dream in Blake's *Four Zoas*." *South Atlantic Quarter-
       ly*, LXIV (1965), 110-124.

       Four Zoas presents a cyclical theory of history,
       one in which man returns to the pastoral garden—a
       theory opposed to the linear-progressive nineteenth-
       century notions of history.

1344. Hoagwood, Terence A. "*The Four Zoas*: The 'Philosophick
       Cabbala.'" *Blake: An Illustrated Quarterly*, XII
       (1978), 87-90.

       Henry More's "The Philosophick Cabbala" and *The
       Four Zoas* are alike in regard to "casts of symbolic
       characters, similar accounts of the cause of the fall,

and similar accounts of certain consequences of the
fall."

1345.   Johnson, Mary Lynn, and Brian Wilkie. "The Spectrous
        Embrace in *The Four Zoas*, VIIa." *Blake: An Illustrated
        Quarterly*, XII (1978), 100-106.

        Blake "leaves an area of disjunction between despair
        and recovery" because recovery from this spiritual dark
        night is not thoroughly explicable.

1346.   Johnson, Mary Lynn, and Brian Wilkie. "On Reading *The
        Four Zoas*: Inscape and Analogy." *Blake's Sublime
        Allegory* (item 118), 203-232.

        A reading which emphasizes "personal verification"
        and hopes "to show that the poem has a demonstrable
        pattern of continuity, though this artistic pattern
        depends significantly on patterns in the psyche that
        we can arrive at only through introspection." Super-
        seded by the authors' 1978 book (item 1363).

1347.   Kaplan, Nancy A. "William Blake's *The Four Zoas*: The
        Rhetoric of Vision." *DAI*, XXXVI (1975), 2846A
        (Cornell University).

        Demonstrates how Blake's art engages the reader in
        The Four Zoas via rhetorical means.

1348.   Kilgore, John. "The Order of Nights VIIa and VIIb
        in Blake's *The Four Zoas*." *Blake: An Illustrated
        Quarterly*, XII (1978), 107-113.

        Recommends a critical order much like Wagenknecht's
        in *Blake's Night* (item 1137).

1349.   Lefebvre, Mark S. "A Note on the Structural Necessity
        of Night VIIb." *Blake: An Illustrated Quarterly*,
        XII (1978), 134.

        Rearranges *Four Zoas* by inserting VIIb between the
        original and added parts of VIIa.

1350.   Lemieux, Gerald A. "The Mantle of Mystery: Its Growth
        from Vala to *The Four Zoas*." *DAI*, XXXVIII (1978),
        6144A (Southern Illinois University, Carbondale).

        Blake's purpose in his changes was to introduce
        Christ who synthesizes all Blake's major themes.

1351. Lincoln, Andrew. "The Revision of the Seventh and Eighth Nights of *The Four Zoas*." *Blake: An Illustrated Quarterly*, XII (1978), 115-133.

Suggests a textual arrangement for the two Nights the Seventh.

1352. Lincoln, Andrew. "*The Four Zoas*: The Text of Pages 5, 6, & 7, Night the First." *Blake: An Illustrated Quarterly*, XII (1978), 91-95.

What is the latest revision of these pages?

1353. Lindsay, David W. "Prelude to Apocalypse: A Short Commentary on Night VIII of Blake's *Vala* or *The Four Zoas*." *Durham University Journal*, LXX (1978), 179-185.

Line-by-line explication.

1354. McNeil, Helen T. "The Formal Art of *The Four Zoas*." *Blake's Visionary Forms Dramatic* (item 139), 373-390.

Argues that the form of this poem reflects the riot within the mind of fallen man.

1355. Myers, Victoria. "The Dialogue as Interpretive Focus in Blake's *The Four Zoas*." *Philological Quarterly*, LVI (1977), 221-239.

The difference in the characters' narration is due to their attempts to "extract themselves from unity and set up independent personalities." Containment of others and self-assertion dominate individual narrations.

1356. Nanavutty, Piloo. "*Materia Prima* in a Page of Blake's *Vala*." *William Blake: Essays for S. Foster Damon* (item 256), 293-302.

Argues that this poem is loaded with hidden emblems of alchemy.

1357. Sanders, Jon. "The Desire of Man: A Reading of Blake's 'The Four Zoas.'" *DAI*, XXXV (1974), 3698A (University of Oregon).

An allegorical reading.

1358. Schotz, Myra G. "The Altering Eye: William Blake and the Art of Parallax: An Approach to *The Four Zoas*." *DAI*, XXXVI (1975), 910A (Brandeis University).

Suggests the term "parallax" be employed to meta-
phorically describe perception contingent upon the
relationship existing at that moment of perception.

1359. Schotz, Myra G. "On the Frontispiece of *The Four Zoas*."
       Blake Newsletter, X (1977), 126-127.

       The figure is a dreamer and his ambiguous position
       is emblematic of the dream world.

1360. See item 1361a.

1361. Smith, Catherine. "Pictorial Language in *The Four
       Zoas* by Blake." *DAI*, XXXIII (1973), 5142A (University
       of North Carolina, Chapel Hill).

       His "drawings are graphic re-statements of verbal
       ideas, and the texts are verbal structures of inter-
       related image patterns."

1361a. Sugnet, Charles J. "The Role of Christ in Blake's
       The Four Zoas." *Essays in Literature*, III (1976),
       167-180.

       Argues for the importance of Christ in the final
       Four Zoas but insists that this does not imply a simple
       return to orthodoxy or a turn away from the natural
       world to pie-in-the-sky.

1362. Wegner, A. Grace. "Blake's *The Four Zoas*, Night the
       Ninth." *Explicator*, XXVII, 7 (1969), Item 53.

       A source for the description of the threshing of the
       nations in Night the Ninth of *Four Zoas* is probably
       Isaiah, xli.15-16.

1363. Wilkie, Brian, and Mary L. Johnson. *Blake's Four
       Zoas: The Designs of a Dream*. Cambridge, Mass.,
       and London: Harvard University Press, 1978.

       A thorough, detailed reading which takes advantage
       of prior scholarship and various analogues.

1364. Leader, Zachery. (rev., *Blake's Four Zoas*).
       Essays in Criticism, XXX (1980), 243, 247.

       "Blake's claims on our interest--both as
       narrative (or prophetic) as well as lyric
       poet--are by now secure: the polemical pre-
       tence that his system or myth is totally co-

herent, or his art without flaw, ought finally
to be dropped...."

The French Revolution

1365. Cherry, Charles L. "The Apotheosis of Desire: Dia-
       lectic and Image in *The French Revolution*, *Visions
       of the Daughters of Albion*, and the *Preludium to
       America*." *Xavier University Studies*, VIII (1969),
       18-31.

       The sexuality theme in these works can be directly
       related to certain formal qualities.

1366. Halliburton, David G. "Blake's *French Revolution*: *The
       Figura* and Yesterday's News." *Studies in Romanticism*,
       V (1966), 158-168.

       Tries to discover the fundamental reasons behind
       the failure of *The French Revolution*.

1367. Halloran, William F. "*The French Revolution*: Reve-
       lation's New Form." *Blake's Visionary Forms Dramatic*
       (item 139), 30-56.

       Argues that to Blake the French Revolution was a
       bloodless apocalypse and that the poem itself is a
       recasting of Revelation.

1368. Halloran, William F. "William Blake's *The French
       Revolution*: A Note on the Text and a Possible
       Emendation." *Bulletin of the New York Public Library*,
       LXXII (1968), 3-18.

       Report on the text of *French Revolution*, its history;
       discussion of a questionable passage; a proposed emen-
       dation and a discussion of how the error might have
       occurred.

The Gates of Paradise

1369. Kmetz, Gail. "A Reading of Blake's *The Gates of Para-
       dise*." *Blake Studies*, III (1971), 171-185.

This poem is as interesting as "The Mental Traveller" or "The Crystal Cabinet."

1370. Parisi, Frank M. "Emblems of Melancholy *for Children*: *The Gates of Paradise*." *Interpreting Blake* (item 245), 70-110.

A plate-by-plate examination of *The Gates of Paradise* in the light of traditional and contemporary analogues. The cycle presents the calamities of fallen man but also points to an apocalyptic breakthrough.

Jerusalem

1371. Adams, Hazard. "Blake and the Muse." *Bucknell Review*, XV (1967), 112-119.

Presents the view that *Jerusalem* and *Milton* are about the creative process and their own creation.

1372. Adlard, John. "Los Enters London." *English Studies*, LIV (1973), 227-230.

Very detailed presentation of what streets in London Los would have walked when in *Jerusalem* he decides to explore the interiors of Albion's bosom.

1373. Bloom, Harold. "Blake's *Jerusalem*: The Bard of Sensibility and the Form of Prophecy." *Eighteenth Century Studies*, IV (1970), 6-20.

Ezekiel is a model but one that Blake does not follow too closely for fear of erring as the poets of sensibility had erred and for fear of imitating a vigorous Hebraic theism.

1374. Bogan, James J., Jr. "A Guidebook to William Blake's *Jerusalem*." *DAI*, XL (1980), 4603A (University of Kansas).

Supposedly provides the reader with all the information he needs to read *Jerusalem*.

1375. Carr, Stephen. "'Striving with Systems': William Blake's Print-Making Process and *Jerusalem*." *DAI*, XL (1979), 867A (University of Michigan). See item 795.

Attempts to relate a Blakean epistemology to his techniques of printmaking. Blake scorned "one central Form" not only in his narrative and rhetorical strategies but also in his printmaking techniques.

1376. Chayes, Irene H. "The Marginal Design of *Jerusalem* 12." *Blake Studies*, VII (1974), 51-76.

After a very lengthy, detailed reading of the marginal design (three figures, a globe and a compass), Chayes concludes that Reason and Desire clash.

1377. Curran, Stuart. "The Structures of *Jerusalem.*" *Blake's Sublime Allegory* (item 118), 329-346.

The architecture of *Jerusalem* is Gothic, distinct, with novel parts which make defining the whole work difficult.

1378. Dargan, Thomas R. "Blake, Stonehenge, and the New Jerusalem." *DAI*, XXXIX (1978), 893A (SUNY, Stonybrook).

Argues that *Jerusalem* is a parody of an eighteenth-century archaeological "biblical habit of mind." For Blake, Stonehenge "becomes the site for a republican resurrection."

1379. Dilgard, Cynthia. "The Structure of *Jerusalem.*" *DAI*, XXXIV (1973), 2553A-2554A (Vanderbilt University).

Focuses on both Blake's method and the poem itself.

1380. Doskow, Minna L. "Structure and Meaning in William Blake's *Jerusalem.*" *DAI*, XXXIII (1972), 2322A (University of Maryland).

Argues that the poem is built around a single theme which is presented in all its variety via both text and design. Therefore, each aspect of the poem is essential.

1381. Easson, Roger. "The Rhetoric and Style of Apocalypse in William Blake's 'Jerusalem.'" *DAI*, XXXI (1970), 2873A (University of Tulsa).

Jerusalem is as much an iconoclastic work in form as Sterne's *Tristram Shandy* is.

1382. Easson, Roger. "William Blake and His Reader in *Jerusalem.*" *Blake's Sublime Allegory* (item 118), 309-327.

Jerusalem is a poem about itself. Argues that Blake is really in search of an honest reader and that the rhetorical density and allegoric opacity of the work are merely ways in which Blake gets the reader to participate in the creative process.

1383. Erdman, David V. "The Suppressed and Altered Passages in Blake's *Jerusalem*." *Studies in Bibliography*, XVII (1964), 1-54.

By superimposition of hypothetical readings of portions of *Jerusalem* which Blake deleted, although leaving crumbs of letters, Erdman is able to select compatible readings.

1384. Erdman, David V. "South Bounding!" *Blake: An Illustrated Quarterly*, XIII (1979), 106-107.

Offers the word "bounding" for a suppressed line in *Jerusalem* 32.

1385. Erdman, David V. "Lambeth and Bethlehem in Blake's *Jerusalem*." *Modern Philology*, XLVIII (1951), 184-192.

Investigates the topographical allusions in *Milton* Plate 25 and *Jerusalem* Plate 31 in order to clear up the Lambeth-Bethlehem confusion as well as date *Jerusalem*.

1386. Erdman, David V. "Blake's *Jerusalem* Plate 3 Fully Restored." *Studies in Bibliography*, XVIII (1965), 281-282.

Plate 3 has been fully restored.

1387. Essick, Robert N. "*Jerusalem* 25: Some Thoughts on Technique." *Blake Newsletter*, VII (1973-74), 64-66.

Describes engraving techniques used on this copper plate.

1388. Ferguson, James. "Prefaces to *Jerusalem*." *Interpreting Blake* (item 245), 164-195.

Argues for coherence in *Jerusalem* by using the prose prefaces as determiners of that coherence.

1389. Harley, A.D. "The English Epic in the Romantic Period." *Philological Quarterly*, 55 (1976), 241-259.

States briefly that Blake's *Jerusalem* is in the
apocalyptic rather than the epic tradition.

1390. Harper, George Mills. "The Odyssey of the Soul in
       Blake's *Jerusalem.*" *Blake Studies*, V (1973), 65-80.

       Blake makes frequent use of the Platonic doctrine
       of the One and the Many.

1391. Harper, George M. "The Divine Tetrad in Blake's
       Jerusalem." *William Blake: Essays for S. Foster
       Damon* (item 256), 235-255.

       Argues that divine numbers are intended to be a key
       to the gates of Paradise.

1392. Helms, Randel. "Ezekiel and Blake's *Jerusalem.*" *Studies
       in Romanticism*, XII (1974), 127-140.

       The continuity of *Jerusalem* is like the organization
       of Ezekiel.

1393. Hower, Harold E. "The Aesthetics of Composite Art
       in William Blake's 'Jerusalem.'" *DAI*, XXXV (1974),
       3683A (Kent State University).

       Outlines a theoretical basis for understanding the
       composite art and demonstrates an application of such.

1394. Kemper, F. Claudette. "The Interlinear Drawings in
       Blake's *Jerusalem.*" *Bulletin of the New York Public
       Library*, LXIV (1960), 588-594.

       Argues that a reading of these drawings contributes
       to one's appreciation and understanding of *Jerusalem*.

1395. Kiralis, Karl. "*London* in the Light of *Jerusalem.*"
       Blake Studies, I (1968), 5-15.

       Contends that the restraints of society described
       in "London" are eventually solved in *Jerusalem*.

1396. Kiralis, Karl. "A Possible Revision in Blake's
       Jerusalem." *Art Bulletin*, XXXVII (1955), 203-204.

       Suggests that the first design to the *Paradiso*,
       "Dante Adoring Christ," was originally intended to
       be the 97th illustration to *Jerusalem*.

1397. Kroeber, Karl. "Delivering *Jerusalem.*" *Blake's Sub-
       lime Allegory* (item 118), 347-367.

Argues that this poem is "an essential document for
understanding the genesis of modern culture." It advocates the individual active creation of belief through
imaginative activity.

1398.   LaFarge, Henry. "Blake's Best Book." *Art News*, LI
        (1952), 36-37.

        A very superficial description of *Jerusalem*.

1399.   Lesnick, Henry G. "Narrative Structure and the Antitheti-
        cal Vision of *Jerusalem*." *Blake's Visionary Forms
        Dramatic* (item 139), 391-412.

        "... the structural antithesis reflects the truly
        paradoxical nature of Blake's vision."

1400.   Lesnick, Henry G. "The Function of Perspective in
        Blake's *Jerusalem*." *Bulletin of the New York Public
        Library*, LXXIII (1969), 49-55.

        Different perspectives reveal different modes of
        perception.

1401.   Lesnick, Henry G. "Blake's Antithetical Vision: A
        Study of the Structure of *Jerusalem*." *DAI*, XXX (1969),
        2533A (SUNY, Buffalo).

        Argues that Blake's antithetical vision is a dominant
        structural as well as thematic factor in *Jerusalem*.

1402.   Lowry, Mark D. "Relationship of Design, Color and Text
        in the Stirling-Keir Copy of William Blake's *Jerusalem*."
        DAI, XXXVI (1975), 2850A (University of Texas, Austin).

        Believes that Blake's composite art does not possess
        a critical category to deal with it. He treats *Jerusalem*
        as a physical object.

1403.   Marks, Mollyanne K. "Despair and Desire: A Study of
        William Blake's *Jerusalem* and Its Relation to Poetic
        Tradition." *DAI*, XXXII (1972), 6987A (Yale Univer-
        sity).

        The struggle between Los and the Spectre is a move
        toward imaginative regeneration from within.

1404.   Marks, Mollyanne. "Self-Sacrifice: Theme and Image
        in *Jerusalem*." *Blake Studies*, VII (1974), 27-50.

Jerusalem is "an allegorical rendering of a vision of self-sacrifice, intended to reveal the nature of the selfhood in man and so to make the prophetic word actuality...."

1405. Mellor, Anne Kostelanetz. "The Human Form Divine and the Structure of Blake's *Jerusalem*." *Studies in English Literature 1500-1900*, XI (1971), 595-620.

"By developing the implications of his early image of 'the human form divine,' Blake found in the bounded figure of Christ the fusion of the finite and the infinite...."

1406. Murray, E.B. "*Jerusalem* Reversed." *Blake Studies*, VII (1974), 11-25.

Applies an explication-of-text method to trace the image of reversed movement in *Jerusalem*.

1407. Nelms, Ben F. "Exemplars of Memory and of Intellect: *Jerusalem* Plates 96-100." *Blake Studies*, V (1973), 81-95.

The two designs reveal the themes of reconciliation and purification.

1408. Nelson, Cary R. "Blake's *Jerusalem*: A Fourfold Vision of the Human Body." *The Incarnate Word*. Urbana: University of Illinois Press, 1973, 129-159.

"*Jerusalem* dramatically enacts Blake's self-deliverance from the womb of his world."

1409. Rose, Edward J. "The Structure of Blake's *Jerusalem*." *Bucknell Review*, XI (1963), 35-54.

The four parts of *Jerusalem* are keynoted by an appropriate Zoa and the imagery associated with that Zoa.

1410. Rose, Edward J. "Wheels Within Wheels in Blake's *Jerusalem*." *Studies in Romanticism*, II (1972), 36-47.

Wheels within wheels--"starry wheels of vision"; wheels without wheels--fallen, Urizenic world.

1411. Rose, Edward J. "Circumcision Symbolism in Blake's *Jerusalem*." *Studies in Romanticism*, VIII (1968), 16-25.

Circumcision equated with "circumscribing" and thus a positive connotation to Blake.

1412.   Rose, Edward J. "Preface: Perspectives on *Jerusalem*." *Blake Studies*, VII (1974), 7-9.

Announces three worthwhile approaches to *Jerusalem*: critical, thematic, pictorial.

1413.   Rose, Edward J. "The Symbolism of the Opened Center and Poetic Theory in Blake's *Jerusalem*." *Studies in English Literature*, V (1965), 587-606.

The present, the moment in each day Satan cannot find, is an opened center to infinity. Creativity leads to such centers.

1414.   Ryan, Robert E. "The Structure and Function of the Cosmogonic Myth in William Blake's *Jerusalem*." *DAI*, XXXVII (1976), 339A (Case Western Reserve).

Intends to prove that Blake utilized a widespread grammar of ancient, archetypal religious symbols to implement his visionary apocalypse.

1415.   Toomey, Deirdre. "The State of Plate 25 of *Jerusalem*." *Blake Newsletter*, VI (1972), 46-48.

Compares various copies of Plate 25.

1416.   Unruh, Donald. "*Jerusalem*: The Primitive Christian Vision of William Blake." *DAI*, XXXI (1970), 1819A.

Jerusalem is different in point of view and system than the works which precede the Felpham experience (University of Southern California).

1417.   Wilkinson, Carolyn. "Perception, Action and Character: The Structure of Blake's *Jerusalem*." *DAI*, XXXV (1974), 1638A (Michigan State University).

What do the characters in *Jerusalem* perceive?

1418.   Witke, Joanne. "*Jerusalem*--A Synoptic Poem." *Comparative Literature*, XXII (1970), 265-278.

Comparisons of *Jerusalem*'s four chapters with the four Gospels in regard to structure and purpose.

1419.   Worrall, David. "Blake's *Jerusalem* and the Visionary History of Britain." *Studies in Romanticism*, XVI (1977), 189-216.

Eternal vision lies beneath fable and fact.

1420. Wyatt, David M. "The Woman Jerusalem: Pictura versus
       Poesis." *Blake Studies*, VII (1975), 105-124.

       Jerusalem's "completed image in text and illustration
       creates a woman who is at once her own contrary, both
       a natural and a visionary form."

                      The Lambeth Books

1421. Noll, Jacqueline A. "Old Testament Prophecy in Blake's
       Lambeth Poems." *DAI*, XXXVIII (1978), 5500A (University
       of Maryland).

       States Blake's intention in the Lambeth Books is to
       destroy misreadings of the Old Testament perpetuated
       by orthodox Christianity.

1422. Roth, James P. "The Bible of Hell: William Blake's
       Lambeth Books." *DAI*, XL (1980), 5454A (University
       of Wisconsin, Milwaukee).

       Treats the seven Lambeth Books as a composite work
       representing Blake's Bible of Hell. Argues that the
       later prophecies are "not radically different from"
       this interpretation of the composite Lambeth Books.

                The Marriage of Heaven and Hell

1423. Baine, Rodney, and M.R. Baine. "*The Marriage of Heaven
       and Hell*, Plate 9." *Explicator*, XXXII (1974), Item
       50.

       Argues that Blake is pointing out that there is no
       real difference between taking a baby's physical life
       and taking his spiritual life, in the proverb "Sooner
       murder an infant in its cradle than nurse unacted
       desires."

1424. Bloom, Harold. "Dialectic in *The Marriage of Heaven
       and Hell*." *PMLA*, LXXIII (1958), 501-504.

       An outstanding essay, both scholarly and imaginative,
       pointing to a dialectic in form in the *Marriage* as
       well as a conceptual dialectic. The best essay around
       on the *Marriage*.

1425.   Casimir, Paul H. "Blake's *Marriage of Heaven and Hell*."
        Contemporary Review, CLXXXIII (1953), 351-355.

        An enthusiastic but superficial discussion of Blake's
        "message" as revealed in the *Marriage*.

1426.   Coon, Stephen W. "Roads of Excess: Towards a Poetics
        of Visionary Writing: Blake, Burroughs, Lautreamont,
        Michaux." *DAI*, XXXVIII (1977), 242A (Brown University).

        Presents a model for visionary writing and contends
        that Blake's *Marriage* is "ultimately more a manifesto
        of vision than an enactment of it."

1427.   Drescher, Timothy. "Art and Alienation in Blake's *The
        Marriage of Heaven and Hell*." *DAI*, XXXII (1971),
        386A (University of Wisconsin).

        Argues for a relationship between Blake's handling
        of a dialectical progression in text and design and
        the destruction of alienation in the reader.

1428.   Eaves, Morris. "A Reading of Blake's *Marriage of
        Heaven and Hell*, Plates 17-20: On and Under the
        Estate of the West." *Blake Studies*, IV (1972), 81-
        116.

        Plates 17-20 present a fictional account of the
        principle of the Prolific and Devourer.

1429.   Erdman, David V., with Tom Dargan and Marlene Deverell-
        Van Meter. "Reading the Illuminations of Blake's
        Marriage of Heaven and Hell." *William Blake: Essays
        in Honour of Sir Geoffrey Keynes* (item 240), 162-
        207.

        A kind of descriptive bibliography of Blake's designs
        to the *Marriage*.

1430.   Frost, Everett C. "The Prophet Armed: William Blake's
        Marriage of Heaven and Hell." *DAI*, XXXII (1971),
        2685A (University of Iowa).

        Blake's persona, that of prophet, is formed in the
        Marriage. He attains reprobate wisdom necessary to
        describing the apocalypse.

1431.   Gleckner, Robert F. "Priestley and the Chameleon Angel
        in *The Marriage of Heaven and Hell*." *Blake: An
        Illustrated Quarterly*, XIII (1979), 37-39.

Believes that the last Memorable Fancy in the *Marriage* is an early effort by Blake to incorporate "the symbol- ism of the new iron age." Joseph Priestley's work, especially *The History and Present State of Discoveries Relating to Vision, Light and Colours*, 1772, represents this new age.

1432. Helms, Randel. "Blake's Use of the Bible in 'A Song of Liberty.'" *ELN*, XVI (1979), 287-291.

Argues that the *Song of Liberty* relates to the *Marriage* as Revelations relates to the Bible. It is also a revision of Revelations.

1433. Holstein, Michael E. "Crooked Roads Without Improve- ment: Blake's 'Proverbs of Hell.'" *Genre*, VIII (1975), 26-41.

These proverbs are within a tradition of gnomic expressions which had stultified in Blake's time and which he tried to revive.

1434. Howard, John. "An Audience for *The Marriage of Heaven and Hell*." *Blake Studies*, III (1970), 19-52.

Argues that the *Marriage* is addressed to the New Jerusalem church and to the Joseph Johnson circle.

1435. Jackson, Mary V. "Prolific and Devourer: From Non- mythic to Mythic Statement in *The Marriage of Heaven and Hell* and *A Song of Liberty*." *Journal of English and Germanic Philology*, LXX (1971), 207-219.

The *Marriage* possesses different genres; *A Song of Liberty* has fused history, religion and psychology into one vision.

1436. Jones, Edward T. "Another Look at the Structure of *The Marriage of Heaven and Hell*." *Blake Newsletter*, X (1977), 115-116.

There are echoes of the Biblical mythos in the *Marriage*--Fall and Exile, the Law, Priesthood, the Coming of the Messiah, the Proclamation of the Gospel, the Life of Jesus and the Apocalypse.

1437. Kline, Alfred A. "Blake's *A Song of Liberty*." *Explica- tor*, XV (1956), Item 4.

A passage in Paine's *Rights of Man* clarifies lines 5-6 of *A Song of Liberty*.

1438. Lipking, Laurence. "Blake's Initiation: *The Marriage
       of Heaven and Hell*." *Woman in the 18th Century and
       Other Essays*. Edited by S. Stevens. Toronto: Hakkert,
       1976, 217-243.

       Dante had Beatrice but Blake was alone. "The savior
       whose way Blake prepares is Blake himself--or each of
       us."

1439. McGann, Jerome J. "Staging *The Marriage of Heaven and
       Hell*." *Blake Newsletter*, V (1972), 182-183.

       Adapting the poem to the stage involved a number of
       problems, including trying to fit Blake's own dramatic
       presentation into workable theatrical motifs.

1440. Nurmi, Martin K. "On the *Marriage of Heaven and Hell*."
       Discussions of William Blake (item 182), 93-101.

       This is a condensation from Nurmi's *Blake's Marriage
       of Heaven and Hell: A Critical Study* (item 1440a).
       One of the best studies of the *Marriage*.

1440a. Nurmi, Martin K. *Blake's Marriage of Heaven and Hell*.
       Kent, Ohio: Kent State University Bulletin Research
       Series III, 1957.

1441. Sabri-Tabrizi, G.R. *The "Heaven" and "Hell" of William
       Blake*. New York: International Publishers, 1973.

       A Marxist interpretation of Blake's *Marriage*. The
       author believes that the *Marriage* was written in re-
       sponse to Swedenborg's hatred for the working class.

       1442. Anon. "The Processes of William Blake" (rev.,
              The "Heaven" and "Hell" of William Blake;
              Blake's Night [item 1137]; *Blake's Sublime
              Allegory* [item 118]; *William Blake: Essays
              in Honour of Sir Geoffrey Keynes* [item 240]).
              Times Literary Supplement, Feb. 15, 1974, 145-
              147.

              Sabri-Tabrizi finds a strong Marxist atti-
              tude in Blake which he examines in a long
              account of the *Marriage*. Wagenknecht's "study
              grinds on with inexorable blandness through
              thick and thin, making ingenious interpreta-
              tions of Blakean lyrics fit tortured readings
              of Spenser's *Shepherd's Calendar* or vice

versa...." The Curran and Wittreich collection
is "a mixed bag," while the Paley and Phillips
collection ranges more widely than the Curran
text and is more informative.

1443.   Johnson, Mary Lynn. (rev., *The "Heaven" and "Hell"*
        of William Blake). *Philological Quarterly*,
        LIII (1974), 653-655.

        "His is another of those keys to Blake's
        thought that closes more doors than it opens."

1444.   Tolley, Michael J. (rev., *The "Heaven" and "Hell"*
        of William Blake). *Blake Newsletter*, VIII
        (1975), 138.

        "This is a pretentious, bad book. The author
        is both ignorant and prejudiced...."

1445. Schicker, Stephen M. "The Rainbow Beneath the Ground:
       A Study of the Descent into Hell Metaphor in William
       Blake's 'The Marriage of Heaven and Hell,' Gerard
       de Nerval's 'Aurelia,' and Arthur Rimbaud's 'Une
       Saison en enfer.'" *DAI*, XXXI (1970), 369A (Syracuse
       University).

       Each poet redefines "the nature of the descent into
       hell as part of a process leading to psychic integra-
       tion. Blake, Nerval, and Rimbaud turned to hermetic
       and alchemical tradition in order to clarify their own
       descents into hell."

1446. Stavrou, Constantine M. "A Reassessment of *The Marriage*
       of Heaven and Hell." *South Atlantic Quarterly*, LIV
       (1955), 381-385.

       The "pretentious" prophetic books are no more than
       an extension of everything that is to be found in the
       Marriage and in the *Songs*.

1447. Stempel, Daniel. "Angels of Reason: Science and Myth
       in the Enlightenment." *Journal of the History of*
       Ideas, XXXVI (1975), 63-78.

       Discusses Blake's fourth Memorable Fancy in the
       Marriage. Blake is rebelling against everything that
       is natural, including natural philosophy, religion,
       history and l'homme naturel.

1448.   Tannenbaum, Leslie. "Blake's News from Hell: *The Marriage of Heaven and Hell* and the Lucianic Tradi- tion." *ELH*, XLIII (1976), 74-99.

"Christian eschatology is applied to Lucianic satire for the purpose of subverting all previous epics and prophecies and of calling for a new epic-prophecy that will be even more revolutionary than Milton's--Blake's projected *Bible of Hell*."

1449.   Taylor, Gary J. "A Critical Edition of *The Marriage of Heaven and Hell* with Annotations." *DAI*, XXXIII (1972), 2345A (University of Arkansas).

Essentially a variorum text.

1450.   Taylor, Gary J. "The Structure of the *Marriage*: A Revolutionary Primer." *Studies in Romanticism*, XIII (1974), 141-145.

The "Primer" mosaic format may have suggested the structure of the *Marriage* to Blake.

1451.   Taylor, Gary J. "Blake's Proverb 67 (from the *Marriage of Heaven and Hell*)." *Explicator*, XXXII (1973), Item 8.

"Sooner murder an infant in its cradle than nurse unacted desires." Argues that there is no real dif- ference between robbing an infant of his physical life or the potential adult of his spiritual life.

1452.   Weissman, Judith. "A Note on the Pleasant Bank by Moonlight in *The Marriage of Heaven and Hell*." *Notes & Queries*, N.S. XXIV (1977), 321-322.

This passage alludes to *Paradise Lost*, Book One, 777-788. Blake transforms Milton's image of moonlight, from Milton's reason to Blake's imagination.

1453.   Widmer, K. "*The Marriage of Heaven and Hell*." *The Literary Rebel*. Carbondale: Southern Illinois Uni- versity Press, 1965.

In the cynic-heretic-épater tradition, with indig- nation and perversity its tone and method. "Blake endlessly opposes the things that supposedly are."

Milton

1454. Adlard, John. "Blake and 'Electrical Magic.'" *Neo-philologus*, LIII (1969), 422-423.

Mr. Birch's Electrical Magic aided Mrs. Blake's recovery, and thus the lines in *Milton*, 20:25-26.

1455. Adlard, John. "Drunkenness at the Mills in Blake's *Milton*." *Notes & Queries*, N.S. XII (1965), 183-184.

Blake's depicted drunks in *Milton* are like the drunks working for Joseph Seagrave, printer for Hayley.

1456. Adlard, John. "Tasso and the Cock and the Lion in Blake's *Milton*." *Symposium*, XX (1966), 5-6.

Perhaps Blake had Tasso, Agrippa and Milton in mind in creating the cock and the lion.

1457. Adlard, John. "The Cock, the Lion and the Spectres in Blake." *Archiv für das Studium der neueren Sprachen und Literaturen*, CCIV (1968), 432-433.

Argues against Damon's view that there is antipathy between cock and lion and insists upon contrariety.

1458. Butler, Peter. "*Milton*: The Final Plates." *Interpreting Blake* (item 245), 145-163.

Looks for an "adequate surface" to carry the inner meanings and concludes that Blake is uneven both going beyond spectrous explication and being himself too much the spectrous explicator.

1459. Carothers, Yvonne M. "Space and Time in *Milton*: The 'Bard's Song.'" *Blake in His Time* (item 149), 116-127.

Blake held a Kantian notion of time and space and thus could not assign painting and poetry to "distinct provinces on the basis of their affinities with empirical space and time." He interrelated verbal and visual forms.

1460. Coomar, Devinder M. "Silence, Language and the Poetry of Criticism in Romantic Expression: Blake, Keats, Foscolo, and Tagore." *DAI*, XXXVII (1976), 3601A (University of California, Riverside).

Believes Blake's *Milton* is an example of meta-poetry,
"a poem that examines the history of mimetic poetry
in the light of the romantic theory of poetics, ex-
plaining the symbolical form of the language of silence."

1461.   Cowling, William H. "Blake and the Redeemer Poet."
        DAI, XXXI (1970), 382A (Indiana University).

        Milton is a depiction of the victory of the redeemer
        poet and imagination over a mechanistic universe.

1462.   Curran, Stuart. "The Mental Pinnacle: Paradise Regained
        and the Romantic Four-Book Epic." *Calm of Mind*.
        Edited by Joseph Wittreich. Cleveland: Press of Case
        Western Reserve, 1971, 133-162.

        The epic continued after Milton and Blake's *Milton*
        and *Jerusalem* are evidence of this. This romantic epic
        involved prophetic truth, a Christ-like hero, self-
        purification and a regaining of Paradise on earth.

1463.   Erdman, David V. "The Steps (of Dance and Stone) That
        Order Blake's *Milton*." *Blake Studies*, VI (1973),
        73-87.

        The work is organized as a two-part dance opera with
        all the world as its stage and the vale of Felpham
        as stage center.

1464.   Fox, Susan C. "Hammer and Loom: The Design of Blake's
        Milton." *DAI*, XXXI (1970), 6547A (Yale University).
        See item 595.

        Only a difference in perception separates the
        temporal elements from the eternal in *Milton*.

1465.   Fox, Susan C. "The Structure of a Moment: Parallelism
        in the Two Books of Blake's *Milton*." *Blake Studies*,
        II (1969), 21-35.

        The struggle in *Milton* is between the constructive-
        creative force of Los and the destructive, pseudo-
        creative force of Urizen-Satan.

1466.   Glausser, Wayne. "*Milton* and the Pangs of Repentance."
        Blake: An Illustrated Quarterly, XIII (1980), 192-
        199.

Argues that the theme of memory in *Milton* is most interesting in regard to memory as repentance. "*Milton* as a whole could be taken as a complicated act of repentance on the part of Blake."

1467. Goslee, Nancy M. "'In Englands Green & Pleasant Land': The Building of Vision in Blake's Stanzas from *Milton*." *Studies in Romanticism*, XIII (1974), 105-125.

Argues that this lyric is a model for the themes of both *Milton* and *Jerusalem*.

1468. Herzing, Thomas W. "Book I of Blake's *Milton*: Natural Religion as an Optical Fallacy." *Blake Studies*, VI (1973), 19-34.

Argues that Book I "shows sensate nature to be a Satanic delusion and Natural Religion to be essentially an optical fallacy."

1469. Howard, John. *Blake's Milton: A Study in the Selfhood*. Rutherford, N.J.: Fairleigh Dickinson University Press, 1976.

Milton is sublime allegory, an allegory which goes beyond the topical and reflects a grand mythology. The Selfhood "is survival-oriented, manifesting itself as a hold-fast defense mechanism toward exterior reality as well as repressive enchainments of the creativity within."

1470. Eaves, Morris. (rev., *Blake's Milton*). *Studies in Romanticism*, XVI (1977), 251-260.

Howard ignores the composite art and provides a "mildly psychoanalytical version of the familiar idea that Romantic poets liked to write about themselves...."

1471. James, David E. "Written Within and Without: Form and Structure in Blake's *Milton*." *DAI*, XXXII (1972), 4614A (University of Pennsylvania).

"Blake's idea of the imagination is the point at which all ways of looking at *Milton* coincide, and the conflict between its form and those of reason is the 'kernel action' of all events in the poem."

1472. Johnson, Mary Lynn. "Recent Reconstruction of Blake's Milton and *Milton: A Poem*." *Milton and the Romantics*, II (1976), 1-10.

A review of Wittreich's *Angel of Apocalypse* (item 1286) and Susan Fox's *Poetic Form in Blake's Milton* (item 595). Wittreich's Blake looked upon Milton as a fellow prophet and not in the "Bloom-sense" (deliberate misreading). Neither Fox's book nor Wittreich's is the last word on Blake's Milton or his poem *Milton*.

1473.   Johnson, Mary Lynn. "'Separating What Has Been Mixed': A Suggestion for a Perspective on *Milton*." *Blake Studies*, VI (1973), 11-17.

Argues for the importance of the person and death of Jesus in all his prophecies.

1474.   Lawson, Mildred. "Creative and Sexual Energy in Blake's *Milton*." *American Notes and Queries*, XV (1976), 68-70.

Milton is depicted in the drawing of 15:48-49 as a star because the Book of Daniel refers to wise leaders as stars. He enters the feet because they are a euphemism for sexual organs in the Bible. Sexual energy is therefore entering Blake.

1475.   Mitchell, W.J.T. "Blake's Radical Comedy: Dramatic Structure as Meaning in *Milton*." *Blake's Sublime Allegory* (item 118), 281-307.

"Radical comedy" because *Milton* reveals Blake as neither a conservative nor a romantic idealist.

1476.   Noer, Philip D. "The Rhetorical Structure of *Milton*: An Introduction to the Reading of Blake's Major Prophecies as Poetry." *DAI*, XXXI (1970), 5418A (University of Minnesota).

Argues that Blake comes into full possession of his technical and creative powers only with *Milton*.

1477.   Reinhart, Charles. "The Universal Brotherhood: Blake, Milton and the Reader in Blake's *Milton*." *DAI*, XXXIX (1979), 4283A (Indiana University).

Demonstrates how Blake went about making the reader participate in the prophecy of *Milton*.

1478.   Rieger, James. "The Hem of Their Garments: The Bard's Song in *Milton*." *Blake's Sublime Allegory* (item 118), 259-280.

"... the pure sublimity of the Bard's Song forces us to abandon every level of traditional exegesis except anagogy."

1479.   Rix, Donna S. "The Function of Biblical Sources in the Structure and Meaning of Blake's *Milton*." *DAI*, XXXVIII (1978), 7349A (University of New Mexico).

Argues that Blake may have modeled *Milton* directly upon the prophecy of second Isaiah.

1480.   Rose, Edward J. "Blake's *Milton*: The Poet as Poem." *Blake Studies*, I (1968), 16-38.

Compares the three later Blake books with Dante's *Inferno*, *Purgatorio*, *Paradiso*.

1481.   Sutherland, John H. "Blake's *Milton*: The 'Bard's Song.'" *Colby Library Quarterly*, XIII (1977), 142-157.

The god-like figures of *Milton* represent universal psychological forces which "may be seen as acting within the psyche of William Blake."

1482.   Tayler, Irene. "Say First! What Mov'd Blake? Blake's *Comus* Designs and *Milton*." *Blake's Sublime Allegory* (item 118), 233-258.

Argues that the *Comus* designs led Blake to *Milton* and that their influence is discernible in that work.

1483.   Taylor, Peter A. "A Reading of Blake's *Milton*." *DAI*, XXX (1969), 737A (University of Connecticut).

Milton is Blake's idea of the Fall, which he arrived at after having read *Paradise Lost*.

1484.   Taylor, Peter A. "Providence and the Moment in Blake's *Milton*." *Blake Studies*, IV (1971), 43-60.

Argues that Blake wound up close to the mature John Milton in regard to the concept of providence.

1485.   Teitelbaum, Eve. "Form as Meaning in Blake's *Milton*." *Blake Studies*, II (1969), 37-64.

The central dramatic experience of the Bard's Song in *Milton* is the Rintrah-Palamabron-Satan myth.

1486.   Wilkie, Brian. "Epic Irony in *Milton*." *Blake's Visionary Forms Dramatic* (item 139), 359-372.

The epic tradition is useful in clarifying much of
Blake's later work but it does not explain everything.

Notebook (Rossetti Ms.)

1487.   Erdman, David V. "Preface to the Revised Edition of
        Blake's *Notebook*." *Blake: An Illustrated Quarterly*,
        XI (1977), 21-23.

        Revises his readings of two of the emblem designs.

1488.   Erdman, David V. "Blake's Transcript of Bisset's 'Lines
        Written on Hearing the Surrender of Copenhagen.'"
        Bulletin of the New York Public Library, LXXII (1968),
        518-552.

        Blake presumably copied this poem from a newspaper
        and transcribed it in his Notebook. It's a "response
        to the shock of the conflagration of a neutral city."

1489.   Erdman, David V. "'Terrific Blake in His Pride': An
        Essay on the *Everlasting Gospel*." *From Sensibility
        to Romanticism*. Edited by F.W. Hilles and Harold
        Bloom. New York: Oxford University Press, 1965.

        Attempts to locate editorial problems in the ms.
        fragments.

1490.   Finch, G.J. "'Never Pain to Tell Thy Love' Blake's
        Problem Poem." *Blake Studies*, IV (1971), 73-79.

        Argues that this poem from the Notebook could not
        express Blake's complex response to the problems of
        sexual love.

1491.   Gleckner, Robert F. "Blake's 'I Saw a Chapel All of
        Gold.'" *Colby Library Quarterly*, XV (1979), 37-47.

        "I Saw a Chapel" is as much influenced by Spenser
        as by Milton, a typical occurrence through the last
        decade of the eighteenth century.

1492.   Grant, Phillip B. "Blake's 'The Everlasting Gospel':
        An Edition and Study." *DAI*, XXXVII (1977), 4366A
        (University of Pennsylvania).

        Argues for an edition of "The Everlasting Gospel"
        "that considers the work as a poem of substance, co-
        herence and vision."

1493. Hall, Jean. "Blake's Everlasting Gospel." *Blake Studies*, IV (1971), 61-72.

 Everlasting Gospel is like *Marriage* except its technique is more direct. "... the *Gospel* is a didactic effort to dispel a conventional and illiberal view of Christ, which Blake wishes to replace with his own visionary conception."

1494. Heinzelman, Kurt. "Blake's Golden Word." *English Language Notes*, XV (1977), 33-38.

 Paraphrases Blake's Notebook entry thus: "... on this day I found the word Golden even though the word, golden, was debased."

1495. Helms, Randel. "The Genesis of *The Everlasting Gospel*." *Blake Studies*, IX (1980), 122-160.

 Argues that "the poem arose as part of Blake's ongoing and sometimes unsuccessful poetic debate with certain interpretations of the nature of Christ presented in the Bible...."

1496. Kettle, Arnold. "The Mental Traveller." *Arena*, No. 3 (1949), 46-52, 93, 94.

 A Marxist interpretation.

1497. Moore, Donald K. "Blake's Notebook Versions of 'Infant Sorrow.'" *Bulletin of the New York Public Library*, LXXVI (1972), 209-219.

 The Notebook variants are so extensive that they almost comprise a separate poem.

Pickering Ms.

1498. Adams, Hazard. "'The Crystal Cabinet' and 'The Golden Net.'" *Blake: A Collection of Critical Essays* (item 155), 79-87. See item 66.

 Discovers a similarity in the two poems by comparing the perspectives of the speakers. Like the cabinet, the "net is associated with a threefold female of delusory powers."

1499. Adamson, Arthur. "Structure and Meaning in Blake's
       'The Mental Traveller.'" *Mosaic*, VII (1974), 41-58.

       The structure of this poem and that of *Jerusalem* are
       comparable. Blake and Spengler held the same theory of
       culture.

1500. Adlard, John. "Blake's Crystal Cabinet." *Modern Language
       Review*, LXII (1967), 28-30.

       A discussion of the poem in relation to *Milton* and
       to Blake's reaction to Locke's concept of the mind as
       initially an "empty cabinet."

1501. Dunlap, Ann Bush. "Blake's 'The Mental Traveller' and
       the Critics." *DAI*, XXXIV (1974), 6586A (University
       of New Mexico).

       Discusses the 27 major commentaries and attempts to
       derive some conclusions regarding critical methodologies
       as well as some ideas as to the meaning of the poem.

1502. Enscoe, Gerald E. "The Content of Vision: Blake's
       'Mental Traveller.'" *Papers on Language and Litera-
       ture*, IV (1968), 400-413.

       Argues that Frye's interpretation limits interpreta-
       tion of this poem to the context of the Orc-Urizen cycle.

1503. Leonard, Harris K. "William Blake and 'The Mental
       Traveller.'" *DAI*, XXXVIII (1978), 6743A (Howard
       University).

       Reviews criticism of the poem and then presents an
       interpretation which takes into account biographical
       facts.

1504. Nurmi, Martin K. "Joy, Love, and Innocence in Blake's
       'The Mental Traveller.'" *Studies in Romanticism*,
       III (1964), 109-117.

       Reviews various interpretations of this poem but
       concludes that it eludes such interpretations.

1505. Reisner, Thomas A., and Mary Ellen Reisner. "Blake's
       'Auguries of Innocence.'" *Explicator*, XXXV (1977),
       32-33.

       Refers to the lines "The strongest Poison ever known
       came from Caesar's Laurel Crown." Toxicity of laurel
       was discovered some 30 years before Blake's birth.

1506. Sutherland, John H. "Blake's 'Mental Traveller.'"
      Discussions of William Blake (item 182), 86-92. Re-
      printed in item 223.

      A reading based on background, situation and point
      of view in the poem.

1507. Warner, Janet. "Blake's 'Auguries of Innocence.'"
      Colby Library Quarterly, XII (1976), 126-138.

      Argues that patterns of language in this poem are
      coherent and reveal a microcosm of Blake's thought.

                        Poetical Sketches

1508. Bogen, Nancy. "An Early Listing of William Blake's
      Poetical Sketches." *ELN*, III (1966), 194-196.

      In John Egerton's *Theatrical Remembrances* (1788).

1509. DuPlantier, R.R. "Method in Blake's 'Mad Song.'" *Blake:*
      An Illustrated Quarterly, XIII (1979), 102-109.

      The speaker's affliction is not impotence but om-
      nipotence. He is inspired.

1510. Hartman, Geoffrey H. "Blake and the 'Progress of Poesy.'"
      Beyond Formalism. New Haven, Conn.: Yale University
      Press, 1970, 193-205.

      Blake's season poems are about poetry.

1511. Knights, L.C. "Early Blake." *Sewanee Review*, LXXIX
      (1971), 376-392.

      Focuses on eight songs in *Poetical Sketches* which
      come midway in the collection of shorter poems pre-
      ceding the dramatic fragment, "King Edward the Third."
      They are an intrinsic part of Blake's work as a whole.

1512. McGowan, James D. "Rising Glories: A Study of William
      Blake's *Poetical Sketches*." *DA*, XXIX (1969), 2221A
      (Rutgers University).

      There is an imagistic consistency in these sketches
      that argues for coherence and unity of vision.

1513.   McGowan, James. "The Integrity of the *Poetical Sketches*:
        A New Approach to Blake's Earliest Poems." *Blake
        Studies*, VIII (1979), 121-144.

        The movement in the *Poetical Sketches*, if they are
        read in the given order, is a movement from calmness
        to the uncertainty of the secular world, to the terrors
        of political chaos, to discontent and frustration.

1514.   Phillips, Michael. "The Reputation of Blake's *Poetical
        Sketches* 1783-1863." *Review of English Studies*, XXVI
        (1975), 19-33.

        Traces H.C. Robinson's attempts to publish *Poetical
        Sketches* and interest others in Blake.

1515.   Phillips, Michael. "Blake's Early Poetry." *William
        Blake: Essays in Honour of Sir Geoffrey Keynes* (item
        240), 1-28.

        States that we can discern Blake's feelings regarding
        his vocation as poet in the *Poetical Sketches*.

1516.   Wilkes, John E. "Aeolian Visitations and the Harp De-
        frauded: Essays on Donne, Blake, Wordsworth, Keats,
        Heine, and James Wright." *DAI*, XXXV (1974), 1129A
        (University of California, Santa Cruz).

        Discusses Blake's season poems to see whether Blake's
        created self-generated world can be sustained.

                          The Song of Los

1517.   Erdman, David V. "The Symmetries of *The Song of Los*."
        Studies in Romanticism, XVI (1977), 179-188.

        Describes the plates of *The Song of Los* as illumina-
        tions of what Erdman calls the "whole four-harp se-
        quence": *America: A Prophecy*, *Europe: A Prophecy*,
        "Africa" and "Asia."

1518.   Lindsay, David W. "'The Song of Los': An Interpreta-
        tion of the Text." *Forum for Modern Language Studies*,
        XIII (1977), 1-5.

        Argues that *The Song of Los* is about the humaniza-
        tion of the material world via energy.

Songs of Innocence and of Experience

1519. Ackland, Michael. "Blake's Problematic Touchstones to
        Experience: 'Introduction' 'Earth's Answer' and the
        Lyca Poems." *Studies in Romanticism*, XIX (1980),
        3-17.

        These poems lead to self-emancipation, an understand-
        ing and even transcendence of the state of Experience.

1520. Adams, Hazard. "Reading Blake's Lyrics: 'The Tyger.'"
        Texas Studies in Literature and Language, II (1960),
        18-37.

        "From the point of view of the visionary, the tiger,
        fearful as he may be, is created form...." He is a
        creature of tremendous life and energy and must be
        accepted in that fashion.
        Introduces the notion of dual speakers--"... it is
        clear that there is also another speaker of the poem
        who presents us with an alternative reading, a speaker
        whose attitude casts an ironic perspective upon the
        words as they are spoken by our Urizenic questioner."
        The tyger should be confronted with "that strange
        gaiety suggested by the visionary intensity of the
        poem itself."

1521. Adlard, John. "The Age and Virginity of Lyca." *Blake
        Newsletter*, VI (1972-73), 73.

        The commentary of Hierocles on the Golden Verses of
        Pythagoras indicates that the number 7, the age of
        Lyca of "The Little Girl Lost," is a virgin.

1522. Adlard, John. "Blake's 'The Little Girl Lost and
        Found.'" *Archiv für das Studium der neueren Sprachen
        und Literaturen*, CCX (1973), 330-334.

        Uses Cornelius Agrippa and Swedenborg rather than
        Thomas Taylor to clarify Lyca's abduction to a lion's
        den.

1523. Adlard, John. "'The Garden of Love.'" *Blake Newsletter*,
        IV (1971), 147-148.

        Binding with briars was common in graveyards in
        Blake's day and until Victorian times.

1524. Adlard, John. "Blake's Indenture and 'The Little Vaga-
       bond.'" *Blake Newsletter*, V (1972), 214.

       Similar lines in poem and document of indenture.

1525. Adler, Jacob H. "Symbol and Meaning in 'The Little
       Black Boy.'" *Modern Language Notes*, LXXII (1957),
       412-415.

       Discusses various complexities in the poem and points
       out that the speaker utters them but does not understand
       them, like those disciples of Jesus who heard Jesus but
       held onto their desires.

1526. Anshutz, Herbert L., and Donald W. Cummings. "Blake's
       'The Sick Rose.'" *The Explicator*, XXIX (1970), Item
       32.

       "The Sick Rose" as a parody of Prior's "A True Maid."

1527. Bacon, M.E. "Blake's 'The Tyger.'" *Explicator*, XXVI
       (1967), Item 35.

       There is a sketch of Orc on the page of the Notebook
       which contains a draft of "The Tyger."

1528. Baine, Mary, and Rodney Baine. "Blake's Other Tygers
       and 'The Tyger.'" *Studies in English*, XV (1975),
       563-578.

       Argues that critics have ignored the design for "The
       Tyger" as well as traditional symbolism of the animal--
       bloodthirsty cruelty.

1529. Baine, Rodney. "Blake's 'Tyger': The Nature of the
       Beast." *Philological Quarterly*, XLVI (1967), 488-498.

       Lamb and tiger are complementary symbols. The tiger
       symbolizes the creation of brutal cruelty in nature
       and in man.

1530. Baine, Rodney M. "Blake's 'The Little Vagabond.'"
       Explicator, XXVII (1968), Item 6.

       The church and the school are equally indicted in
       this poem.

1531. Baine, Rodney M., and Mary R. Baine. "Blake's 'Blossom.'"
       Colby Library Quarterly, XIV (1978), 22-27.

       Argues that the speaker is a mother with her child.

1532.   Bass, Eben. *"Songs of Innocence and of Experience*: The
        Thrust of Design." *Blake's Visionary Forms Dramatic*
        (item 139), 196-213.

        Illustration often merges into decoration, into pure
        compositional effects. In "The Divine Image" the design
        actually divides the poem into two portions.

1533.   Bentley, G.E., Jr. "A Piper Passes: The Earliest Parody
        of Blake's *Songs of Innocence." Notes & Queries*, N.S.
        XI (1964), 418-419.

        This parody of "Piping Down the Valleys Wild" was not
        Blake's or Swinburne's.

1534.   Bloom, Harold. "Blake and Revisionism." *Poetry and Re-
        pression*. New Haven, Conn.: Yale University Press,
        1976, 28-51.

        Argues that accepted readings of "London" and "The
        Tyger" are canonical misreadings alien to Blake's strong
        misreading of Ezekiel and Job.

1535.   Bowden, William R. "Blake's 'Introduction' to *Songs of
        Innocence." Explicator*, XI (1953), Item 41.

        The poem is a proud poetic credo.

1536.   Bowen, Robert O. "Blake's 'The Tyger,' 7-8." *Explicator*,
        VII (1949), Item 62.

        Daedalus, Icarus and Prometheus as sources for lines
        in "The Tyger."

1537.   Bowra, C.M. *"Songs of Innocence and Experience." The
        Romantic Imagination*. Cambridge, Mass.: Harvard
        University Press, 1949, 25-50.

        A good introduction to the *Songs* with frequent
        reference to the differences between them and the
        prophecies.

1538.   Brennan, Joseph X. "The Symbolic Framework of Blake's
        'The Tyger.'" *College English*, XXII (1961), 406-407.

        The poem moves from a description of the tiger's power
        to speculation regarding who could have created him.

1539.   Chayes, Irene H. "Blake and Tradition: 'The Little
        Lost' and 'The Little Girl Found.'" *Blake Newsletter*,
        IV (1970), 25-28.

Corrects Raine's imposition of Thomas Taylor on these two poems.

1540.   Chayes, Irene H. "Little Girls Lost: Problems of a
        Romantic Archetype." *Bulletin of the New York Public
        Library*, LXVII (1963), 579-592.

        Blake's Lyca poems join with "Lucy Gray" and "The Eve
        of St. Agnes" in presenting the Romantic version of the
        paradox that "in order to gain life it is necessary
        to lose it; in order to be 'found' one must first be
        irretrievably lost."

1541.   Combs, William W. "Practical Minstrelsy: Some English
        Songs and Their Settings." *Mad River Review*, II
        (1966), 20-36.

        Stresses the necessary interdependence of words and
        music, pointing out that Blake was a good songwriter.
        Contextual critics aren't interested in simple lyrics
        and ignore the transformation that music creates.

1542.   Connolly, Thomas B. "The Real 'Holy Thursday' of
        William Blake." *Blake Studies*, VI (1976), 179-187.

        Not Ascension Thursday or Maundy Thursday but the
        day of the yearly meeting of the Charity School chil-
        dren.

1543.   Connolly, Thomas E. "A Blakean Maze." *Blake Studies*,
        III (1970), 61-68.

        Points out that the four copies of the *Songs* in the
        British Library are to some extent inaccurate.

1544.   Connolly, Thomas E., and George R. Levine. "Pictorial
        and Poetic Design in Two Songs of Innocence." *PMLA*,
        LXXXII (1967), 257-264.

        "The Little Boy Lost" has to do with disillusionment
        due to the pursuit of a false ideal. "The Little Boy
        Found" is concerned with the mother-son relationship
        and the protection of innocence from a destructive
        experience.

1545.   Deck, Raymond, Jr. "An American Original: Mrs. Colman's
        Illustrated Printings of Blake's Poems, 1843-4."
        Blake: An Illustrated Quarterly, XI (1977), 4-18.

        She's interesting because she represents American
        Swedenborgians' interest in Blake and because her work

typifies the genre of American children's books in the 1840's.

1546. Dike, Donald. "The Difficult Innocence: Blake's Songs and Pastoral." *ELH*, XXVIII (1961), 353-375.

Argues that the *Songs of Innocence* do not describe an Edenic state, but are struggling against the "gross moral and perceptual reality of the reader."

1547. Dillon, Ralph G. "Source for Blake's 'The Sick Rose.'" *American Notes and Queries*, XII (1974), 157-158.

Jeremiah iv:30.

1548. Dilworth, Thomas. "Blake's Argument with Newberry in 'Laughing Song.'" *Blake: An Illustrated Quarterly*, XIV (1980), 36-37.

Suggested prototype for "Laughing Song" is "How to Laugh" by John Newberry, 1761.

1549. Doherty, F.M.J. "Blake's 'The Tyger' and Henry Needler." *Philological Quarterly*, XLVI (1967), 566-567.

Is Needler's *Copy of Verses* the target for Blake's poem?

1550. Donaldson, Ian. "The Satirist's London." *Essays in Criticism*, XXV (1975), 101-122.

Blake's "London" mentioned briefly.

1551. Doxey, William S. "William Blake and William Herschel: The Poet, and Astronomer, and 'The Tyger.'" *Blake Studies*, II (1970), 5-13.

Astronomy, which Blake may have picked up from Herschel's astronomical reports, provides an interpretation of certain passages in "The Tyger."

1552. Doyno, V. "Blake's Revision of 'London.'" *Essays in Criticism*, XXII (1972), 58-63.

A number of postulations as to why certain changes were made. The author concludes that it all doesn't amount to a great deal.

1553. Draper, R.P. "Blake's Early Poems: Experiments in Romantic Style." *Revue des Langues Vivantes*, XXXII (1966), 587-597.

Songs are the only truly original embodiment of Blake's imaginative perception.

1554. Dyson, A.E., and J. Lovelock. "The Road of Excess: Blake's *Songs of Innocence and Experience*." *Masterful Images*. New York: Barnes & Noble, 1976, 125-135.

Reading of "The Shepherd" and "The Sick Rose."

1555. Dyson, A.E. "'The Little Black Boy': Blake's Song of Innocence." *Critical Quarterly*, I (1959), 44-47.

"... it is through the acceptance of outpoured love as a universal norm that he [the little black boy] goes beyond the bitterness of experience."

1556. Eaves, Morris. "'Songs of Innocence and Experience' by William Blake Tuned by Allen Ginsberg." *Blake Newsletter*, IV (1971), 90-97.

Poetry, designs and music make up the *Songs*.

1557. Eberly, Ralph D. "Blake's 'The Tyger,' 17-18." *Explicator*, VIII (1949), Item 12.

Image of the celestial smithy discussed.

1558. Eberly, Ralph D. "Blake's 'The Little Black Boy.'" *Explicator*, XV (1957), Item 42.

"... it is a shocking violation of 'poetic logic' for the little black boy to say that he will become like the English boy."

1559. England, Martha W. "Blake and the Hymns of Charles Wesley." *Hymns Unbidden: Donne, Herbert, Blake, Emily Dickinson and the Hymnographers*. New York: New York Public Library, 1966, 93-112. See item 1190.

Blake's *Songs* are compared to Wesley's. Wesley's are simple in every respect while Blake's are simple only in form. Both Blake and Wesley read the Bible--and read it differently.

1560. Fairchild, B.H., Jr. "Melos and Meaning in Blake's Lyric Art." *Blake Studies*, VII (1975), 125-141.

"Blake's lyric mode is tripartite: music (melos), poetry, and visual art (opsis)...." Yet melos is most direct, communicating Eternity to the listener without words or images.

1561. Forsyth, R.A. "Europe, Africa and the Problem of
       Spiritual Authority." *Southern Review* (Adelaide),
       III (1969), 294-323.

       Africa is the Dionysian sea which Europe, the boat,
       resists. Blake's "The Tyger" among other works is a
       potentially destructive force in the heart of Apollonian
       Europe.

1562. Franz, Rolaine. "All the Ship's Company: A Wesleyan
       Paradigm for the Poetry of Christopher Smart,
       William Cowper and William Blake." *DAI*, XXXIX (1979),
       5523A (Brown University).

       Views Wesleyan theology as a good gloss for reading
       these poets. *Songs* used the hymn tradition.

1563. Frye, Northrop. "Blake's Introduction to Experience."
       Huntington Library Quarterly, XXI (1957), 57-67.

       Argues that Blake is consistent in "his theory and
       practice as an artist" and that an examination of the
       "Introduction" to the *Songs of Experience* is also an
       introduction to some of the main principles of Blake's
       thought.

1564. Gallagher, Phillip J. "The Word Made Flesh: Blake's
       'A Poison Tree' and the Book of Genesis." *Studies
       in Romanticism*, XVI (1977), 237-249.

       Argues that "A Poison Tree" is a countermyth which
       exposes the biblical narrative of the Fall as a fraud
       by giving "the true etiology of the Tree of the Knowl-
       edge of Good and Evil."

1565. Ginsberg, Allen. "To Young or Old Listeners: Setting
       Blake's *Songs* to Music, and a Commentary on the
       Songs." *Blake Newsletter*, IV (1971), 98-103.

       States that he heard Blake recite "The Sun Flower"
       and "The Little Girl Lost."

1566. Giovannini, Margaret. "Blake's 'Introduction' to *Songs
       of Innocence*." *Explicator*, VII (1949), Item 5.

       The Songs of Innocence reflect the joy issuing from
       a perfectly innocent faith.

1567. Glazer, Myra, and Gerda Norvig. "Blake's Book of
       Changes: On Viewing Three Copies of *The Songs of*

Innocence and of Experience." Blake Studies, IX (1980), 100-121.

Copies A, B and T.

1568.   Gleckner, Robert. "'The Lamb' and 'The Tyger'--How Far with Blake?" *English Journal*, LI (1962), 536-543.

How Blake should be taught in the high school class-room.

1569.   Gleckner, Robert. "Irony in Blake's 'Holy Thursday.'" *Modern Language Notes*, LXXI (1956), 412-415.

Blake's attack upon charity is similar to Mandeville's in regard to the colorful uniforms they wear. Blake's irony is further extended to the "wise guardians of the poor" and Ascension Day.

1570.   Gleckner, Robert. "William Blake and the Human Abstract." *PMLA*, LXXVI (1961), 373-379.

Contrasts "The Human Abstract" with "The Divine Image."

1571.   Glen, Heather. "Blake's Criticism of Moral Thinking in *Songs of Innocence and of Experience." Interpreting Blake* (item 245), 32-69.

Blake displays a mistrust of moral thinking in these poems and advocates an energy which challenges conventional standards of judgment.

1572.   Grant, John E., and Fred C. Robinson. "Tense and the Sense of Blake's 'The Tyger.'" *PMLA*, LXXXI (1966), 596-603.

Argue that the verb tense in this poem reveals meaning.

1573.   Grant, John E. "Interpreting Blake's 'The Fly.'" *Bulletin of the New York Public Library*, LXVII (1963), 593-615.

A very exhaustive account which states that the speaker of this poem presents a limited point of view.

1574.   Grant, John E. "Two Flowers in the Garden of Experience." *William Blake: Essays for S. Foster Damon* (item 256), 333-367.

Detailed interpretation of "My Pretty Rose Tree" and
"The Lilly" and study of other important concurrences
of this flower imagery throughout Blake's literary and
pictorial work.

1575. Grant, John E. "The Art and Argument of 'The Tyger.'"
       Texas Studies in Literature and Language, II (1960),
       38-60.

       A close reading of the poem in which Grant states that
       "the illustration to 'The Tyger' primarily depicts the
       divorce of heaven and hell, the split between the Eagle
       and the Tyger...."

1576. Grant, John E. "Misreadings of 'The Fly.'" *Essays in
       Criticism*, XI (1961), 481-487.

       Grant corrects Kirschbaum and makes a criticism of
       F.W. Bateson's postscript to Kirschbaum's essay.

1577. Grimes, Ronald L. "'The Fly.'" *William Blake: Essays
       for S. Foster Damon* (item 256), 368-382.

       A detailed reading.

1578. Grimes, Ronald L. "William Blake's 'The Clod' & 'The
       Pebble.'" *Restoration and Eighteenth Century Litera-
       ture: Essays in Honor of Alan Dugald McKillop*. Edited
       by Carroll Camden. Chicago: University of Chicago
       Press, 1963, 381-388.

       Argues that the Pebble and not the Clod, as is fre-
       quently maintained, is Blake's *raisonneur*.

1579. Harper, George M. "The Source of Blake's 'Ah! Sunflower.'"
       Modern Language Review, XLVIII (1953), 139-142.

       Suggested source is Taylor's translation of *Hymns of
       Orpheus*.

1580. Harrison, James. "Blake's 'The Chimney Sweeper.'"
       Explicator, XXXVI (1978), 2-3.

       Irony is more devastating since the tone of the poem
       is that of an innocent child.

1581. Hill, A.A. "Imagery and Meaning: A Passage from *Lycidas*
       and a Poem by Blake." *Constituent and Pattern in
       Poetry*. Austin: University of Texas Press, 1976,
       71-82.

       A reading of "London."

1582. Hirsch, E.D. *Innocence and Experience: An Introduction
       to Blake*. New Haven, Conn.: Yale University Press,
       1964.

       Hirsch opposes Frye's view that each of Blake's works
       represents the total vision of Blake.

       1583. Anon. "Meet the Mystic" (rev., *Innocence and
              Experience*). *Times Literary Supplement*, Feb.
              11, 1965, 108.

              "Mr. Hirsch's study of the development of
              Blake's ideas ... comes as a most welcome anti-
              dote to the prevailing view of Blake which in-
              sists upon seeing even his juvenilia as a
              'microcosm' of his later prophecies...."

       1584. Bentley, G.E., Jr. (rev., *Innocence and Experi-
              ence*). *Modern Philology*, LXIII (1965), 77-79.

              "In short, Mr. Hirsch has investigated a very
              promising thesis which requires by its nature
              the most exacting standards of scholarship,
              but by a frequent disregard of the distinction
              between accepted fact and tendentious hypothe-
              sis, and by an insufficient examination of the
              facts available, he often forfeits the reader's
              confidence in the reliability of what he is
              saying."

       1585. Bostetter, Edward E. (rev., *Innocence and Ex-
              perience*). *College English*, XXVI (1965), 580.

              "This study will be wonderful therapy for
              those who have been intimidated by the elaborate
              critical attempts of recent years."

       1586. Goldman, Arnold. (rev., *Innocence and Experience*).
              Notes & Queries, N.S. XIII (1966), 234-235.

              "Mr. Hirsch has ... written, I venture, not
              only the best book on the *Songs*, but perhaps
              the best introduction to Blake before *Milton*...."

       1587. Nurmi, Martin K. (rev., *Innocence and Experience*).
              Journal of English and Germanic Philology,
              LXV (1966), 201-202.

              "Hirsch's book is not an introduction but a
              polemical re-introduction; criticisms of Blake
              have gone astray, he argues, by reading him

as if he had some kind of system in mind, and
Hirsch proposes to set things right, by showing
how Blake should be read."

1588. Schulz, Max F. (rev., *Innocence and Experience*).
       Modern Language Quarterly, XXVI (1965), 339-341.

       "... the limited insights of most of these
       commentaries are indirectly an eloquent justi-
       fication of the intuitive approach of Damon
       et al." Hirsch rejects most of Blakean criti-
       cism and scholarship.

1589. Ure, Peter. (rev., *Innocence and Experience*).
       Review of English Studies, XVIII (1967), 83-87.

       "He [Hirsch] believes that *Innocence* was
       composed without thought for *Experience* and
       that the latter gives continual evidence of
       'self-satire.' He believes also that the ap-
       parent orthodoxies and pieties of *Innocence* ...
       need to be taken more at their face value than
       it is nowadays at all common to take them."

1590. Hirst, Desiree. "Once More Continuing 'The Tyger.'"
       Blake Studies, VII (1975), 177-179.

       Robert Fludd's *Mosaicall Philosophy*, 1659, a work on
       the Cabbala, is a source for this poem.

1591. Hobsbaum, Philip. "A Rhetorical Question Answered:
       Blake's Tyger and Its Critics." *Neophilologus*, XLVIII
       (1964), 151-155.

       Argues that Blake did not know who made the tiger.

1592. Jackson, Wallace. "William Blake in 1789: Unorganized
       Innocence." *Modern Language Quarterly*, XXXIII (1972),
       396-404.

       Argues that the poems are distinct, separate entities.

1593. Jeffrey, Lloyd N. "Blake's 'The Little Black Boy.'"
       Explicator, XVII (1958), Item 27.

       Clear interpretation of this poem depends on a recog-
       nition of two speakers in it.

1594. Justin, Howard. "Blake's 'Introduction' to *Songs of
       Innocence*." *Explicator*, XI (1952), Item 1.

       Argues that art is disparaged in this poem.

1595.   Kaplan, Fred. "The Tyger and Its Maker: Blake's Vision
        of Art and the Artist." *Studies in English Literature
        1500-1900*, VII (1967), 617-627.

        The tiger is an "experience" which "Blake-framer"
        frames by creative process.

1596.   Keating, Ruth A. "A Fourth Dimension in Word and Picture:
        William Blake's Theory of Imagination." *DAI*, XXXVI
        (1975), 6115A (Texas Woman's University).

        The beginnings of Blake's vision are in the *Songs*.
        Lines from the later works are used as a gloss.

1597.   Keynes, Geoffrey L. "Blake's 'Holy Thursday' in Anne
        and Jane Taylor's *City Scenes*." *Book Collector*, IX
        (1960), 75-76.

        The Taylors pirated Blake's poem, rewrote the first
        line and omitted the title.

1598.   Kirschbaum, Leo. "Blake's 'The Fly.'" *Essays in Criti-
        cism*, XI (1961), 154-162.

        Flies are idiotic and children have an untested inno-
        cence.

1599.   Landry, Hilton. "The Symbolism of Blake's Sunflower."
        Bulletin of the New York Public Library, LXVI (1962),
        613-616.

        Derides the Platonic interpretation of Blake's "Ah,
        Sunflower," and points to the obvious sensuousness of
        the imagery and the goal of the flower as total Blakean
        fulfillment.

1600.   Lindop, Grevel. "Blake: 'The Little Girl Lost' and 'The
        Little Girl Found.'" *The Critical Survey*, VI (1973),
        36-40.

        The poems were switched from Innocence to Experience
        because they're transitional.

1601.   Long, Kay Parkhurst. "Unity in William Blake's 'Songs
        of Innocence and of Experience': A Review and Dis-
        cussion." *DAI*, XXXI (1970), 2884A (University of
        Tulsa).

        Argues that it is preferable to treat each song in-
        dividually rather than attempt to fit it into a scheme
        for the whole.

1602. Mabbott, Thomas O. "Blake's 'A Poison Tree.'" *Explicator*, VI (1948), Item 19.

> Open quarrel as opposed to a concealed quarrel.

1603. McElderry, B.R., Jr. "Coleridge on Blake's *Songs.*" *Modern Language Quarterly*, IX (1948), 298-302.

> Argues that Coleridge's objections were moralistic, that he didn't admire any unconventionality in these poems. The younger Coleridge might have applied more critical subtlety to the *Songs*.

1604. McGlynn, Paul D. "Blake's 'The Chimney Sweeper' (from *Songs of Innocence*)." *Explicator*, XXVII (1968), Item 21.

> Distinction is made between Blake and the speaker of the poem.

1605. Manlove, C.N. "Engineered Innocence: Blake's 'The Little Black Boy' and 'The Fly.'" *Essays in Criticism*, XXVII (1977), 112-121.

> "The Little Black Boy" describes the preservation of innocence by falsification of experience and in this it is very like "The Fly."

1606. Mikkelson, Robert. "William Blake's Revisions of the *Songs of Innocence and of Experience*." *Concerning Poetry*, II (1969), 60-71.

> Manuscripts of the *Songs* show meticulous care and craftsmanship.

1607. Miner, Paul. "'The Tyger': Genesis and Evolution in the Poetry of William Blake." *Criticism*, IV (1962), 59-73.

> Symbol cracking in this poem is not pertinent.

1608. Nathan, Norman. "Blake's 'Infant Sorrow.'" *Notes & Queries*, N.S. VII (1960), 99-100.

> Birth of an infant also brings sorrow to those already in this world.

1609. Nurmi, Martin K. "Fact and Symbol in 'The Chimney Sweeper' of Blake's *Songs of Innocence*." *Bulletin of the New York Public Library*, LXVIII (1964), 249-256.

Nurmi believes that increased knowledge of the plight of the chimney sweep increases our sense of Blake's use of irony in the poem and also defines the circumference of symbolic interpretation.

1610.   Ober, Warren. "'Poor Robin' and Blake's 'The Blossom.'" *Blake Newsletter*, IX (1975), 42-43.

"Poor Robin" is a bawdy ballad which may have been in Blake's mind when he composed "The Blossom."

1611.   O'Brien, Michael W. "Between Language and Voice: A Study of Aesthetic Experimentation in Blake, Whitman, Cummings and Concrete Poetry." *DAI*, XXXIV (1973), 5985A (University of Illinois, Urbana-Champaign).

The states of the *Songs* are defined by psycholinguistic opposition to each other.

1612.   O'Higgins, Elizabeth. "Blake's Joy of the Yew." *Dublin Magazine*, XXXI (1956), 21-29.

Translates "Infant Joy" into Gaelic, which she feels was the original language Blake wrote in. Analyzes the poem in relation to Irish history.

1613.   Paley, Morton D. "Tyger of Wrath." *PMLA*, LXXXI (1966), 540-555.

A survey of "Tyger" commentary plus a reading in relation to various traditions.

1614.   Parsons, Coleman O. "Tygers Before Blake." *Studies in English Literature 1500-1900*, VII (1968), 573-592.

Blake's tyger transcends all others and suggests the moral ambiguities of Job without having the questioner "intimidated into accepting the unknowable."

1615.   Parsons, Coleman O. "Blake's 'Tyger' and Eighteenth Century Animal Pictures." *Art Quarterly*, XXXI (1968), 296-312.

Blake was directly influenced by George Stubbs.

1616.   Peterfreund, Stuart. "The Name of Blake's Lyca Re-examined." *American Notes and Queries*, XIII (1974-75), 133-136.

Considers the name as Greek for she-wolf and as Greek for harlot.

1617. Phillips, Michael. "William Blake's *Songs of Innocence and Songs of Experience* from Manuscript Draft to Illuminated Plate." *Book Collector*, XXVIII (1979), 17-59.

  Attempts to illustrate Blake's own description of his method and its significance.

1618. Pottle, Frederick A. "Blake's 'The Tyger,' 17-18." *Explicator*, VIII (1950), Item 39.

  Lines mean "When the stars faded out in the dawn and the dew fell."

1619. Primeau, Ronald. "Blake's Chimney Sweeper as Afro-American Minstrel." *Bulletin of the New York Public Library*, LXXVIII (1975), 418-430.

  "... Blake's representation of the sweep places him in a revolutionary tradition and links him with later black writers from Richard Wright to LeRoi Jones."

1620. Rawlinson, D.H. "An Early Draft of Blake's 'London.'" *The Practice of Criticism*. Cambridge: Cambridge University Press, 1968, 45-51.

  Discusses changes in drafts.

1621. Reisner, Mary Ellen. "Folcroft Facsimile of the *Songs*." *Blake Newsletter*, X (1977), 130.

  Mary Lynn Johnson recommended the use of the Folcroft facsimile posthumous copy (b) but that contains an unwarranted alteration of Blake's text of "The Blossom."

1622. Riffaterre, Michael. "The Self-Sufficient Text." *Diacritics*, III (1973), 39-45.

  An analysis of "The Sick Rose."

1623. Robinson, Fred C. "Verb Tense in Blake's 'The Tyger.'" *PMLA*, LXXIX (1964), 666-669. See item 1572.

  "Dare" is in the past tense, according to the usage of the day, as are other verbs in the poem.

1624. Robinson, Paul. "What Psychology Won't Explain." *Michigan Quarterly Review*, XIX (1980), 36-50.

  On "The Sick Rose." Sexuality reveals the most primitive dialectic of innocence and experience.

1625.   Rose, Edward J. "The 1839-Wilkinson Edition of Blake's
        Songs in Transcendental America." *Blake Newsletter*,
        IV (1971), 79-81.

        "The Houghton Library of Harvard University has in
        its collection two copies of the second issue of the
        1839 edition [of *Songs of Innocence and of Experience*],
        one owned by Ralph Waldo Emerson and another owned by
        Thomas Wentworth Higginson." Higginson was the self-
        appointed teacher of Emily Dickinson.

1626.   Roti, Grant C., and Donald L. Kent. "The Last Stanza
        of Blake's 'London.'" *Blake: An Illustrated Quarterly*,
        XI (1977), 19-21.

        The "Harlot's curse" refers to venereal disease based
        on a reading of the phrase "blasts a tear."

1627.   Salter, Thomas N. "Toward a Symbology of Form in the
        Illuminations of Blake's *Songs of Innocence and of
        Experience*." *DAI*, XXXV (1975), 3737A (University of
        Massachusetts).

        Surveys past critical approaches to the illuminations
        of the *Songs* and offers a discussion of symbolic mean-
        ing as a new principle of description.

1628.   Schulz, Max F. "Point of View in Blake's 'The Clod and
        the Pebble.'" *Papers on Language and Literature*, II
        (1966), 217-224.

        Both the Clod and the Pebble have "fallen" views.

1629.   Shea, James P. "Blake's Archetypal Tyger: A More Compre-
        hensive View." *DAI*, XXXV (1974), 2242A (Marquette
        University).

        A view that can be found elsewhere, in Gleckner in
        particular. See item 1568.

1630.   Shrimpton, Nick. "Hell's Hymn Book: Blake's *Songs of
        Innocence and of Experience* and Their Models." *Litera-
        ture of the Romantic Period, 1750-1850*. Edited by
        R.T. Davies and B.G. Beatty. New York: Barnes &
        Noble, 1976, 19-35.

        The *Songs* are strange in form because they come from
        a specialized branch of the lyric--children's hymns.

1631.   Siemens, Reynold. "Borderers in Blake's 'The Little
        Girl Lost' Found." *Humanities Association Bulletin*,
        XXII (1971), 35-43.

It is Lyca's parent who, in searching for Lyca, ascends the Blakean ladder and finally achieves four-fold vision.

1632. Simpson, David. "Blake's Pastoral: A Genesis for 'The Ecchoing Green.'" *Blake: An Illustrated Quarterly*, XIII (1979), 116-138.

Blake was affected by and in turn altered the vocabulary of the pastoral tradition. The readings of Hirsch (item 1582), Gillham (item 168) and Gleckner (item 180) are discussed. Language and punctuation do not offer as much revelation in this poem as iconography, especially in regard to the image of the tree.

1633. Smith, David J. "Blake's 'The Divine Image.'" *Explicator*, XXV (1967), Item 69.

Neither "The Divine Image" nor "A Divine Image" presents a Blakean dialectical understanding since they are from fallen states.

1634. Somerville, Elizabeth S. "The Application of an Ontological Perspective to the Literary Interpretation of Works Drawn from Several Periods." *DA*, XXVIII (1968), 3158A (Ohio University).

Discusses Blake's "The Little Black Boy" from an existential ontological perspective. "... the ontological perspective offers a critical attitude that avoids the subject-object dilemma by establishing how the work focuses the transcendent quality of being."

1635. Stepto, Michele L. "Mothers and Fathers in Blake's *Songs of Innocence*." *Yale Review*, LXVII (1978), 357-370.

The roots of the Female Will lie in the "gentle mothers and nurses of Innocence and generally in the parental love, typified by mothers but embracing fathers as well...."

1636. Stevenson, Stanley Warren. "'The Tyger' as Artefact." *Blake Studies*, II (1969), 5-19.

Summary of "Tyger" criticism and some suggestions for future study. No unanimity in "Tyger" criticism. There are four groups of critics: moralists, synoptists, rhetoricians and revisionists.

1637. Stevenson, Stanley Warren. "Artful Irony in Blake's
       'The Fly.'" *Texas Studies in Language and Literature*,
       X (1968), 77–82.

1638. Swingle, L.J. "Answers to Blake's *Tyger*: A Matter of
       Reason and of Choice?" *Concerning Poetry*, II (1969),
       61–71.

       Berates scholarly forays into this poem and sees it
       as an existential experience in which "the answers
       have to be created by man himself out of a nature of
       things which in itself is only a chaos of possibili-
       ties...."

1639. Thompson, E.P. "London." *Interpreting Blake* (item 245),
       5–31.

       A discussion of the changes Blake made in the drafts
       of this poem. A postscript discusses Swedenborg's view
       of London as a symbol of a human hell.

1640. Tolley, Michael J. "Blake's Blind Man." *Blake Studies*,
       II (1969), 77–84.

       Discusses Hagstrum's and Grant's readings of "The
       Fly." Prefers Grant's. See items 1573 and 1674.

1641. Trilling, Lionel. "William Blake: Tyger! Tyger!"
       Prefaces to the Experience of Literature. New York:
       Harcourt Brace Jovanovich, 1979, 215–219.

       The tyger stands for, among other things, the Christ
       who brought a freedom too terrible to accept.

1642. Trout, Henry R. "A Reading of Blake's 'The Little Girl
       Lost' and 'The Little Girl Found.'" *West Virginia
       University Philological Papers*, XXIII (1977), 37–46.

       These poems logically belong to both groupings, Inno-
       cence and Experience.

1643. Van Doren, Mark. "On 'The Little Black Boy.'" *Discus-
       sions of William Blake* (item 182), 83–85.

       The paraphrase is complex but the poem itself is
       simple.

1644. Welch, Dennis M. "Blake, Nehemiah and Religious Re-
       newal." *Christian Scholars Review*, II (1973), 308–
       310.

A reading of "The Little Vagabond" in which England's institutionalized religion is deemed not as humane as Nehemiah's Judaism.

1645. Wilkie, Brian. "Blake's Innocence and Experience: An Approach." *Blake Studies*, VI (1976), 119-137.

Argues that point of view and persona are revealed in the *Songs* and that there is enough evidence in the *Songs* to define the speaker. Such personae must be used as lenses.

1646. Wilkinson, A.M. "Illuminated or Not? A Note on Blake's *Songs of Innocence and of Experience*." *Modern Language Review*, LVII (1962), 387-391.

Discovers an essential basic unity of poem and engraving.

1647. Williams, Harry. "The Tyger and the Lamb." *Concerning Poetry*, V (1972), 49-56.

Answers questions in the fifth stanza by referring to *Jerusalem*. Tyger and lamb mutually forgive, become contraries and go forward.

1648. Williams, Porter, Jr. "'Duty' in Blake's 'The Chimney Sweeper' of *Songs of Innocence*." *ELN*, XII (1974), 92-96.

Argues that the closing line be interpreted ironically and that society be condemned for making such advice necessary.

1649. Wittreich, Joseph A. "Blake's 'The Little Girl Lost,' Stanzas 9-11." *Explicator*, XXVII (1969), Item 61.

Blake was thinking of Canto I of Dante's *Inferno* and the lonely lady of Milton's *Comus*. See also item 460.

Tiriel

1650. Behrendt, Stephen C. "'The Worst Disease': Blake's *Tiriel*." *Colby Library Quarterly*, XV (1979), 175-187.

A reading based on a study of the poem and the drawings.

1651.   Bogen, Nancy. "A New Look at Blake's *Tiriel*." *Bulletin of the New York Public Library*, LXXIV (1970), 153-165.

Questions whether or not Bryant's *New System* may have been an influence on *Tiriel*.

1652.   Essick, Robert N. "The Altering Eye: Blake's Vision in the *Tiriel* Designs." *William Blake: Essays in Honour of Sir Geoffrey Keynes* (item 240), 50-65.

The designs of *Tiriel* reveal Blake's later interests.

1653.   Gleckner, Robert. "Blake's *Tiriel* and the State of Experience." *Philological Quarterly*, XXXVI (1957), 195-210.

Argues that *Tiriel* "is an experiment in the ways of the state of experience, poetically ineffective for the most part, crude, even turgid, yet a valuable aid in understanding the working out in Blake's mind of the contrary to innocence."

1654.   Hall, Mary S. "Blake's *Tiriel*: A Visionary Form Pedantic." *Bulletin of the New York Public Library*, LXXIV (1970), 166-176.

Bryant's *A New System* contains the myth of titans of Mauritania which may have influenced *Tiriel*.

1655.   Halloran, William F. "Blake's *Tiriel*: Snakes, Curses, and a Blessing." *South Atlantic Quarterly*, LXX (1971), 161-179.

Overview of the poem based on the Bible and *Paradise Lost* and related to the other narratives of late 1780's and early 1790's.

1656.   Metcalf, Francis Wood. "Toward a More Accurate Description of the *Tiriel* Manuscript." *Blake Newsletter*, IV (1970), 10-11.

"... it is clear from a study of the facsimile that Professor Bentley mistakes Blake's sectional numberings for foliations...."

Visions of the Daughters of Albion

1657. Cherry, Charles L. "William Blake and Mrs. Grundy: Suppression of *Visions of the Daughters of Albion*." *Blake Newsletter*, IV (1970), 6-10.

The Victorians got the drift of this overtly sexual work and protested.

1658. Cherry, Charles L. "Critical Edition of William Blake's *Visions of the Daughters of Albion*." *DAI*, XXIX (1969), 4452A (University of North Carolina, Chapel Hill).

1659. Duerksen, Roland A. "A Crucial Line in *Visions of the Daughters of Albion*." *Blake Newsletter*, VI (1972-73), 72.

"Bound back to back in Bromion's caves, terror and meekness dwell" *Visions*, 2:5. Author suggests that the two bound figures in the frontispiece illustration are terror and meekness.

1660. Erdman, David V. "Blake's Vision of Slavery." *Journal of the Warburg and Courtauld Institute*, XV (1952), 242-252.

Looks upon *Visions* as a poetic counterpart to the parliamentary and editorial debates of 1789-93 on the bill to abolish the British slave trade.

1661. Gillham, D.G. "Blake: *Visions of the Daughters of Albion*." *Wascana Review*, III (1968), 41-59.

Attempts to prove that *Visions*, outside of the *Songs* and the *Auguries* (perhaps the Proverbs), is "notorious."

1662. Hinkel, Howard H. "From Energy and Desire to Eternity: Blake's *Visions of the Daughters of Albion*." *Papers on Language and Literature*, XV (1979), 278-289.

Visions is the key to understanding Blake's concept of time. The human experience of time arises from within, as do visions of eternity. Time only as a measurement is an imposition of a mechanistic intelligence upon reality.

1663. Moss, John G. "Structural Form in Blake's *Visions of the Daughters of Albion*." *Humanities Association Bulletin*, XXII (1971), 9-18.

Argues that *Visions* is a shrewdly modeled forensic oration which must be appreciated as such if an objective interpretation is sought.

1664. Peterson, J.E. "*The Visions of the Daughters of Albion*: A Problem in Perception." *Philological Quarterly*, LII (1973), 252-264.

Argues that Oothoon perceives with the inward eye and thus perceives the truth.

1665. Reisner, Mary Ellen. "The Rainbow in Blake's *Visions of the Daughters of Albion*." *Notes & Queries*, N.S. XVIII (1971), 341-343.

Symbolizes pleasure and austerity.

1666. Sherry, Margaret. "The Human Form Divine, the Marionette and the Actor: Articulation of the Subject in William Blake, Heinrich von Kleist and Bertolt Brecht." *DAI*, XXXIX (1979), 5494A (Johns Hopkins University).

Analysis of *Visions of the Daughters of Albion* in terms of "the transformations of the notion of the subject from its classical ontology of unity and transparence to precise alternative figurations, based upon observation of tensions between language and the notion of presence."

1667. Waxler, Robert P. "William Blake: The Sexual Dynamics of His Early Illuminated Works." *DAI*, XXXVII (1976), 995A (SUNY, Stonybrook).

Argues that Blake in *Visions* and *First Book of Urizen* is "primarily concerned with the sexual dynamics of the fallen body of man."

1668. Burke, Joseph. "The Eidetic and the Borrowed Image:
An Interpretation of Blake's Theory and Practice of
Art." *The Visionary Hand* (item 144), 253-302.

Refers to E.R. Jaensch's *Eidetic Imagery and Typologi-
cal Methods of Investigation*, 1930, as the basis of
Blake's visions. "The optical reality of the visions
involved no act of credence on Blake's part, because
the eidetic image is actually seen." Argues that these
eidetic images were to some extent determined by a
variety of artistic influences.

1669. Digby, George Wingfield. *Symbol and Image in William
Blake*. Oxford: Clarendon Press, 1967 (c.1957).

The book is a study of the meaning of Blake's art
based on *The Gates of Paradise* and the newly found picture at Arlington Court, with reference to nearly sixty
other designs and paintings by him, all of which are
reproduced here. Refers to Jung.

1670. England, Martha. "Apprenticeship at the Haymarket?"
Blake's Visionary Forms Dramatic (item 139), 3-29.

"My hypothesis is that Blake knew of Haymarket
procedures and wrote a Haymarket piece of his own
modeled on *Tea*." *Tea in the Haymarket* is a "generic
name for a variable product of the satiric personality
and dramatic genius of the actor Samuel Foote."

1671. Essick, Robert. *William Blake Printmaker*. Princeton:
Princeton University Press, 1980.

"Most studies of Blake's pictorial works attempt to
interpret their symbolic meaning. The emphasis in this
book lies elsewhere: In the broadest sense, it is a
study that asserts the importance of method when imagination addresses itself to life through art." 148 pages
of plates plus an excellent bibliography of related items.

1672.   Gleckner, Robert. "Point of View and Context in Blake's
        Songs." *Blake: A Collection of Critical Essays* (item
        155), 8-14.

        Blake's *Songs* must be read with great sensitivity to
        context and point of view. One of the best essays on
        the *Songs*.

1673.   Hagstrum, Jean H. "Babylon Revisited, or the Story of
        Luvah and Vala." *Blake's Sublime Allegory* (item 118),
        101-118.

        The story of Luvah and Vala but also a very fine
        account of Blake's views of sexuality and the spiritual
        body.

1674.   Hagstrum, Jean H. "The Fly." *William Blake: Essays for
        S. Foster Damon* (item 256), 368-382.

        "Man was made for thought, or imaginative vision;
        when we rightly know this, we go safely through the
        world, come what may."

1675.   Knight, G. Wilson. "The Chapel of Gold." *William Blake:
        Essays in Honour of Sir Geoffrey Keynes* (item 240),
        157-161.

        A reading which intends to demonstrate how poetry
        should be interpreted.

1676.   Kostelanetz, Anne T. "Blake's 1795 Color Prints: An
        Interpretation." *William Blake: Essays for S. Foster
        Damon* (item 256), 117-130.

        Same argument she pursues in *Blake's Human Form Divine*
        (item 610): Blake advocated definite outline in art
        but rebelled against the imposition of form in the
        fallen world.

1677.   LaBelle, Jenijoy. "Words Graven with an Iron Pen: The
        Marginal Texts in Blake's *Job*." *The Visionary Hand*
        (item 144), 527-550.

        Argues that all the marginalia is intentional and
        goes through *Job* illustrations plate by plate.

1678.   Mitchell, W.J.T. "Poetic and Pictorial Imagination in
        Blake's *The Book of Urizen*." *The Visionary Hand*
        (item 144), 337-380.

Applies his criticism of *ut pictura poesis* specifically to *The Book of Urizen*.

1679. Nanavutty, Piloo. "A Title-Page in Blake's Illustrated Genesis Manuscript." *The Visionary Hand* (item 144), 127-146.

A detailed reading of the title page which concludes with a summary of all of Blake's vision.

1680. Nurmi, Martin K. "Blake's Revisions of 'The Tyger.'" *Twentieth Century Interpretations of the Songs of Innocence and of Experience* (item 238), 104-106.

Traces the drafts of the poem and makes appropriate comments.

1681. Roe, Albert S. "A Drawing of the Last Judgment." *The Visionary Hand* (item 144), 201-232.

A reading of "A Vision of the Last Judgment."

1682. Schorer, Mark. *William Blake: The Politics of Vision*. New York: Henry Holt, 1946.

An historical focus, similar to Bronowski's (item 108) and Erdman's (item 130).

INDEX

Authors of books, articles and reviews are
listed. Titles of all Blake's works are listed
as well as titles of books about Blake (titles
of articles about Blake are not listed). Subject terms are in full capitals, as are titles
of works neither by nor about Blake.